T0301673

European Energy Policy

European Energy Policy

An Environmental Approach

Edited by

Francesc Morata and Israel Solorio Sandoval

Universitat Autònoma de Barcelona, Spain

Edward Elgar
Cheltenham, UK • Northampton, MA, USA

Published by
Edward Elgar Publishing Limited
The Lypiatts
15 Lansdown Road
Cheltenham
Glos GL50 2JA
UK

Edward Elgar Publishing, Inc.
William Pratt House
9 Dewey Court
Northampton
Massachusetts 01060
USA

A catalogue record for this book
is available from the British Library

Library of Congress Control Number: 2011942554

ISBN 978 0 85793 920 3

Typeset by Cambrian Typesetters, Camberley, Surrey
Printed and bound by MPG Books Group, UK

Contents

Contributors

Adelle, Camilla is a Senior Research Associate at the University of East Anglia, in Norwich, UK.

Bechberger, Mischa is an expert on renewable energy promotion policies. Since 2009, he has been in charge of the international relations of the Spanish Renewable Energy Association (APPA) in Barcelona, Spain.

Busch, Per-Olof is Post-Doctoral Researcher and Lecturer at the Chair of International Organisations and Public Policy in the Faculty of Economics and Social Sciences of the University of Potsdam, Germany.

Carafa, Luigi is a PhD candidate at the universities of Toulouse, France and Catania, Italy.

Ciambra, Andrea is a PhD Student at the School of International Studies, University of Trento, Italy.

Dobbins, Michael is a Senior Researcher at the Chair of Comparative Public Policy and Administration at the University of Konstanz, Germany.

Escribano-Francés, Gonzalo is Senior Researcher at the Real Instituto Elcano and Senior Lecturer of Applied Economics at the Spanish Open University-UNED, Spain.

Fischer, Severin is Associate Fellow at Stiftung Wissenschaft und Politik (SWP) in Berlin, Germany, where he is working on topics related to EU energy and climate policy.

Herranz-Surrallés, Anna is a Juan de la Cierva Researcher (Ministry of Science and Innovation) at the Institut Barcelona d'Estudis Internacionals (IBEI), Spain.

Jörgens, Helge is Lecturer at the Department of Political and Social Sciences of the Freie Universität Berlin and Managing Director of the Environmental Policy Research Centre (FFU), Germany.

Knudsen, Jørgen K. is a political scientist from the University of Oslo, Norway. He obtained his Doctoral degree at the University of Twente, the Netherlands.

Morata, Francesc is Professor at the Department of Political Science and Administration of the Universitat Autònoma de Barcelona, Spain and has been an *Ad Personam* Jean Monnet Chair on European Politics since 2005.

Natorski, Michal is a Postdoctoral Researcher in International Relations at the Universitat Autònoma de Barcelona, Spain.

Pallemaerts, Marc is Professor of European Environmental Law at the University of Amsterdam, the Netherlands, and Senior Fellow at the Institute for European Environmental Policy (IEEP) in Brussels, Belgium, where he is head of the Global Issues and External Action Programme.

Russel, Duncan is a Lecturer in the Politics of Climate Change and Sustainable Futures at the University of Exeter, UK. His research focuses on United Kingdom and European Union environmental policy.

San Martín González, Enrique is a Lecturer in the Department of Applied Economics, Spanish Open University (UNED), Spain.

Solorio Sandoval, Israel is a Research Fellow at the University Institute of European Studies (IUEE), Universitat Autònoma de Barcelona, Spain.

Tosun, Jale is a Senior Researcher at the Chair of Comparative Public Policy and Administration at the University of Konstanz, Germany.

Zapater, Esther is a Senior Lecturer of International Public Law at the Universitat Autònoma de Barcelona, Spain.

Foreword: EU energy policy and the strategic value of renewable energy promotion

Mischa Bechberger

As demonstrated in the Copenhagen climate summit, the approach of a global climate regime based on strong and binding greenhouse gas (GHG) reduction targets for industrialized countries, as well as on growing reduction commitments for emerging and developing countries, has largely failed (Scheer, 2010). Besides, the most prominent climate mitigation option of the conventional power industry, nuclear energy, will probably lose government support after the 2011 Fukushima power plant nuclear disaster in Japan, as demonstrated by the decision of the German Government to phase out nuclear until 2021/2022 (Greenpeace, 2011). Therefore, the most efficient, effective and least costly solution for rapidly reducing global GHG emissions is clearly through a very rapid expansion of renewable energy sources (RES) in the global and European energy mix. This would also help to decrease significantly Europe's growing fossil fuel energy import dependency, which in 2008 had already reached 54.8% for the EU-27 (Eurostat, 2011, p. 26).

The strategic importance of RES for the EU energy policy has been demonstrated lately through the political upheavals in the Arab World, involving some of the main oil and/or gas suppliers of Europe (Eurostat, 2011, pp. 40ff.). The EU RES promotion policy should therefore be seen as the only strategic option for rapidly reducing European GHG emissions and the aforementioned energy import dependency. Bearing in mind also that, owing to the 2011 political upheavals in North Africa and the Middle East, June 2011 oil prices – at around US$115 per barrel – have already reached the second-highest levels since the historical peak of summer 2008 (*Manager Magazine*, 2011). In this sense, RES can avoid a lot of GHG emission rights and fossil fuel import costs, which would be much higher in total than the financial support required for a massive deployment of RES.

At the same time, RES could create a lot of new jobs, a very important factor in times of global economic downturn. The best way to do this, as shown in various recent studies (EREC, 2010; ECF, 2010; Jacobson and

Delucchi, 2009; EREC and Greenpeace, 2010), would be through stable (macro-) legal frameworks and binding mid- and long-term targets, combined with strong energy efficiency measures. Whereas there are still many doubts as to when and what extent a new global climate regime might be established (Scheer, 2010), RES is growing at a fast pace, both at a European and a global level, thereby constituting one of the most important means of GHG reductions in recent years.

According to the European Photovoltaic Industry Association (EPIA), in 2010 the growth of the photovoltaic (PV) markets worldwide reached a newly installed capacity of 16.7 gigawatts (GW), experiencing a 132% growth compared with 2009. The total installed global PV capacity has therefore reached 39.6 GW. In Europe in 2010, PV became for the first time the RES electricity (RES-E) technology with the largest amount of newly installed generation capacity, ahead of wind energy and outperformed only by gas-fired plants (EWEA, 2011, p. 6). This also translated into investments of over €50 billion in 2010. PV technology has reduced its unit costs to roughly a third of what they were five years ago, thanks to continuous technological progress, productive efficiency and its wide implementation. The trend of decreasing unit costs will also continue into the future. Thus, PV technology has all the potential to meet a double-digit percentage of the electricity supply needs in every major region of the world.

Looking ahead, a share of over 20 percent of world electricity demand in 2050 appears feasible. Such amounts of PV would avoid a cumulative total of 65 billion tonnes of CO_2 emissions between 2020 and 2050 (EPIA and Greenpeace, 2011, pp. 3ff.). As for wind, according to the Global Wind Energy Council (GWEC), despite being hit by the financial crisis of 2008–09, the global wind market nevertheless grew by 22.5 percent in 2010, with an investment growth of 31 percent, reaching a record level of US$ 96 billion and an overall installed global wind capacity of 194.4 GW. By 2015, annual market additions are expected to reach 60.5 GW, up from 35.8 GW in 2010. This will lead to a doubling of the overall installed worldwide wind capacity to nearly 450 GW by 2015 (GWEC, 2011, pp. 10ff.). Regarding global investments in RES, the Renewable Energy Policy Network for the 21st Century (REN21) showed in its 2010 Global Status Report that investment in renewable energy power capacity (excluding large hydro) in 2009 was comparable to that in fossil-fuel generation, with both at around $100 billion. If the estimated $39 billion of investment in large hydro is included, then total investment in RES exceeded that in fossil-fuel generation for the second successive year. According to REN21, in 2012, the world as a whole will add more capacity to the electricity supply from renewable than non-renewable sources (REN21, 2010).

At the European level, the original capacity targets for RES-E for 2010 (established for the first time in 1997 through the RES White Paper) have been widely exceeded. In the case of wind, at the end of 2010, more than 84 GW had been installed, instead of the forecasted 40 GW. Regarding PV, the 3 GW target has been exceeded more than nine times over, reaching an installed capacity above 27 GW (EREC, 2011, p. 11). How has this impressive development been possible?

At a European level, the focus is mainly on Germany's successful PV development, reaching more than 17 GW of installed capacity at the end of 2010, representing 43 per cent of the cumulated world PV market. This has been achieved thanks to an exemplary feed-in tariff (FIT) law since 2000, which always guaranteed a high level of planning and investment security and allowed small private investors to invest in clean, smart and locally distributed generation facilities. Germany is also still leading the European ranking in wind energy, with 27.2 GW of installed capacity at the end of 2010 (GWEC, 2011, p. 11).

And it is not only Germany showing an impressive growth of RES-E capacity, but also other EU member states, like Italy (at least 2.3 GW), the Czech Republic (1.4 GW) and France (0.7 GW) in the case of PV capacity newly installed in 2010, or Spain (1.5 GW), France (1.1 GW), the UK (1 GW) and Italy (0.9 GW) in newly installed wind capacity in 2010 (GWEC, 2011, p. 11). On the one hand, this is based on strong national RES-E support schemes, while on the other hand it is basically thanks to an ambitious and forward-looking EU RES policy, which began as early as 1997 through the first White Book on RES, followed by two important Directives to promote RES-E in 2001 and biofuels in 2003 (including indicative European and national targets for 2010) and, lately, the new EU RES framework Directive of 2009, which for the first time comprised all RES subsectors (including RES heating and cooling) and relatively ambitious binding targets for RES at EU and country levels (Bechberger, 2009, pp. 536ff.). To ensure these targets are fulfilled, the RES Directive also included the obligation for member states to draft and then submit so-called national renewable energy action plans (NREAP) to the European Commission, following general guidelines and using a template in which they had to forecast the overall RES share of final energy consumption (at least meeting the minimum overall RES target fixed within the RES Directive for each member state and the various subsector and single technology targets) and, most importantly, describing the measures already established or still necessary to adopt in order to meet the different RES targets by 2020. Interestingly, while the member states had to submit their NREAPs by the end of June 2010, it was not until the end of 2010 that all 27 NREAPs were delivered.

As a first analysis of all the NREAPs, the following main results can be highlighted: altogether, the member states expect to exceed the minimum target of 20 percent of RES in final energy consumption by 0.7 percent in 2020. Regarding subsector targets, the NREAPs foresee achieving a share of

RES to meet 34.3 percent of electricity demand, 21.3 percent of heating and cooling demand and 11.3 percent of transport consumption (ECN, 2011, pp. 6ff.). According to these numbers, it looks at first glance like the ambitious EU RES policy has been reaffirmed by a majority of the member states.

The EU REPAP 2020 project (www.repap2020.eu), in its first phase, provided strong scientific input to the authors of the NREAPs by preparing the national RES industry road maps. In a second phase, the project is both closely following the transposition of the RES Directive into national legislation and also evaluating the national NREAPs. A recently published analysis of the NREAPs states that substantial optimization potential exists for all five categories (administrative procedures and spatial planning, infrastructure development and electricity network operation as well as support measure for RES-E, heating and cooling and within the transport sector). The strongest deficits exist in the field of administrative procedures and spatial planning followed by the category support measures for RES heating and cooling. The highest optimization potentials exist in these two areas. Even the section of support measures in the electricity sector receives only a neutral evaluation on average, showing room for improvement in many EU member states (Ragwitz et al., 2011, p. 2). Therefore the same project showed that even higher shares of RES in the EU energy mix could be reached by 2020.

The European RES industry (based on the NREAPs' energy demand scenarios) shows that 24.4 percent of RES in final energy demand can be achieved, provided always that appropriate policies are in place, such as: clear, stable (never retroactive!), technology-specific promotion schemes for RES-E technologies, new incentives for combined heat and power plants and district heating and cooling, priority access/dispatch of RES in all member states, and improved storage capacity planning; the streamlining of permit procedures (mainly for small(er) RES installations, including one-stop-shop approaches), re-established access to equity finance for small and medium enterprises, as well as small private-investor and project bonus and national RES funds, to be fed by the proceeds of auctions under the European Emissions Trading Scheme (EU ETS) from 2013 onwards; strong infrastructure investments based on the new EC infrastructure package of late 2010, including several priority projects (such as new interconnection lines); and last but not least, and of utmost importance, the adoption of ambitious, binding and long-term energy-efficiency targets (which, as a first step might be established within the recasting of the Energy Service Directive), to mention just a few of the policy recommendations of the Repap2020 project (Fouquet, 2011). Moreover, the NREAPs anticipate that the share of RES will meet 34.3 percent of electricity demand, 21.3 percent of heating and cooling and 11.3 percent of transport consumption, while the RES industry (based on the NREAPs' energy demand scenarios and supposing the introduction of the aforementioned measures) suggests that 42.3 percent of electricity consumption, 23.5 percent of heating and cooling and 12.2 percent of transport consumption is attainable by 2020 (EREC, 2011, p. 6).

Although these estimates for 2020 might already look ambitious and would require the deployment of at least a larger part of said measures, they could only signify a first, yet very important, intermediate step towards a complete ecological transformation of the European and global energy mix based entirely on RES by 2050. To make such a transformation come true, what would be needed besides the aforementioned supportive measures, on the one hand, are a fast and complete transposition of the RES Directive and a close and effective monitoring by the European Commission, including infringement procedures in case of non-compliance with the main provisions and targets of the Directive. On the other hand, what is also needed is an adoption of 2030 (and at a later stage also 2040) EU targets for RES as early as possible, in order to give these completely carbon-free energy sources the strategic importance they deserve in the future EU energy mix.

Such a complete switch to RES at EU level, by 2050 at the latest, not only is already possible with the latest RES technologies available today but also would lead to huge overall macroeconomic benefits, as was shown in 2010 through the 100% RES scenario for 2050 by EREC called 'Re-Thinking 2050'. In this report, EREC demonstrated that, even without an aggressive energy efficiency policy, the EU could achieve an effective 96 percent share of renewable energy in final energy consumption by 2050 (the remaining 4 percent stems from the assumption of remaining fossil fuel uses in aviation and inland navigation by 2050). Based on this almost 100 percent RES share by 2050, the avoided CO_2 costs in 2050 alone (assuming a CO_2 price of €41 per tonne in 2020, €45/t in 2030 and €100/t by 2050) would exceed the cumulative investment of €2800 billion necessary to reach 100% RES share by 2050 by €1000 billion. When taking into account the fossil fuel costs avoided (expecting an oil price of $100 per barrel in 2020, $120/bl in 2030 and $200/bl in 2050) the economic benefit would increase to €2090 billion in 2050. Therefore, higher upfront investment needs will certainly pay off in the long run for European citizens. Besides, more than 6 million jobs would be created in the EU RES sector (EREC, 2010, pp. 3ff.).

Last but not least, there is an urgent need for strong and binding energy efficiency targets, not only for 2020 but also for 2030, 2040 and 2050, as these would strongly help to secure the increase of RES in overall energy consumption and bring down the total GHG emissions of Europe. The recasting of the Energy Service Directive planned for 2011–12 should be a good window of opportunity for finally establishing binding energy efficiency targets, the only pillar still missing in the EU's strongly interdependent energy and climate strategy, based on RES, GHG reductions and energy efficiency.

REFERENCES

Bechberger, Mischa (2009), *Erneuerbare Energien in Spanien*, Stuttgart, Germany: ibidem.

Energy Research Centre of the Netherlands (2011), *Renewable Energy Projections as Published in the National Renewable Energy Action Plans of the European Member States – Executive Summary*, accessed 15 June 2011 at www.ecn.nl/docs/library/report/2010/e10069_summary.pdf.

European Climate Foundation (2010), *Roadmap 2050: A Practical Guide to a Prosperous, Low-Carbon Europe*, accessed 15 June 2011 at www.roadmap2050.eu/attachments/files/Volume1_fullreport_PressPack.pdf).

European Commission (2011), *Impact Assessment of 'A Roadmap for Moving to a Competitive Low Carbon Economy in 2050*, SEC(2011) 288 final, accessed 15 June at http://ec.europa.eu/clima/documentation/roadmap/docs/sec_2011_288_en.pdf.

European Photovoltaic Industry Association (2010), 'Market outlook 2010–2015', Brussels.

EPIA and Greenpeace (2011), 'Solar Generation 6 – solar photovoltaic electricity empowering the world – 2011', accessed 10 June at www.greenpeace.org/international/Global/international/publications/climate/2011/Final%20SolarGeneration%20VI%20full%20report%20lr.pdf.

European Renewable Energy Council (EREC) (2010), Re-thinking 2050: A 100% Renewable Energy Vision for the European Union – Executive Summary, accessed 10 June 2011 at www.rethinking2050.eu/fileadmin/documents/Rethinking2050 ExecutiveSummary_final.pdf.

EREC (2011), *Mapping Renewable Energy Pathways Towards 2020 – EU Roadmap*, accessed 10 June at www.repap2020.eu/fileadmin/user_upload/Roadmaps/EREC-roadmap-V4_final.pdf.

EREC and Greenpeace (2010), *Energy (R)evolution – A Sustainable World Energy Outlook*, accessed 10 June 2011 at www.energyblueprint.info/fileadmin/media/documents/2010/0910_gpi_E_R_full_report_10_lr.pdf.

European Wind Energy Association (2011), Wind in Power – 2010 European Statistics, accessed 10 June at www.ewea.org/fileadmin/ewea_documents/documents/statistics/EWEA_Annual_Statistics_2010.pdf.

Eurostat (2011), *Energy, Transport and Environment Indicators – 2010 Edition*, accessed 10 June at http://epp.eurostat.ec.europa.eu/cache/ITY_OFFPUB/KS-DK-10-001/EN/KS-DK-10-001-EN.PDF.

Fouquet, D. (2011), *Overview on the National Renewable Energy Actions Plans of the EU Member States with Focus on PV*, accessed 10 June at www.repap2020.eu/fileadmin/user_upload/Roadmaps/Recommendations_BBH.pdf.

Global Wind Energy Council (2011), *Global Wind Report – Annual Market Update 2010*, accessed 15 June at http://www.gwec.net/fileadmin/documents/Publications/Global_Wind_2007_report/GWEC%20Global%20Wind%20Report%202010%20low%20res.pdf.

Greenpeace (2011), *Fukushima 1 (Daiichi) Radiation Briefing*, accessed 12 June at http://www.greenpeace.org/international/en/campaigns/nuclear/safety/accidents/Fukushima-nuclear-disaster/Fukushima-radiation-briefing/.

Jacobson, M.Z. and M.A. Delucchi (2009), *A Path to Sustainable Energy by 2030*, accessed 1 July at www.solaripedia.com/files/399.pdf.

Manager Magazin (2011), *Brent Oil Spot*, accessed 18 June 2010 at http://boersen.manager-magazin.de/spo_mmo/kurse_einzelkurs_uebersicht.htm?s=BRENTDAT.RSM&b=400&l=276&n=OIL%20in%20USD.

Renewable Energy Policy Network for the 21st Century (2010), *Global Trends in Green Energy 2009: New Power Capacity from Renewable Sources Tops Fossil Fuels Again in US, Europe*, accessed 1 June 1011 at www.ren21.net/Portals/97/ documents/Media%20Resources/REN21_GSR_2010_Press_Release.pdf.

Ragwitz, M. et al. (2011), *Assessment of National Renewable Energy Action Plans*, accessed 1 July at www.repap2020.eu/fileadmin/user_upload/Roadmaps/ Assessment_of_NREAPs__REPAP_report_-_interim_status_.pdf.

Scheer, H. (2010), 'Global reden, national bremsen', *Le Monde Diplomatique*, 12 February 2010, accessed 10 March at www.eurosolar.de/de/index.php?option= com_content&task=view&id=1297&Itemid=340.

Preface and acknowledgements

To truly appreciate European integration development, it is crucial to understand the role energy has played (and still has the potential to perform) throughout the 50-year-plus history of this process. Indeed, given energy's trajectory in this process it is accurate to argue that energy is not only deeply rooted in European construction, but that energy itself, with more or less success, has also been a driver of integration. Paradoxically the integration process has never developed so far as to lay the foundations for a fully-fledged and coherent Common Energy Policy (CEP), which has instead become one of the weakest policy areas to date.

But after years of persistent neglect at the core of EU policies, energy is today a hot topic on the EU's political agenda, also attracting the attention of scholars. Even though the EU's participation in energy policy really took off in the 1990s through contiguous areas (primarily the environment and the liberalization of the internal market), it was not until recently that the barriers hindering Brussels's action in this policy area were finally broken down. Against this backdrop, while the past years have seen an unprecedented development of the European energy policy, the understanding of this process has lagged behind.

Alongside the scarce literature on this emergent policy, there is also a gap regarding the attention paid to its different components. This book stems from the perception of a mismatch between the valuable debate that certain dimensions of energy policy have triggered (namely energy security and the market and competition framework) and the neglect of its environmental and climate change dimensions. The book highlights the significance of environmental policy concerns, instruments and objectives *vis-à-vis* the competing security and market dimensions in order to achieve an all-embracing European energy policy perspective for the future.

This book has its roots in the seminar 'European Energy Policy: the Environmental Dimension' organized by the University Institute of European Studies (IUEE) in November 2009 and financially supported by the Spanish Ministry of Science and Innovation. Held on the campus of the Autonomous University of Barcelona, this event was attended by a long list of scholars dealing with the European energy policy. This volume is a product of that enriching experience and so far it has facilitated the development of a network of scholars working in the field of energy policy at the EU level. The editors of this volume are especially grateful to all the participants who attended our research seminar. We extend our special thanks to Professor Christoph Knill and Dr Esther Zapater for their support in organizing the panels of the event and we also want to express our gratitude to all our contributors for the patience they have shown us.

Moreover, none of what we have accomplished here would have been possible without the support of the IUEE team and in particular its projects department. In this regard we would like to thank Lucia Popartan, the head of the department, for her full-time dedication and support both before and during the seminar and in the follow-up publication project. Last but not least this book could not have been a reality without the support of Nikole Ottolia, our research assistant. We must thank all of them for their indispensable support.

Francesc Morata and **Israel Solorio Sandoval**
December 2011, Barcelona

Abbreviations

AFD	French Development Agency
Btu	British thermal unit
CCS	carbon capture and storage
CDM	clean development mechanism
CEE	Central and Eastern Europe
CEPS	Centre for European Policy Studies
CO_2	carbon dioxide
COP	Conference of the Parts
CSP	concentrated solar power
DLR	German Aerospace Center
DG	Directorate General
ECCP	European Climate Change Program
ECJ	European Court of Justice
ECSC	European Coal and Steel Community
EC	European Community
ECO	European Coal Organization
ECT	Energy Charter Treaty
EDAM	Centre for Economics and Foreign Policy Studies
EEA	European Environment Agency
EEC	European Economic Community
EECB	Energy Efficiency Coordination Board
EERA	European Energy Research Alliance
EIB	European Investment Bank
EIT	European Institute of Innovation and Technology
EMRA	Energy Market Regulatory Authority
EnC	Energy Community
ENP	European Neighborhood Policy
ENPI	European Neighborhood and Partnership Instrument
EPE	Energy Policy for Europe
EREC	European Renewable Energy Council

ESTELA	European Solar Thermal Electricity Association
EPI	Environmental Policy Integration
EPIA	European Photovoltaic Industry Association
EU	European Union
EU-15	Austria, Belgium, Denmark, Finland, France, Germany, Greece, Ireland, Italy, Luxembourg, Netherlands, Portugal, Spain, Sweden, United Kingdom
EU ETS	European Emissions Trading Scheme
EUROSTAT	Statistical Office of the European Union
EWEA	European Wind Energy Association
FDI	foreign direct investment
FEMIP	Facility for Euro-Mediterranean Investment and Partnership
FIT	feed-in tariff(s)
FYROM	Former Yugoslavian Republic of Macedonia
GCC	Gulf Cooperation Council
GDP	gross domestic product
GHG	greenhouse gases
GW	gigawatts
GWEC	Global Wind Energy Council
HVDC	high voltage direct current
IA	impact assessment
IEA	International Energy Agency
IEEP	Institute for European Environmental Policy
IMF	International Monetary Fund
IPP	independent power producers
IPPC	Intergovernmental Panel on Climate Change
KfW	Kreditanstalt für Wiederaufbau, the German development bank
MC	Ministerial Council
Med-Emip	Euro-Mediterranean Energy Market Integration Project
MENA	Middle East and North Africa
MoU	memorandum of understanding
MPCs	Mediterranean Partner Countries
Mtoe	millions tons of oil equivalent
MW	megawatts

NGO's	Non-governmental organizations
NO_x	nitric oxide
NREAPs	National renewable energy action plans
OECD	Organisation for Economic Co-operation and Development
OEEC	Organisation for European Economic Co-operation
OME	Observatoire Méditerranéen de l'Energie
ONE	Office National de l'Electricité
PPA	power purchasing agreements
PPP	public private partnership
PTC	production tax credits
PV	photovoltaic
RECSs	Renewable Energy Certificate System
REN21	Energy Policy Network for the 21st Century
RES	renewable energy sources
RES-E	renewable energy electricity
SAP	stabilization and association process
SD	sustainable development
SDS	EU Sustainable Development Strategy
SEA	Single European Act
SEM	Single European Market
SET-Plan	Strategic Energy Technology Plan
SO_2	sulphur oxide
TACIS	technical assistance to the CIS countries
TEC	Treaty establishing the European Community
TEN-E	Trans-European Energy Network
TFEU	Treaty on the Functioning of the European Union
TREC	Trans-Mediterranean Renewable Energy Cooperation
TSO	transmission system operator
UCTE	Union for the Coordination of Transmission of Electricity
UfM	Union for the Mediterranean
UNFCCC	United Nations Framework Convention on Climate Change
US	United States (of America)
USD	United States (of America) dollars
VAs	voluntary agreements
WCED	World Commission on Environment and Development

1. Introduction: the re-evolution of energy policy in Europe

Israel Solorio Sandoval and Francesc Morata

> Putting more abundant energy at a cheaper price at the disposal of the European economies constitutes a fundamental element of economic progress.
>
> *Messina Declaration, 1955*

> The energy challenge is indeed one of the greatest tests of Europe.
>
> *Speech by EU Commissioner for Energy Günther H. Oettinger, on preparation of Energy Strategy 2011–2020, Brussels, September 2010*

1.1 INTRODUCTION

To truly appreciate European integration development, it is crucial to understand the role energy has played (and has still the potential for) throughout the more than 50 years' history of this process. Indeed, it is hardly possible to explain the origins of the European Union (EU) without considering what happened in Europe just after the end of World War II (Lucas, 1977). Starting with the establishment of the European Coal Organisation (ECO) in 1946 and then the Organisation for European Economic Co-operation (OEEC) in 1948, energy was a cornerstone of European integration. The rationale for establishing the first Community organization in 1951, the European Coal and Steel Community (ECSC), lay explicitly with the energy-related challenges that Europe had to face during those years. A similar motivation lay behind the creation of the European Atomic Energy Community (Euratom) in 1957, with both the latter and the ECSC constituting the basic pillars of the European Economic Community (EEC). Thus, it is accurate to argue that energy is not only deeply rooted in European construction, but that it has been in itself – with more or less success – a driver of integration.

That said, it is fairly paradoxical that the integration process has never developed so far as to lay the foundations for a fully fledged and coherent common energy policy, which has instead become one of the weakest policy areas to date. During the 1980s, energy policy was considered a 'spectacular failure' of integration (Andersen, 2000). However, this condition has been

gradually changing. Even when the EU's participation in energy policy really
took off in the 1990s by means of contiguous areas (primarily environment
and liberalization of the internal market), it was not until recently with the
Lisbon reform and the Treaty on the Functioning of the European Union
(TFEU) that the formal barriers that hindered Brussels's action in this policy
area were finally broken down. The overriding result is that energy now
pertains formally to the 'family' of EU policies.

By building a forward-looking 'European energy policy'[1] (the term is used
throughout this book to refer to the coordinated efforts between the EU and its
member states in this policy field), the EU is preparing the ground to face
twenty-first-century global challenges such as climate change and the explod-
ing demand for energy (Pielbags, 2009, p. 3). For this, the EU has arranged
what are meant to be their policy goals in the field (that is what we refer
throughout this book as the 'energy trinity'): (1) increasing security of supply;
(2) ensuring the competitiveness of European economies and the availability
of affordable energy; (3) promoting environmental sustainability and combating climate change (Council of the European Union, 2007, p. 11). Energy
policy is no longer a matter exclusive to the national administrations, as nowadays Brussels performs an active, although still limited, role in this field.

This transition in the governance of energy policy in Europe is reflected in
the chapter 4 of the TFEU, where energy appears as a 'shared competence'
between the EU and its member states – as in the case of the internal market,
the environment and the trans-European networks (art. 4.2, TFEU). This effort
to better coordinate actions in the energy field is reflected in art. 194 of the
TFEU on energy, which argues as follows:

> In the context of the establishment and functioning of the internal market and with
> regard for the need to preserve and improve the environment, Union policy on
> energy shall aim, in a spirit of solidarity between Member States, to:
> (a) ensure the functioning of the energy market;
> (b) ensure security of energy supply in the Union;
> (c) promote energy efficiency and energy saving and the development of new
>   and renewable forms of energy; and
> (d) promote the interconnection of energy networks. (art. 194.1, TFEU)

In this regard, in spite of the 'misleading debut' of energy in the European integration (Buchan, 2009, p. 6), '[t]oday's leaders have [finally] come back to the
philosophy which Europe started off with in the 1950s – namely that the best
way to deal with energy challenges is European cooperation' (Oettinger,
2010b). After decades of boosting cooperation in the energy field by means of
alternative paths (see Lucas, 1977; Matláry, 1997), nowadays the European
energy policy can rely on a stronger legal framework in order to pursue the
energy trinity. It is notable that even though this article refers to objectives

previously contained in the Treaty establishing the European Community (TEC), these objectives were actually disseminated throughout the treaty according to distinct policy areas (for example internal market or environment) (Zapater, 2009).

The fact that these energy policy goals are now laid down in the Lisbon Treaty is aimed at facilitating the advancement towards policy coherence. Indeed, the expected outcome of this new governance framework is to reduce existent contradictory signals between the EU and its member states' policies together with the trade-offs derived from the energy trinity and the matching areas of the European energy policy (internal market, external relations and environmental/climate protection), which is one of the biggest concerns for the EU. As pointed out by David Buchan (2009, p. 16), '[i]ndeed it is ironic that Brussels should devote so much rhetoric denying the existence of such conflicts when it spends so much time actually dealing with them'.

While this governance framework presents new opportunities to the EU, it must be clarified that there is still an essential constraint to its performance. This critical limit stems from the member states' 'right to determine the conditions for exploiting its energy resources, its choice between different energy sources and the general structure of its energy supply' (art. 194.2, TFEU). To be clear, this exception, which derives from an identical one imported from the environment chapter, leaves a narrow yet significant space that protects member states' sovereignty in a core aspect: the energy supply structure. The result is that 'the EU has no power over member states' energy mix, depletion policy or taxation' (Buchan, 2009, p. 9).

Therefore, five main aspects of the emergent European energy policy need to be emphasized in relation with the European integration process:

1. For now, it is the coordinated action both of the EU and of its member states that defines the European energy policy.
2. Its governance essentially relies on the cooperation between the EU and its member states.
3. It is still 'a work in progress'.
4. Its final outcome is uncertain.
5. Consequently, it is still far from being a common policy.

This unprecedented period for energy policy in Europe has drawn attention to EU performance in this policy area for the first time (traditionally under the member states' control, except for the deregulation policy and the Euroatom-related issues). Against this backdrop, the argument of Janne Matláry sounds fairly outdated: '[e]nergy policy in the European Union has never been one of the main areas of integration, and for this reason this policy area has attracted little scholarly attention among analysts of the EU' (Matláry, 1997, p. 1).

Today, energy policy is a 'hot topic' in the EU's political agenda, also attracting the attention of scholars. The growing number of articles and academic
works dealing with energy policy in Europe is proof of this trend (for example Buchan, 2009). Yet there is a lack of understanding of the effects this
process is producing, especially with regard to the 'green component' of the
European energy policy (see below).

In spite of the current financial and economic crisis, the energy policy area
remains one of the key concerns both at European and national levels. Since
energy is the 'blood' of modern societies and the whole economic and social
well-being of the European peoples and European industry relies on safe,
secure, sustainable and affordable energy (European Commission, 2011a, p.
2), there are those in Europe who argue that energy policy is to be 'the next
great European integration project' (European Commission, 2011b, p. 2). The
pressing importance of current challenges such as climate change and energy
security has made the creation of European energy policy an essential prerequisite for the construction of the Europe of the twenty-first-century, and the
European institutions have therefore called for a 'revolution in the energy
systems' to face the challenging global context that hastens the decarbonization of the European economy (European Commission, 2011b, p. 1).

1.2   ENERGY AND ENVIRONMENT: AN OPEN-ENDED HISTORY?

To begin with, we must stress that what we are now witnessing is the realization of a process that entailed the progressive transition of governance towards
the EU. In the words of David Buchan (2009, p. 7), energy policy in the EU is
characterized by an 'organic' growth, where 'policymakers borrowed legal
competence from the economic and environmental parts of the EU treaties in
order to justify proposing and passing energy measures'. Hence, it is not
surprising to notice that a peculiarity of the emergent energy policy in Europe
is that the EU already possesses a significant number of instruments for attain-
ing its energy trinity goals (see Chapter 6 by Solorio and Zapater).

There is a broad consensus regarding the fact that the environmental
concerns of the energy chain have been some of the most significant drivers to
influence EU energy policy (Damro et al., 2008; Buchan, 2009; Solorio, 2009,
2011). The integration between environment and energy policies has been an
outstanding platform upon which the EU has influenced energy governance, a
process that gathered pace as the 'antidote' to global warming concerns
(Collier, 2002, p. 177). Climate change has been a key element in leading the
EU to debate its energy policy at a more practical level (Piebalgs, 2009), and
the link between environment and energy policies has gradually transformed

the energy policy in Europe (Buchan, 2009). On the one hand the integrated approach between climate and energy policies is one of the most innovative features, adopted after the 2007 spring European Council. On the other, the 2009 Climate and Energy Package is considered the flagship instrument of the EU's forward-looking perspective on a sustainable energy model (Oberthür and Pallaemarts, 2010).

While there are few doubts regarding the energy chain's environmental concerns as a driver behind the European energy policy (that is behind the cooperation in the energy field between the EU and its Member States), there is still a lack of clarity as to how the intrinsic relationship between both policies has transformed and ultimately shaped energy policy in Europe. Accordingly, even when the environment–energy relationship has received considerable political and scientific attention (for example Collier, 1994, 1997, 2002), what we are still missing is a picture to help us understand how the increasing proximity of both policies has contributed to the transformation of energy policy.

Broadly speaking, we can distinguish four phases through which the relationship between both policies has passed and which explain how the progressive integration[2] of environmental concerns has influenced European energy policy construction.

1.2.1 Phase 1: Environmental Awakening

From its early beginnings, European integration has demonstrated a propensity to react to emergent problems (Jordan et al., 1999). With the growing concern over environmental issues in the 1970s, the Community did not hesitate to focus on the ecological impact of the energy chain. The Commission's reflections as well as the Council's resolutions reflected the reality of increasing environmental awareness (for example Commission of the European Communities, 1972, 1974; European Council, 1974, 1975). The institutional flexibility allowed environmental issues to become one of the earliest and most remarkable goals of the free movement of goods policy (Pollack, 1994, p. 124). However, the oil crisis of the 1970s contributed to making energy security one of Europe's paramount policy goals (Natorski and Herranz-Surrallés, 2008). This scenario increased the necessity of formulating and developing policies together in order to tackle the energy problems. Specifically regarding the environment, the Council (1975) provided the following statement:

> [I]t is the duty of the Communities and the Member States to: (a) take environmental protection requirements into account in all energy policy strategy by taking effective measures. (Council of the European Communities, 1975)

The recognition of environmental policy integration (EPI) as a policy objective was translated into a considerable number of environment-related measures and recommendations. On the energy efficiency side, there were numerous acts such as the action program on the rational use of energy and the recommendations on the energy consumption of road vehicles and on the rational use of electrical household appliances. Resolutions were also adopted on setting a short-term target for the reduction of oil consumption and for energy savings. On the other hand the development of renewable energy sources (RES) was delayed, given the immediate need to solve the supply problems (Twidell and Brice, 1992). Thus the Community's activities were limited to granting financial support for projects to exploit alternative energy sources.

This first phase was characterized by an increasing awareness of environmental issues within Europe and the very first reactions in this regard. EPI began to be recognized as a policy objective in energy policy-making, and the Community adopted a considerable body of legislation consisting of EPI-related instruments years before the Single European Act (SEA). The Commission's main success was to bring energy issues back onto the European agenda and to trace a path that in the following years appeared to be a useful driver for the evolution of energy governance: the environmental policy.

1.2.2   Phase 2: Environmental Formal Competence

The year 1986 was of great significance for European integration as well as for EPI issues. The main shift upon the SEA's arrival came through internal market performance (McGowan, 2008) as well as the institutionalization of other significant areas such as environmental policy. The new environmental policy emerged with the task of protecting the environment 'through the prudent and rational utilization of natural resources' such as oil products, natural gas and solid fuels (Article 191, TFEU). The Community environmental policy was supported by two particular features from the start: (1) its success in terms of expansion, and (2) its efforts towards integration in other policies, mainly in the energy field.

Regarding its expansion, this can be measured by the number of legislative acts adopted, as well as the successive governance modifications in the following treaty revisions. With regard to integration, it is worth commenting that the new competence emerged nearly parallel with the fourth Action Programme (1987–92), which declared that the 'integration of the environmental dimension in other major policies will be a central part of the Commission's efforts' (Owens and Hope, 1989, p. 97). The initial years of environmental competence were characterized by a lack of remarkable results in energy policy, perhaps with the exception of the large combustion plant directive. However climate change emerged as a hot topic at the international level, which proved beneficial for the relationship between energy and environment (Damro et al., 2008). Since the first EU target for stabilizing carbon dioxide emissions was adopted by the Joint Council of Energy and the Environment in October 1990 (Skjaerseth, 1994), the European climate policy has become increasingly intertwined with energy policy. This second phase led to the institutionalization of environmental policy as a path for intervening in the energy field. The results of this second phase became more evident in the following years.

1.2.3 Phase 3: Formal Integration

EPI was legally codified by the Maastricht Treaty in 1992 and incorporated into TEC art. 6 (art. 11, TFEU), which contains the integration principle as a core EU objective (Lenschow, 2002). It recognized that the environmental protection requirements must be integrated into the definition and implementation of the Union's policies and activities, in particular with a view to promoting sustainable development. In parallel with these governance changes, climate change placed more pressure on the integration process of both policies. While this issue has moved to the mainstream of the international political agenda, Europe has also accelerated efforts to reduce global warming, thus improving its energy consumption practices (Henningsen, 2008; Solorio, 2009, 2011)

With the intention of presenting the European Community negotiators with strong arguments for the Rio Conference in 1992, the Commission proposed a 'Climate Package' for the first time that included a directive proposal on renewable electricity (RES-E); regulatory measures in the field of efficiency and energy savings, and a tax on energy-using products (Skjaerseth, 1994). However this package was diluted by the Council, which ultimately adopted pilot programs such as ALTENER and SAVE and excluded the possibility of taxation on energy use and a regulatory framework for RES-E (Collier, 1997). Nevertheless this involved the development of the first Community strategy to fight climate change in the early 1990s, the emergence of the climate policy to the core of the EU agenda and the creation of a new stage for EPI issues (Andersen, 2000).

Given the growing awareness of climate change, it is understandable that limiting carbon dioxide emissions by improving energy efficiency was a significant step forward. The Directive SAVE (closely related to the homonym program) emerged with the intention of drawing up and implementing programs in fields related to energy efficiency. Regarding RES, the Commission decided to boost their development with the Green Paper of 1996 on RES, a document that provided the basis for the White Paper in this area.

The initiation of the so-called 'Cardiff Process' in 1998 represented a step forward to the practical application of EPI, calling to Council formations to prepare strategies and programs focused on integrating environmental considerations into its own policies (See Chapter 2 by Adelle et al.). Regarding energy, the Commission upheld that 'given the important impact on the environment, environmental integration cannot be achieved without adapting energy policy' (European Commission, 1998, p. 3). This way, energy efficiency and RES came to form the cornerstone of a sustainable energy system (Collier, 2002). Soon new environmental measures were adopted at the EU level, such as the RES-E Directive, and the biofuels Directive (see Chapter 3 by Knudsen). Moreover, once the Kyoto Protocol was ratified in 2002, the adoption of concrete measures to fight against climate change accelerated. Soon after, the directive establishing a scheme for greenhouse gas emission allowance trading within the Community was adopted and a consensus was even reached to adopt a measure restructuring the Community framework for the taxation of energy products and electricity. EPI's third phase was characterized by a double impetus to its integration within energy. On the one hand, the consolidation of environmental governance facilitated its influence in energy. On the other hand, climate change as an outstanding issue in international as well as in European politics sped up this process (Damro et al., 2008).

1.2.4   Phase 4: European Energy Policy Emergence

In 2005, the EU began a new stage in its climate change program in order to prepare a mid- and long-term strategy to confront this challenge. In this context, the European Council perceived 'the need to demonstrate that the EU's commitment to meet Kyoto … is practical and not just a paper one' (Piebalgs, 2009, p. 2). In response, the Commission began pushing forward the energy debate with the paramount goal of laying down the foundations of a new energy policy of global character as an indispensable step towards effectively tackling climate change (European Commission, 2006, 2007).

The first step was the Green Paper entitled *A European Strategy for Sustainable, Competitive and Secure energy*, in which the Commission put forward concrete proposals for implementing a European energy policy (European Commission, 2006). In the following year, 2007, the Commission launched a strategic review of the current energy challenges as a guide to Europe's energy policy, in which the 'triple twenty' (RES, energy efficiency and greenhouse gas emissions reductions) were specified as a necessary goal to limit climate change. In this document, the Commission argued that '[m]eeting the EU's commitment to act now on greenhouse gases should be at the centre of the new European Energy Policy' (European Commission, 2007).

As a turning point, the 2007 spring European Council highlighted the

Action Plan (2007–2009) Energy Policy for Europe 'as a milestone in the creation of an Energy Policy for Europe and as a springboard for further action' (Council of the European Union, 2007, p. 13). An imperative goal was set to achieve *integration* between climate and energy policies (Council of the European Union, 2007, p. 11). The European Council also recognized the importance of EPI by stating that 'a substantive development of energy efficiency and of renewable energies will enhance energy security, curb the projected rise in energy prices and reduce greenhouse gases emissions' (Council of the European Union, 2007, p. 20).

Responding to the Council's move, the Commission launched the Communication '20 20 by 2020: Europe's Climate Change Opportunity' on January 2008. The Commission proposed a set of measures 'designed in a way so that they are mutually supportive', in order to translate 'political direction into action' (European Commission, 2008). The economic crisis was certainly an added obstacle during the legislative process. However, after the hard inter-governmental negotiations, the Climate and Energy Package became law in early 2009. The package comprises four main measures: (1) a revision of the Emissions Trading System (EU ETS); (2) an 'Effort Sharing Decision' governing emissions from sectors not covered by the EU ETS, such as transport, housing, agriculture and waste; (3) binding national targets for RES; and (4) a legal framework to promote the development and safe use of carbon capture and storage (see Chapter 5 by Fischer). With all these measures, it represents the most concrete expression of the new European energy policy and the most convincing proof that the win–win solutions between energy and environment are more than possible.

When the internal dimension of the EU energy policy has apparently been moving easily towards a more sustainable approach, the picture regarding its external dimension is dominated by a great concern for exporting its market model and securing energy supply. The European Commission has often emphasized that 'the same collaboration and common purpose that has led to the adoption of the EU's headline energy and climate targets is not yet evident in external energy policy' (European Commission, 2011a, p. 17). However, in order to pursue this paramount goal regarding the external dimension of its energy policy, the EU has to 'face up to' its own nature. In other words, given that 'EU external energy policy stems from the complex and hybrid nature of the European integration' (Belyi, 2008, p. 203), the goal of a single approach and speaking with a single voice is an overarching need that has been a constant cause of frustration in Brussels.

The EU Commissioner for Energy, Günther Oettinger, recently stated that 'the EU still hesitates to commit itself to a coherent and common external voice' (Oettinger, 2010a, p. 3). In this sense, it is essential to acknowledge that the 'Lisbon Treaty will lend the EU more weight and a clearer profile in its external relations' (Müller-Kraenner, 2010, p. 2). A new window of opportunity has been opened for pulling together a broad range of policies, touching upon cooperation with third countries, humanitarian aid, common commercial policy, development, and cooperation policy and, needless to say, security and foreign policy, under the broader umbrella of energy policy. Nevertheless, it is still too early to predict how these changes in the EU's external profile will impact on policy-making in the energy field.

To sum up, from this historical review there are at least three main issues to note regarding EPI in energy and the development of the European energy policy. First of all, there is a clear continuity of the environmental component as a result of sector-specific actions within energy, encouraged mainly in the framework of the European fight against climate change. Second, the wider concept of EPI has, at least within energy policy, been centered on the environmental subsector of climate policy (see Chapter 2 by Adelle et al.). Third, after this historical review the link between the environmental policy development impelled by EPI and the Europeanization of energy governance remains clearer (that is facilitating the emergence of the European energy policy) (see Chapter 6 by Solorio Sandoval and Zapater). In this context, the former commissioner on energy, Andris Pielbags, seems to have been correct in defining the EU's shift in energy policy as the 'third industrial revolution' (Pielbags, 2009, p. 5).

1.3 AIMS OF THIS BOOK AND OVERALL ANALYTICAL FRAMEWORK

While the past years have contemplated an unprecedented development of the energy policy at the European level, the understanding of this process has lagged behind. Alongside the scarce literature on this emergent policy, there is also a gap regarding the attention paid to its different components. On the one hand, too much interest has been paid to the member states' actions, deflecting the EU efforts to boost European coordinated action in this field. On the other, there is certainly a mismatch between the valuable debate that certain dimensions of energy policy – namely, energy security and the market and competition framework – have triggered and the neglect of its environmental and climate change dimensions (although the several attention paid to the EU's climate policy). This book is intended to highlight the significance of environmental policy concerns, instruments, and objectives *vis-à-vis* the competing security and market dimensions in order to achieve an all-embracing EU energy policy perspective for the future.

How to understand in depth the EU energy policy and its 'green component'? As seen with the historical analysis presented above, EPI is a useful tool for understanding the closeness between energy and environmental policies in the EU. It is known that the concept of EPI as a principle of environmental policy stems from the wider theoretical concept of sustainable development. There are two fundamental ways of looking at EPI: one based on rationality and the effectiveness of policy-making, the other on normative and principled assumptions. Irrespective of the chosen approach, it is worth reminding that '[e]nergy presents a major challenge for the concept of integration ... because of its political and economic significance and because of the complexity of energy–environment interactions' (Owens and Hope, 1989, p. 97). Accordingly, this book copes with the matter of integration between environment and energy policies (see Chapters 2 and 3). Following the challenge to undertake the European energy policy, Europeanization is an indispensable analytical instrument to penetrate in the 'adaptive process triggered by European regional integration' (Vink and Graziano, 2007, p. 7). The Europeanization of energy policy governance has radically changed its conception. What have been the main changes and driving forces behind this process? This book has been written to tackle this issue. Last but not least, the EU not only has the obligation to go forward in its effort to integrate climate and energy policies, but also has to confront the apparent disassociation between what the EU is doing at home and the bulk of its external relations. In this sense, external governance and/or external Europeanization are by far the most useful analytical devices to approach the EU external relations regarding energy policy and the promotion of a sustainable energy system. In sum, the chapters included here move between different approaches to EPI, Europeanization and external governance in order to carry out the overriding task of explaining the dynamics affecting both the internal and the external dimensions of European energy policy.

This introductory chapter proposes a three-step model of 'green Europeanization' for energy policy (Figure 1.1) as an explanatory tool for contextualizing the changes that have occurred in European energy policy. Our model here attempts to illustrate: (1) how energy governance was Europeanized before formal competence was granted by means of environmental performance (a process illustrated in the first part of this book) and (2) the emergence of the EU as a 'green-model' exporter referring to energy policy (a process captured in the second part).

As shown before, the environmental concerns regarding the energy chain were a useful 'excuse' in order to facilitate Community intervention. This is the *first step* of our model: EPI in energy. Just after the oil crisis shocked Europe in the 1970s the European institutions led by the Commission began to facilitate the 're-entry' of energy onto the Community's political agenda (Andersen, 2000, p. 2). Certainly energy security was the main concern

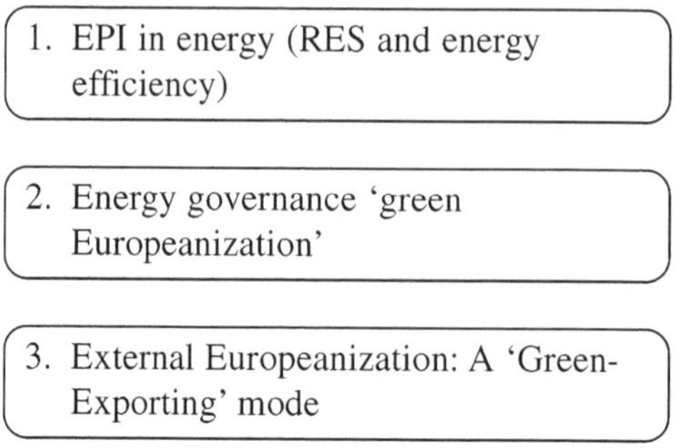

1. EPI in energy (RES and energy
   efficiency)

2. Energy governance 'green
   Europeanization'

3. External Europeanization: A 'Green-
   Exporting' mode

Source: Own interpretation.

Figure 1.1   'Green Europeanization' model.

between the energy policy goals at that time (Natorski and Herranz-Surrallés, 2008, p. 75). It was also undeniably the positive step that opened the door to Community participation in energy policy and the adoption of a number of Regulations – primarily concerning energy efficiency but also trying to boost RES at the European level.

The awakening of environmental concerns regarding the energy chain (and the need for urgent action) led eventually to the institutionalization of EPI as a concept guiding EU environmental policy-making. Of particular note here is the fact that when EPI generated enough consensus regarding the urgency of greening the energy policy (Collier, 2002), the number of strategies and choices to make integration a reality became considerably more widely debated. Against this background we need to clarify that even though nowadays EPI is largely considered as a 'dead process' in EU policy-making, its heritage in energy policy is self-evident (see Chapter 2 by Adelle et al., Chapter 3 by Knudsen and Chapter 6 by Solorio Sandoval and Zapater).

The analysis of the greening of energy policy has been well documented by Ute Collier in her publications on EPI (Collier, 1994, 1997, 2002). Nevertheless, there is a 'black hole' in the understanding of how the increasing proximity between both energy and environment has contributed to Europeanizing energy policy in Europe. This represents the *second step* of our model: the 'green Europeanization' of energy policy. In this context, it is noticeable that although the Europeanization research agenda recently received considerable attention in European studies (Bulmer, 2007), energy policy has been a largely neglected area. It is certainly reasonable to acknowledge that numerous elements of energy policy have been examined during this period of expansion of the Europeanization research agenda. However, they have frequently been limited to a sector-based perspective and have by no means covered the broader picture of energy policy. In other words, if this sector-based perspective is required, given the role of energy in European integration, these studies have yet to succeed in expanding the Europeanization approach to overall energy policy because of their research foci.

Research concentrated on the Europeanization of the internal energy market has attracted most of the attention (McGowan, 2008). It is possible to find earlier examples, such as the study by Andersen (1999) on natural-gas liberalization, the work of Eising and Jabko (2001) on the changing objectives of the French energy policy as a result of the market liberalization negotiations, the well-known publication by Levi-Faur (2002) on the Europeanization of the electric and telecommunications regime and the research of Humphreys and Padgett (2006) on globalization, EU and domestic governance, as well as other relevant works (Jordana et al., 2005; Bartle, 1999, 2002). Oddly though, despite the considerable political attention to climate change in the EU (Damro et al., 2008), it is hard to find studies linking the environmental performance of the EU and the Europeanization of energy policy (Solorio Sandoval, 2009, 2011). Such a link therefore provides an emerging research agenda, which is addressed in Part I of this volume.

One of the main tasks this book attempts is to analyze how the EU governance system has been centralizing many policy-making activities regarding energy in Brussels, while relying on national administrative actors for implementation (Knill and Lenschow, 2005). However, the 'adventure' of analyzing EU influence on energy policy entails certain risks. First of all, this task involves considerable risks inherent in the application of the Europeanization framework, which has been quite 'contested as to its usefulness for the study of European politics' (Vink and Graziano, 2007, p. 3). Second and as already mentioned, our research topic distinguishes itself from other policy fields since the Europeanization of energy governance has been mainly driven by competences in related areas. Hence it becomes necessary to follow the 'green Europeanization' model in order to understand the indirect Europeanization of energy policy through EU environmental performance.

When approaching the Europeanization of energy policy, a fundamental step towards understanding it is to categorically separate the 'process in which countries pool sovereignty' from what follows 'once EU institutions are in place and produce their effects' (Radaelli, 2000, p. 6). In other words, it is essential to identify the limit between Europeanization and political integration. Nevertheless the boundary between both can become blurred by the fact that Europeanization has a dual function: (1) 'as an independent variable in domestic politics' and (2) 'as the processes by which domestic structures adapt to European integration' (Caporaso, 2007, p. 27). In particular, this book is interested in exploring function (1). The goal pursued is to understand the European energy policy as a transformation variable. However, it is also true that a key element in this process is to shed light on the interaction between Europeanization and political integration, and this is therefore a principal task throughout the entire book.

While the first part of this book is centered on the European energy policy as a variable of change for its member states, the second is dedicated to understanding the EU's role as an exporter of its energy model – that is external Europeanization, the *third step* of our model. The bulk of literature that focuses on the export of ideas, rules and norms beyond EU borders has grown significantly in recent years (for example Lavenex and Schimmelfenning, 2009; Barbé et al., 2009). Energy being a core interest of the EU's external policy, it has occupied an increasingly central place on the agenda in this particular case. As put forward by Sandra Lavenex and Adam Stulberg (2007, pp. 135–36),

> [h]arbouring no illusions that energy security can be attained through self-sufficiency, expanding alternative (renewable and sustainable) energy resources, or managing internal consumption alone, the EU has placed priorities on managing the diversification of external supply and market stability in Europe.

Paradoxically, in this sense, it is remarkable that even when climate change has been a main concern of EU external action (Wurzel and Connelly, 2010), most of the literature referring to EU external governance has focused on the projection of the internal energy market rules (see Escribano, 2010; Herranz Surrralés and Zapater, 2010), on the geopolitical dimension of EU energy policy (see Correljé and Van der Linde, 2006) and on issues concerning the security of supply (see Umbach, 2010).

Contrary to this tendency, this book stems from the understanding that the EU's policy actors have sought climate change not only as a challenge but also as an opportunity in order to become an exporter of its energy model with the expected political and economic advantages (Wurzel and Conelly, 2011). In this context the *third step* of our 'green Europeanization' model focuses on the EU's foreign behavior and the emergent role as an exporter of its 'green-energy' model. That is to say, the second part of this work focuses on the neglected side of external European energy policy: the promotion of a sustainable energy model beyond European frontiers. This book also serves as a piece of evidence on how the increasing concern for energy security and/or the internal market rules in the external dimension of the European energy policy affect the promotion of a 'green-energy' model abroad.

To sum up, this book aims to contribute to the scarce literature regarding the European energy policy by putting the emphasis on its environmental component (that is by highlighting the significance of environmental policy concerns, instruments, and objectives *vis-à-vis* the competing security and market dimensions in order to achieve an all-embracing EU energy policy perspective for the future). Finally, moving beyond the mere descriptive analysis, the authors contributing to this volume have been encouraged to emphasize the green element of the European energy policy (in its internal as well as in its external dimension), a frequently neglected yet essential element for building a forward-looking energy policy for twenty-first-century Europe.

1.4   STRUCTURE OF THE BOOK

This volume is in two main parts covering the internal and the external dimensions of the European energy policy, besides the introductory and conclusive chapters. In Chapter 2, Camilla Adelle, Duncan Russel and Marc Pallemaerts touch upon the sensitive issue of the integration in the EU of policies on energy, on climate change and on the environment in general. The chapter draws on the longer-standing difficulties of translating the concept of EPI in policy and administrative terms. While climate change challenges stress the need to improve the existing cross-sectoral coordination mechanisms or to introduce new structures and procedures, the fact remains that generally speaking, effective linkages are still missing both at the EU and the domestic level. The chapter focuses on the European Commission's strategies as regards climate and energy policy. Based on the evaluation framework designed by the EEA, it both assesses the progress achieved and also surveys the shortcomings still hampering the integration of climate change issues into the energy sector.

Starting with the theoretical implications of EPI for European energy policy from the dual horizontal (cross-sectoral policies) and vertical (multilevel governance) perspective, in Chapter 3 Jørgen K. Knudsen examines how EPI has been incorporated into the promotion of RES in the EU. The empirical analysis of the implementation process in the Nordic countries (Denmark, Finland, Norway and Sweden) provides an assessment of the extent to which EPI and RES-E have been connected and followed up in these states. Despite a high level of market integration in the electricity sector among the four countries, both domestic contextual and institutional specificities reveal different approaches to EPI's effective implementation. The chapter concludes with a discussion about the potential of EPI for contributing to a stronger common EU RES policy.

In Chapter 4 Per-Olof Busch and Helge Jörgens put the spotlight on the diffusion of RES policies in the EU. More precisely, their contribution attempts to assess the impact of EU programs on the degree of convergence achieved in this field by the member states as a form of Europeanization (that is 'green Europeanization'). Drawing on an analytical scheme based on three classic modes of international policy coordination (cooperation, coercion and diffusion), the authors examine the cross-national spread of support schemes for electricity generation from RES sources from 1988 to 2005. These consist of feed-in tariffs and green certificate systems. The analysis highlights the interactions between the domestic implementation of these incentives and the mechanisms of Europeanization promoted by the European Commission.

In Chapter 5, Severin Fischer also applies the Europeanization approach to the issue of carbon capture and storage (CCS). The author stresses the high expectations raised by this new technology, especially in some coal-producing countries, but also the uncertainties about the environmental risks that it may entail. The chapter examines in depth the complex policy process followed by the CCS system in the EU. It sheds light on the relevant role played the European Commission and the European Parliament in setting the environmental standards to be respected (that is 'green Europeanization' of energy policy alternative technologies), the pressures from some member states acting as front-runners and the multilevel interactions between political and economic actors to get public financial support to private operators.

To close Part I, dedicated to the internal dimension, in Chapter 6 Israel Solorio Sandoval and Esther Zapater address the Europeanization of energy governance in the EU and the relative importance of the 'green driver' (that is the 'green Europeanization' of energy governance). Importantly in this sense, the chapter constitutes a broad picture of the institutionalization of energy policy at the European level and the predominant forms of governance in this process.

Part II, dealing with the external dimension, starts with Chapter 7 and the exploration of the marketization of energy policy in central and eastern Europe (CEE). Starting from the ill-known environmental regulatory legacy of these countries before their accession to the EU, Michael Dobbins and Jale Tosun review the marked-based instruments put in practice in CEE, showing up the differences with regard to the EU-15 (that is the limits of the EU as a 'green-energy' model exporter towards the CEE countries). The empirical analysis is focused on the application of environmental taxes related to one particular source of energy (fuels). Dobbins and Tosun's main assumption is that 'market-based policy instruments should be more prominent in the CEE countries than in the EU-15'. The justification lies both in the regulatory legacies and the opportunity structures for environmental policy actors operating in the industrial and energy sectors.

Chapter 8 is focused on the EU's energy security issue with regard to its eastern neighbors and the southern Caucasus as the most relevant areas in terms of supply and transit of natural gas. The main research question put forward by Anna Herranz-Surrallés and Michal Natorski is about the extent to which the EU's concerns over energy security have affected its foreign policy, impacting also on other strategic areas (that is testing the role of the EU as a 'green-energy' model exporter towards the east). The analytical approach builds on the three dimensions of the EU's external energy relations: promoting market-oriented policies, Europeanization beyond the EU' (fostering environmental protection and RES, and combating climate change) and security of supply. The chapter illustrates the growing importance of the third dimension as a result of the strong energy dependency of the EU, exacerbated by recent disputes with Russia relating to the supply of natural gas. Particular attention is paid to bilateral relations with three strategic countries; Russia, the main supplier of hydrocarbons to the EU; Ukraine, the most important transit country for the transport of gas; and Azerbaijan, regarded as one of the alternative suppliers of natural gas via the Nabucco pipeline. The last point focuses on the recent European attempts to develop a more institutionalized cooperation framework in the region through a number of multilateral initiatives such as INOGATE–Baku and the Eastern Partnership.

Andrea Ciambra (Chapter 9) addresses the question of whether – and how – the EU's external relations policy combines its twofold strategy towards promoting competitiveness and sustainability concerns with regard to energy issues. With this aim, the study reviews, from a sociological institutionalist approach, the theoretical fundamentals of the EU's market-oriented external energy relations. Subsequently, the author identifies the instruments set up by the EU to achieve its strategic objectives. These are empirically applied to the neighboring countries in the western Balkans. Drawing on the creation of the Energy Community (EnC), Ciambra evaluates the degree of socialization achieved in this area through the penetration of the energy's *acquis* (that is the EU as a 'green-energy' model exporter towards the western Balkan countries). He underlines the relevance of economic and political expectations, but also the sharing of common values as explanatory variables.

In Chapter 10, Luigi Carafa turns to the EU's influence on energy sector reform in Turkey. The analytical focus draws on the transformative power of the EU in the international system and the impacts of Europeanization beyond its borders. The enlargement policy is a main driver to promote changes in the energy policy sector of candidate countries, like Turkey, that must adapt their domestic regulations to comply with the requirements of the *acquis communautaire*. However, the impacts of these changes are still poorly understood. The chapter examines the implementation of EU-based energy reforms in Turkey, arguing that the principle of conditionality is not sufficient by itself to explain the reforms operated in this country (that is the EU as a 'green-energy' model exporter towards Turkey). Other factors, such as the impacts of European energy Regulations together with key domestic concerns, also play a considerable role. Such a statement is empirically rooted on three case studies related, respectively, to energy competitiveness, energy security and sustainability.

As an interesting example of an experimental external European energy policy, Chapter 11 explores the efforts of the EU to foster the deployment of

RES in the southern shore of the Mediterranean. Gonzalo Escribano-Francés and Enrique San Martín González investigate the reasons behind the launching of the Mediterranean Solar Plan, paying particular attention to the case of Morocco as the best-positioned country in the region to implement the Plan (that is the EU as a 'green-energy' model exporter towards the southern Mediterranean). In addition to the important financial and technological challenges that project entails, the discussion also revolves around two interrelated issues: the implications of the Mediterranean Solar Plan as a potential economic driver for Morocco's development and its EU-centric design tailored to the requirements of European environmental and technological priorities.

In Chapter 12, in their concluding remarks, Francesc Morata and Israel Solorio Sandoval assess the overall 'green contribution' to the construction of European energy policy and the perspectives for further research in the field.

NOTES

1. The bulk of official documents dealing with energy policy in the EU have also used the wording 'EU's energy Policy' and energy Policy for Europe'. In this volume we rely mainly on the use of 'European energy policy' as a term to refer to this emergent policy. However, the use of any one of these phrases is correct and, in any case, some authors also alternatively adopt one of the other options for referring to the subject of this book.
2. In order to trace out this process, we adopt the environmental policy integration (EPI) definition put forward by Ute Collier (1994), which regards EPI as a concept aimed at 'achieving sustainable development and preventing environmental damage; removing contradictions between policies as well as within policies; and realizing mutual benefits and the goal of making policies mutually supportive' (Collier, 1994, p. 36).

REFERENCES

Andersen, S. (1999), 'European integration and the changing paradigm of energy policy: the case of natural gas liberalization', *Arena Working Papers*, **99** (12), accessed 18 November 2010 at www.sv.uio.no/arena/english/research/publications/arena-publications/workingpapers/.

Andersen, S. (2000), 'EU energy policy: interest interaction and supranational authority', *Arena Working Papers*, **100** (5), accessed 18 November 2010 at www.sv.uio.no/arena/english/research/publications/arena-publications/workingpapers/.

Barbé, E., O. Costa, A. Herranz Surrales and M. Natorski (2009), 'Which rules shape EU external governance? Patterns of rule selection in foreign and security policies', *Journal of European Public Policy*, **16** (6), 834–52.

Bartle, I. (1999), 'Transnational interests in the European Union: globalization and changing organization in the telecommunications and electricity', *Journal of Common Market Studies*, **37** (3), 363–83.

Bartle, I. (2002), 'When institutions no longer matter: reform of telecommunications and electricity in Germany, France and Britain', *Journal of European Public Policy*, **22** (1), 1–27.

Belyi, Andrei (2008), 'EU external energy policies: a paradox of integration', in Jan Orbie (ed.), *Europe's Global Role*, London: Ashgate, pp. 203–16.

Buchan, D. (2009), *Energy and Climate Change: Europe at the Crossroads*, Oxford: Oxford University Press.

Bulmer, Simon (2007), 'Theorizing Europeanization', in P. Graziano and V. Vink (eds), *Europeanization: New Research Agendas*, New York: Palgrave Macmillan, pp. 3–20.

Caporaso, James (2007), 'The three worlds of regional integration theory', in P. Graziano and V. Vink (eds), *Europeanization: New Research Agendas*, New York: Palgrave Macmillan, pp. 23–34.

Collier, Ute (1994), *Energy and Environment in the European Union: The Challenge of Integration*, Aldershot: Avebury.

Collier, U. (1997), 'Prospects for a Sustainable Energy Policy in the European Union' European University Institute working paper, Robert Schuman Centre no. 97/29, London.

Collier, Ute (2002), 'EU energy policy in a changing climate', in A. Lenschow (ed.), *Environmental Policy Integration: Greening Sectoral Policies in Europe*, London: Earthscan Publications, pp. 175–92.

Commission of the European Communities (1972), *Necessary Progress in Community Energy Policy*, COM(72) 1200, 4 October, *Supplement to Bulletin of the European Communities*, no. 11.

Commission of the European Communities (1974), *Towards a New Energy Policy Strategy for the European Community*, Com(74) 550 final/2, Brussels, 26 June.

Council of the European Communities (1974), *Council Resolution of 17 December 1974 on a Community Action Programme on the Rational Utilization of Energy*, accessed 18 November 2010 at http://eur-lex.europa.eu/en/legis/latest/chap121010.htm. .

Council of the European Communitues (1975), *Council Resolution of 3 March 1975 on Energy and the Environment*, accessed 18 November 2010 at http://eur-lex.europa.eu/en/legis/latest/chap121010.htm.

Council of the European Union (2007), *Action Plan (2007–2009): An Energy Policy for Europe*, *Presidency Conclusions*, Brussels, 8–9 March, accessed 18 November 2010 at http://register.consilium.europa.eu/ pdf/en/07/st07/ st07224–re01.en07. pdf

Correljé, A. and C. van der Linde (2006), 'Energy supply security and geopolitics: a European perspective', *Energy Policy*, **34** (5), 532–43.

Damro, C., Hardie, I. and D. MacKenzie (2008), 'The EU and climate change policy: law, politics and prominence at different levels', *Journal of Contemporary European Research*, **4**, 179–92.

Eising, R. and N. Jabko (2001), 'Moving targets: national interests and electricity liberalization in the European Union', *Comparative Political Studies*, **34** (7), 742–67.

Escribano, G. (2010), 'Convergence towards differentiation: the Europeanization of Mediterranean energy corridors', *Mediterranean Politics*, **15** (2), 211–29.

European Commission (1998), *Communication from the Commission of 14 October 1998: Strengthening Environmental Integration within Community Energy Policy*, accessed 18 November 2010 at http://eur-lex.europa.eu/smartapi/cgi/sga_doc?smartapi!celexplus!prod!DocNumber&lg=en&type_doc=COMfinal&an_doc=1998&nu_doc=571.

European Commission (2006), *Green Paper of 8 March 2006: A European Strategy for*

Sustainable, Competitive and Secure Energy, Brussels, 8 March, accessed 18 November 2010 at http://eur-lex.europa.eu/smartapi/cgi/sga_doc?smartapi!celex-plus!prod!DocNumber&lg=en&type_doc=COMfinal&an_doc=2006&nu_doc=105

European Commission (2007), *Communication from the Commission to the European Council and the European Parliament of 10 January 2007: An Energy Policy for Europe*, accessed 18 November 2010 at http://eur-lex.europa.eu/smartapi/cgi/sga_doc?smartapi!celexplus!prod!DocNumber&lg=en&type_doc=COMfinal&an_doc=2007&nu_doc=1.

European Commission (2008), *Communication from the Commission to the European Parliament, the Council, the European Economic and Social Committee and the Committee of the Regions – Second Strategic Energy Review: An EU Energy Security and Solidarity Action Plan*, accessed 18 November 2010 at http://eur-lex.europa.eu/LexUriServ/LexUriServ.do?uri=CELEX:52008DC0781:EN:HTML:NOT.

European Commission (2011a), Communication from the Commission to the European Parliament, the Council, the European Economic and Social Committee and the Committee of the Regions: Energy 2020: A Strategy for Competitive, Sustainable and Secure Energy, COM(2010) 639, Brussels.

European Commission (2011b), *Background Paper: Energy Roadmap 2050 – State of Play*, Brussels, 3 May.

Henningsen, J. (2008), 'EU energy and climate policy – two years on', European Policy Centre, issue paper, **55**, September, Brussels.

Herranz-Surrallés, A. and E. Zapater (2010), 'A toda luz y a medio gas: relaciones energéticas entre la Unión Europea y su entorno próximo', in *La Unión Europea más allá de sus fronteras ¿Hacia la transformación del Mediterráneo y Europea oriental?*, Madrid: Tecnos.

Humphreys, P. and S. Padgett (2006), 'Globalization, the European Union, and domestic governance in telecoms and electricity', *Governance: An International Journal of Policy Administration and Institutions*, **19** (3), 383–406.

Jordan, A., R. Brouwer and E. Noble (1999), 'Innovative and responsive? A longitudinal analysis of the speed of EU environmental policy-making, 1967–97',*Journal of European Public Policy*, **6** (3), September, 376–98.

Jordana, J., D. Levi-Faur and I. Puig (2005), 'The limits of Europeanization: regulatory reforms in the Spanish and Portuguese telecommunications and electricity sectors', *European Integration online Papers (EIOP)*, **9** (10), accessed 18 November 2010 at http://eiop.or.at/eiop/texte/2005–010a.htm.

Knill, C. and A. Lenschow (2005), 'Compliance, competition, and communication: different approaches of European governance and their impact on national institutions', *Journal of Common Market Studies*, **43** (3), 583–606.

Lavenex, S. and F. Schimmelfennig (2009), 'EU rules beyond EU borders: theorizing external governance in European politics', *Journal of European Public Policy*, **16** (6): 791–812.

Lavenex, Sandra and Adam Stulberg (2007), 'Connecting the neighborhood: energy and environment', in Weber, K., M.E. Smith and M. Baun (eds), *Governing Europe's New Neighborhood: Partners or Periphery*? Manchester: Manchester University Press, pp. 134–55.

Lenschow, A. (2002), 'Greening the European Union: an introduction', in A. Lenschow (ed.), *Environmental Policy Integration: Greening Sectoral Policies in Europe*, London: Earthscan Publications, pp. 3–21.

Levi-Faur, D. (2002), 'On the "net impact" of Europeanization: the EU's telecoms and electricity regimes between the global and the national', *European Integration online Papers (EIOP)*, **6** (7), accessed 18 November 2010 at http://eiop.or.at/eiop/texte/2002–007a.htm.

Lucas, N.J.D. (1977), *Energy and the European Communities*, London: Europa.

Matláry, J. (1997), *Energy Policy in the European Union*, New York: St Martin's Press.

McGowan, F. (2008), 'Can the European Union's market liberalism ensure energy security in a time of economic nationalism?', *Journal of Contemporary European Research*, **4** (2), 90–106.

Müller-Kraenner, S. (2010), 'The external relations of the EU in energy policy', *European Community for Renewable Energy (ERENE)*, issue paper 6.

Natorski, M. and A. Herranz-Surrallés (2008) 'Securitizing moves to nowhere? The framing of the European Union's energy policy', *Journal of Contemporary European Research*, **4** (2), 71–89.

Oberthür, S. and M. Pallemaerts (2010), 'The EU's internal and external climate policies: an historical overview', in S. Oberthür and M. Pallemaerts (eds), *The New Climate Policies of the European Union: Internal Legislation and Climate Diplomacy*, Brussels: VUB Press.

Oettinger, G. (2010a), 'Energy challenges of the next ten years: the need for a European common policy', speech at the Stakeholder Conference on Preparation of Energy Strategy 2011–2020, Brussels, 30 September, accessed 18 November at http://europa.eu/rapid/pressReleasesAction.do?reference=SPEECH/10/504.

Oettinger, G. (2010b), 'Europeanization of energy policy', speech of Commissioner Oettinger at the Dinner Debate with the European Energy Forum, Strasbourg, 19 October, accessed 18 November at http://europa.eu/rapid/ pressReleasesAction. do?reference=SPEECH/10/573&format=HTML&aged=0&language=EN.

Owens, S. and C.W. Hope (1989), 'Energy and environment: the challenge of integrating European policies', *Energy Policy*, **17** (2), 97–102.

Piebalgs, A. (2009), 'How the European Union is preparing the third industrial revolution with an innovative energy policy', *EUI Working Papers*, RSCAS 2009/11.

Pollack, M. (1994), 'Creeping competence: the expanding agenda of the European Community', *Journal of Public Policy*, **14** (2), 95–145.

Radaelli, C.M. (2000), 'Whiter Europeanization? Concept stretching and substantive change', *European Integration online Papers (EIOP)*, **4** (8), accessed 18 November 2010 at http://eiop.or.at/eiop/texte/2000–008a.htm.

Skjaerseth, J. (1994), 'The climate policy of the EC: too hot to handle', *Journal of Common Market Studies*, **32**, (1), 25–42.

Solorio Sandoval, I. (2009), 'La construccion de la política energética europea desde el area medioambiental', in F. Morata (ed.), *La Energía del siglo XXI: perspectivas europeas y tendencias globales*, Barcelona: Institut Universitari d'Estudis Europeus, pp. 99–118.

Solorio Sandoval, I. (2011) 'Bridging the gap between environmental policy integration and the EU's energy policy: mapping out the "Green Europeanisation" of energy governance', *Journal of Contemporary European Research*, **7** (3), 396–415.

Twidell, John and Robert Brice (1992), 'Strategies for implementing renewable energy: lessons from Europe', *Energy Policy*, **12** (5), 464–79.

Umbach, F. (2010) 'Global energy security and the implications for the EU', *Energy Policy*, **38** (3), 1229–40.

Vink, M. and P. Graziano (2007), 'Challenges of a new research agenda', in P. Graziano, and V.M. Vink (eds), *Europeanization: New Research Agendas*, New York: Palgrave Macmillan, pp. 3–20.

Wurzel R.K.W. and J. Connelly (eds.) (2011), *The European Union as a Leader in International Climate Change Politics*, New York: Routledge.

Zapater, E. (2009), 'La seguridad energética de la Unión Europea en el contexto de la nueva política energética y el tratado de Lisboa', in F. Morata (ed.), *La Energía del siglo XXI: perspectivas europeas y tendencias globales*, Barcelona: Institut Universitari d'Estudis Europeus, pp. 49–79.

PART I

The internal dimension of the European energy
policy

2. A 'coordinated' European energy policy? The integration of EU energy and climate change policies

Camilla Adelle, Duncan Russel and Marc Pallemaerts[1]

2.1 INTRODUCTION

Energy production and consumption as practiced by Europeans has enormous environmental impacts. Energy-related emissions pollute air, water and soil, and pose risks to human health and biodiversity. However, it is the relationship between energy and climate change that mainly commands political and scientific attention. Recognizing the importance of climate change, the European Union (EU) has positioned itself as a global champion against climate change, backed up with substantive internal policy (see Chapter 1 by Solorio Sandoval and Morata; Chapter 6 by Solorio Sandoval and Zapater). However, producing policy to mitigate climate change is no easy task. Mitigating climate change requires a complex combination of improving energy efficiency, switching to less carbon-intensive fossil fuels and carbon-free energy sources and carbon capture and storage (CCS) – at least in the medium term (see Chapter 5 by Fischer for further information on CCS policies). Moreover the root causes of climate change are embedded across a number of sectors (for example energy, transport, industry, housing and agriculture) and associated actors each with differing priorities and interests (on climate change and other issues). Given the complex cross-sector nature of the climate problem there is a compelling case for climate and energy policy to be coordinated to produce a coherent EU approach.

One proposed strategy for following a more coordinated approach to environmental issues such as climate change is environmental policy integration (EPI) (Jordan and Lenschow, 2008, 2010; see also Chapter 1 by Solorio Sandoval and Morata, Chapter 3 by Knudsen). The EU has a longstanding interest in EPI to better mainstream environmental issues into its sectoral policymaking (Jordan et al., 2008). With the signing of the Amsterdam Treaty in 1997 the legal status of the principle of EPI was augmented, bringing pressure on heads of state and governments to put this clause into practice (Lenschow, 2002). However, the EU's efforts at implementing EPI have been viewed as largely ineffective, with little systematic integration of environmental issues into its sectoral policy-making (Jordan et al., 2008). Given, on the one hand, these difficulties over implementing EPI and, on the other, the emergence of the European energy policy, what are the prospects for better integration of EU energy and climate change policies?

The issue of integrating energy and environmental policies has been on the European political agenda since the 1980s. However, the first real attempts at 'greening' EU energy policy were not made until the 1990s. The initial, results were disappointing (even when facilitating the 'green Europeanization' of energy policy; see Chapter 1 by Solorio Sandoval and Morata, Chapter 6 by Solorio Sandoval and Zapater) Measures on renewable energy sources (RES) and energy efficiency had little impact, while more significant decisions in terms of energy policy were connected to liberalizing the EU energy market with little consideration given to the environment (Collier, 2002). On the back of heightened concerns about climate change and fears over energy security, the EU has more recently endeavored to better link climate change and energy. Consequently, in March 2007 heads of state and governments agreed to a set of legally binding climate and energy targets (see Chapter 1 by Solorio Sandoval and Morata). These are to, by 2020, reduce greenhouse gas (GHG) emissions by 20 percent, increase the proportion of RES in the energy mix to 20 percent and to increase the use of liquid fuels in transport energy to 10 percent.[2] Political agreement on the so-called 'Climate and Energy Package' was then reached in December 2008. Implementation of these new policies is still at an early stage, but already it is recognized that many member states will find it difficult to meet the targets (IEEP, 2009). Moreover, it is becoming increasingly clear that the 20 percent cut in GHG emissions is not enough to stabilize global temperatures at $2\,°C$ above pre-industrial levels, the EU's ultimate climate goal. Therefore, the extent to which energy and climate policy are adequately coordinated is still questionable despite the Climate and Energy Package.

In the framework of the emergent European energy policy, this chapter explores the integration of the EU's climate and energy policies. Section 2.2 briefly sets out the EPI concept and draws the European Environment Agency (EEA) framework as a means to evaluate EPI. Section 2.3 sets out the EU's efforts to integrate climate change and energy policy across different categories of processes in the EEA framework, namely: drivers, pressures and changes; political commitments; administrative culture and practices; assessment and consultation; policy instruments; and monitoring and learning. Section 2.4 reflects on both the strengths and weaknesses of the EU's approach to integrate these two policy areas. In conclusion, Section 2.5 focuses on the usefulness of the evaluation framework as well as the prospects for future integration.

2.2 EPI AND ITS EVALUATION

Prior to the publication of the Brundtland Report (WCED, 1987), environmental policy's goal was regulating end-of-pipe emissions of pollutants (Lenschow, 2002, pp. 4–5; Hertin and Berkout, 2003, pp. 41–4). As the concept of sustainable development (SD) gained momentum in the late 1980s and early 1990s, the regulatory approach began to 'face a legitimacy crisis, as it seemed to impose high costs on the economic actors without producing the desired environmental improvements' (Lenschow, 2002, p. 21). Moreover, there was 'a fundamental recognition that the environmental sector alone will not be able to secure environmental objectives and that each sector must take on board environmental policy objectives' (Lafferty and Hovden, 2003, p. 1). EPI has been advocated as a strategy to achieve a shift in governance so that the environment is placed at the heart of policy-making in non-environmental sectors (Jordan and Lenschow, 2008, 2010).

While EPI has become a more mainstream political concept employed by many political systems, there is still a lack of clarity over its precise meaning (Jordan and Lenschow, 2008). Researchers such as Lafferty and Hovden (2003) have argued that the concept entails giving principled preference to environmental protection during sectoral policy-making (see Chapter 3 by Knudsen). Contrary to this, others – for example the EEA (2005), Collier (1994) and to some extent Lenschow (2002) – suggest EPI is more of an exercise for balancing trade-offs between the environmental, social and economic pillars of SD so that environmental protection is given due consideration in policy processes but not principled priority.

Some authors have focused on EPI as a process to encourage communication and learning between different actors across different policy sectors (for example Lenschow, 2002; Nilsson and Persson, 2003; Jordan and Lenschow, 2008; Russel and Jordan, 2009). With a focus on processes, emphasis is placed on the development and performance of various communicative, procedural and organizational instruments. Studies employing this approach tend to be less concerned with policy outcomes (that is whether a policy is more or less sustainable) and more with how well these various instruments have performed to make sectoral policymakers give due consideration to environmental impacts (see Jordan and Lenschow, 2008). For the purpose of this chapter, the focus is on the European Commission's EPI strategies in relation to climate and energy policy, not on how integrated or sustainable final policy outcomes are (that is we are concerned with the process of integration). The reasons for this are twofold. First, focusing on the final policy output (that is whether or not climate and energy policy are more or less integrated) would be difficult because of the counterfactual of whether or not policy outcome would have occurred in the absence of an official EPI strategy.

Second, defining and rating the level of integration in final policy outcome would be highly subjective.

Having established that this chapter focuses on the process of EPI, the obvious question is how to analyze the process. In the existing literature, there are a number of attempts to construct frameworks for the analysis of EPI. Lafferty and Hovden (2003) suggest that analysis should be based around horizontal and vertical aspects of EPI (see also Chapter 3 by Knudsen). By horizontal they imply analyzing cross-cutting support for EPI across a political system, including the level of authority the concept has, how conflicts between objectives and sectors are managed, and how the importance of EPI concept is communicated across sectors. By vertical EPI they imply focusing on the analysis of how particular government sectors have sought to implement environmental objectives as part of their core activities. While this framing offers insights into different dimensions of integration it does not suggest ways in which to assess whether EPI processes have been effectively implemented. Nilsson and Persson (2003) devised a framework focusing on policy-making rules and assessment processes alongside background factors such as problem characteristics and the international policy context to define whether EPI is weaker or stronger in character. Their approach provides a strong analytical base for studying EPI; but for our purposes the framework is too narrow, as we wish to focus on a wider set of processes than policy-making rules and assessment to fully cover the breadth of the European Commission's strategy for integrating energy and climate policy (that is EPI in the European energy policy).

This chapter uses the evaluation framework proposed by the EEA (2005). The framework consists of six broad areas that can be evaluated from a cross-sector (that is horizontal) and sectoral perspective (that is vertical) (see Table 2.1). The value of the EEA's framework is that it encompasses a broad spectrum of EPI processes and allows us to evaluate EPI on a cross-sectoral, sectoral and process-by-process basis. Thus, rather than by a broad-brush approach to evaluate whether EPI is or is not occurring, it should be possible to produce a more nuanced evaluation which identifies those parts of the processes where EPI is quite strong and others where it is weaker.

2.3   PROGRESS ON INTEGRATION

This section examines the EU's efforts to integrate climate change and energy policy in the six categories of the EEA's evaluation framework in turn. The findings are summarized below in Table 2.2.

Table 2.1   A checklist for evaluating sectoral and cross-sectoral EPI

Context for EPI	Cross-sectoral	Sector-specific
1. Trends in drivers, pressures, changes in state of the environment, impacts	1a. What are the main economic and social driving factors facing the administration? 1b. What are the magnitude and trends of socioeconomic impacts? 1c. Is society becoming more eco-efficient, i.e. decoupling its economic activities and outputs from environmental pressures and impacts? 1d. Is progress being made towards key overarching SD/environmental targets and objectives?	1a. What are the trends in the sector's main economic and social driving factors? 1b. What is the magnitude and trend of the sector's socioeconomic impacts? 1c. Is the sector becoming more eco-efficient, i.e. decoupling its economic activities and outputs from environmental pressures and impacts? 1d. Is the sector contributing appropriately to key overarching SD/environmental targets and objectives?

EPI categories	Cross-sectoral	Sector-specific
2. Political commitments and strategic vision	2a. Is there a high-level (i.e. constitutional/ legal) requirement for EPI in general? 2b. Is there an overarching EPI or sustainable development strategy, endorsed and reviewed by the prime minister or president? 2c. Is there political leadership for EPI and/or sustainable development?	2a. Are there high-level i.e. constitutional/ legal requirements for EPI in the sector? 2b. Is the sector included in an overarching strategy for EPI and/or for sustainable development? 2c. Does the sector have its own EPI or sustainable development strategy? 2d. Is there political leadership for EPI in the sector?
3. Administrative culture and practices	3a. Do the administration's regular planning, budgetary and audit exercises reflect EPI priorities? 3b. Are environmental responsibilities reflected in the administration's internal management regime?	3a. Does the sector administration's mission statement reflect environmental values? 3b. Are environmental responsibilities reflected in the sector administration's internal management regime?

Table 2.1 Continued

	Cross-sectoral	Sector-specific
	3c. Is there strategic department/unit/committee in charge of coordinating and guiding EPI across sectors? 3d. Are there mechanisms for cooperation with higher or lower levels of governance?	3c. Are there cooperation mechanisms between the sector and environmental authorities? 3d. Are there mechanisms for cooperation with higher or lower levels of governance?
EPI categories	**Cross-sectoral**	**Sector-specific**
4. Assessments and consultation to underpin policy design and decisions	4a. Does the sector have a process for *ex-ante* environmental assessment of its proposed policies or programmes? 4b. Are environmental authorities and stakeholders engaged in mechanisms for consultation and participation in the sector's policy-making process? 4c. Is environmental information available for and used to inform policy-making?	4a. Does the sector have a process for *ex-ante* environmental assessment of its proposed policies or programmes? 4b. Are environmental authorities and stakeholders engaged in mechanisms for consultation and participation in the sector's policy-making process? 4c. Is environmental information available for used to inform policy-making?
EPI categories	**Cross-sectoral**	**Sector-specific**
5. Use of policy instruments to deliver EPI	5a. Do market-based mechanisms support environmental objectives (e.g. by removing damaging subsidies or introducing measures to 'get the prices right')? 5b. Is spatial planning used to integrate sectoral and environmental issues?	5a. Do the sector's financial assistance programmes support environmental objectives (e.g. by introducing positive incentives or removing damaging subsidies)? 5b. Are other market-based instruments (e.g. taxes and emissions trading) used to internalize external environmental costs?

	Cross-sectoral	Sector-specific
	5c. Are environmental management instruments used for EPI e.g. EMAS, EIS, SEA, Eco-labeling, access to information/participation/justice? 5d. Are other instruments used to promote EPI?	5c. Are there technical or other standards to promote environmental objectives in the sector? 5d. Are other instruments used to promote EPI?
EPI categories	**Cross-sectoral**	**Sector-specific**
6. Monitoring and learning from experience	6a. Is progress towards sectoral and cross-sectoral EPI objectives and targets regularly monitored? 6b. Is there a systematic evaluation of the effectiveness of the policies that have been put in place? 6c. Are there mechanisms for exchanging good practices?	6a. Is the sector's progress towards its EPI objectives and targets regularly monitored? 6b. Is there a systematic evaluation of the effectiveness of the policies that have been put in place? 6c. Are there mechanisms for exchanging good practice?

Source: EEA (2005).

2.3.1 Drivers, Pressures, Changes

A number of policy drivers have created a favorable context for the integration of climate and energy policies in the past decade, creating synergies and propelling climate change and energy issues up the political agenda. This has provided a boost for the integration of climate change issues across all sectors of EU policy-making, including energy policy since energy is one of the biggest GHG-producing sectors. As mentioned in Chapter 1, this increased pressure for integration has been driven by a number of factors: First, the high-profile international processes such as the United Nations Framework Convention on Climate Change (UNFCCC), the related Kyoto Protocol (and its potential successor) and the Intergovernmental Panel on Climate Change have helped to raise the climate agenda into the arena of high politics both internationally and at an EU-level. Second, the imperative for the EU level action (both internationally and domestically) in climate change has been given a boast by the EU's legitimacy crisis in the wake of the rejection of the constitutional treaty in 2005. Climate change appeared to provide a useful narrative to convince public opinion of the need to continue the process of European integration (Oberthur and Pallemaerts, 2010), and this was supported by surveys of public opinion of EU citizens, which have shown increasing support for climate change policy (European Commission, 2008a).[3] Finally, on the back of the EU's Lisbon Agenda for Growth and Jobs and its focus on innovation, the EU has framed the climate problem as an opportunity for Europe to become a leader in low-carbon technologies (for example European Commission, 2010, p. 15).

There have also been significant non-climate challenges within the energy sector in the last two decades). Oil prices have risen and become volatile, the EU dependence on imported energy supplies has increased and there have been political disruptions of supplies (such as between Russia and the Ukraine in 2006 and again in 2009). Therefore, member states have begun to overcome their longstanding reluctance to delegate powers over energy matters to the EU (Pallemaerts, 2008). A political consensus has emerged in recent years to establish a stronger role for the EU in energy policy leading to the inclusion of an energy title in the Lisbon Treaty which came into force in December 2009 (see Chapter 1 by Solorio Sandoval and Morata).

The focus on energy policy, and specifically energy security issues, not only raises the profile of energy policy but also serves to emphasize the synergies between energy and climate change (for a perspective on the relationship between energy and climate change, see Chapter 8 by Herranz-Surrallés and Natorski). Heavy reliance on fossil fuels contributes to climate change and increases European dependency upon a handful of suppliers, many of which are volatile politically or economically. Accordingly, energy security and

Table 2.2 Summary evaluation of sectoral and cross-sectoral EPI aActivities in the energy sector

Context for EPI	Cross-sectoral	Sector-specific
1. Trends in drivers, pressures, changes in the state of the environment, impacts	– The high-profile international climate change agenda and the EU's leadership aspirations in this. – The EU's legitimacy crisis in the wake of the rejection of the constitutional treaty in 2005. – Increasing scientific evidence supporting the case for climate change and action seen as imperative. – Increasing public support for EU climate change policy. – Synergies between climate change policies and the EU's Lisbon Agenda for Growth and Jobs.	– Increased concern over energy security due to energy price volatility; high prices; political stoppages of energy supplies affecting some member states. – Formal (limited) powers given to the EU on energy policy in the Lisbon Treaty. – Synergies between energy security issues and climate change policy.

EPI categories	Cross-sectoral	Sector-specific
2. Political commitment and strategic vision	– Article 11 implicitly includes the integration of climate change into energy policy but no such specific sectoral legal commitment reinforces this. – The integration of energy and climate policy was explicitly included in the Cardiff Process but the results were disappointing. – The integration of climate change into energy policy is included in the SDS but the impact of this has been 'hardly discernible'.	– The EU's international leadership role on climate change has been increasingly supported by high-level political commitment for internal action leading. – Important sector-specific energy strategies (e.g. the Energy Green Papers in 2000 and 2006) have included environmental objectives (including climate change) as one of the three objectives of EU energy policy. – The creation of a new Climate Action DG could increase the profile of climate change but may not necessarily result in better integration, especially since it was not amalgamated with the Energy DG as originally proposed.

Table 2.2   Continued

EPI categories	Cross-sectoral	Sector-specific
3. Administrative culture and practices	– The Cardiff Process failed to embed in the practices of the Council formations.	

EPI categories	Cross-sectoral	Sector-specific
4. Assessments and consultation to underpin policy design and decisions	– Impact assessment has been established in the day-to-day activities of the Commission. However, this does not necessarily lead to the integration of environmental issues into sectoral policies in practice. – The Commission follows 'minimum standards of consultation'. However, imbalances of stakeholder engagement are still reported.	– Modelling employed in the IA for the 2007 Climate and Energy package led to the 'tweaking' of a pre-determined broad policy position, rather than driving policy development. – Privileged access to the Commission outside the consultation process was evident in the 2007 Climate and Energy Package.

EPI categories	Cross-sectoral	Sector-specific
5. Use of policy instruments to deliver EPI	– A number of horizontal environmental policy instruments aimed at implementing EPI could potentially contribute to the integration of climate change and energy policy. These include the EU's Eco-Management and Audit Scheme as well as its Eco-Label initiative. However, these schemes are currently limited in their effectiveness due to their low take-up by EU businesses and industries.	– The Emissions Trading Scheme, the EU's flagship policy instrument to tackle GHGs emissions in the energy sector, has had teething problems but some of these have been resolved in recent revision. – Traditional command-and-control instruments have been widely used but not yet very effectively. Recent revisions of these as part of the Climate and Energy Package will be critical.

EPI categories	Cross-sectoral	Sector-specific
6. Monitoring and learning from experience	– Neither the Cardiff Process nor the Sustainable Development Strategy provided a satisfactory monitoring and review system.	– The failure of the Commission's early proposed carbon tax has been a weakness in the EU's policy tool kit which has only partly been resolved with the ETS. – Voluntary Agreements have been widely used by the Commission but the effectiveness of these instruments has been questioned. – Evidence of lesson learning in the sectoral policy instruments to effect climate change integration into energy policy.

Source: Authors.

climate change linkages have been emphasized in a number of Commission documents such as the European Commission's 2006 Green Paper *A European Strategy for Sustainable, Competitive and Secure Energy* (European Commission, 2006) and more recently in the Commission's energy strategy *Energy 2020 – A Strategy for Competitive Sustainable and Secure Energy* (European Commission, 2010; see also Chapter 9 by Ciambra).

2.3.2 Political Commitment

Political commitment, strategic vision and leadership towards EPI can be expressed in different ways, such as a legal requirement for EPI and high-level integration strategies (EEA, 2005). While there is no specific legal requirement in the EU Treaties for climate change issues to be integrated into energy policy, the EU is legally committed to EPI more generally in all its policy sectors, through art. 11 of the Treaty on the Functioning of the European Union (TFEU) (ex-art. 6). Article 11 thus includes (though not explicitly) the integration of climate change into energy policy.

The integration of energy and climate policy was explicitly included however in two of the EU's high-level environmental strategies: the Cardiff Process launched in 1998, and the EU's Sustainable Development Strategy (SDS) originally proposed by the Commission in 2001. The Cardiff Process initiative required the Council of Ministers (including the Energy Council) to develop strategies to give effect to 'environmental integration and sustainable development' in their sector. The Energy Council was in the first wave of strategy development to put the Cardiff Process into action (see Chapter 1 by Solorio and Morata). However, the results were rather disappointing and the Energy Strategy did not contain any concrete supplementary plans or targets beyond what was already in progress (Fergusson et al., 2001). The original SDS included the headline objective of meeting the EU's Kyoto commitment to further reduce GHG emissions by an average of 1 percent per year from 1990 levels up to 2020 (European Commission, 2001a). The renewed SDS adopted in 2006 confirmed this objective and added that the average global temperature should not rise more than 2 °C compared with the pre-industrial level (Council of the European Union, 2006). However, measures put forward in the SDS either were also existing policy initiatives (for example the Emissions Trading Scheme which was first proposed in 2000) or else when developed did not mention the SDS as a background motivation at all (for example the Directives on eco-design and energy performance in buildings) (Pallemaerts et al., 2007).

The changes in pressures and drivers described above have also created a favorable context for an increased political commitment to integrate *climate change* considerations more specifically across all EU policy sectors and especially the energy sector (see Chapter 3 by Knudsen for the RES case). In particular, the EU has had to underpin its international leadership role with domestic action (Jordan et al., 2010). Much of this action has focused on the energy sector. In 1992 during the negotiations on the UNFCCC in Rio, the EU argued (unsuccessfully) that all industrialized countries should sign up to a commitment to stabilize CO_2 emissions at 1990s levels by 2000. The EU's Environment and Energy Councils had agreed to this very target in October 1990 in response to the Intergovernmental Panel on Climate Change's First Assessment report. Shortly afterwards the Commission published its early Communication, *A Community Strategy to Limit Carbon Dioxide Emissions and Improve Energy Efficiency* (European Commission, 1992), in which it proposed an EU carbon tax (see below).

When the Commission published its original proposals for the targets in the Climate and Energy Package in January 2007 (see above) it claimed that they were to demonstrate the EU's 'commitment to leadership and a long-term vision for a new Energy Policy for Europe that responds to climate change' (European Commission, 2007, p. 1). The importance of the targets, and of Europe having a clear unified position, was reiterated repeatedly in terms of bolstering Europe's international leadership in the run-up to negotiations to replace the Kyoto Protocol in Copenhagen. The swift political agreement by heads of state and governments and the European Parliament on the 'Climate Action and Energy Package' (11 months from when it was published in January 2008) illustrates the high level of political commitment.[4]

Finally, the increased political importance of climate change is demonstrated by the Commission's decision in December 2008 to establish a new DG for energy as well as the creation of a DG Climate Action in November 2009. However, whether the Commission's eventual failure to create a 'super' energy-and-climate DG, after heavily speculation that it would do so, was a missed opportunity or a close shave for policy integration remains to be seen (for example ENDS Report, 2009; ENDS Daily, 2009a; ENDS Daily, 2009b).

This high-level political commitment to climate change, especially in relation to energy policy, has led to implications for important sector-specific strategies and activities (in contrast to the lack of progress achieved through horizontal strategies such the Cardiff Process and the SDS). For example, the Commission's 2006 Green Paper, *A European Strategy for Sustainable, Competitive and Secure Energy* (European Commission, 2006), put forward sustainability as one of the three priorities for a potential EU energy policy (in addition to energy security and competitiveness) as part of a 'new energy landscape for the twenty-first century'. This led eventually to the Commission unveiling the 'package' of energy and climate change policy proposals in January 2007, thereby formally underlining the link between these two policy fields. Moreover, one of the latest energy strategy publications in 2010 *Energy,*

2020 – A Strategy for Competitive Sustainable and Secure Energy, goes even further, stating that energy efficiency is 'one of the [EU's] central objectives for 2020 as well as a key factor in achieving our long-term energy and climate goals' (European Commission, 2010, p. 6).

2.3.3   Administrative Culture and Practices

Given that integrating energy and climate policy suggests that policy-making needs to be conducted in a more coordinated manner, there is an implication that administrative culture and practices may need to change (EEA, 2005). The cross-sector Cardiff Process should have provided an important strategic framework to encourage these changes. However, this process did not become sufficiently embedded in the cultural and administrative practices of the EU institutions, owing mainly to lack of leadership from either the Environment Council or the DG Environment (Jordan et al., 2008).

By contrast, the Commission's Impact Assessment (IA) procedure has become firmly embedded in the bureaucratic procedures of the Commission since it was first established across all Directorates-General in 2003. The intention of the IAs is to improve the quality of policy-making through analyzing the potential impacts of a policy proposal and adjusting policy accordingly. Thus every major Commission proposal (including those in the energy sector) now has such an assessment carried out coordinated by the responsible desk officer. While earlier attempts to embed environmental policy impact assessments (the Green Star Assessments) did not lead to any serious action by Commission services beyond DG Environment, this later IA procedure received strong political support within the Commission on the basis of its Better Regulation remit. However, this procedure has not necessarily led to the better integration of environmental considerations into sectoral policies, including those in the energy sector (see below for more detail).

2.3.4   Assessment and Consultation

According to the EEA (2005), ex-ante environmental assessments and consultation mechanisms are the most obvious examples of mechanisms in this category. As mentioned above, an IA process has now been well established within the Commission's policy formulation and development processes. Information produced by IAs (both in the analysis and through consultation) is intended to serve as a point of communication and ultimately coordination between policy-makers from different sectors. Early IAs conducted by the Commission were fraught with difficulties, including weak analysis and the fact that they were used to justify predetermined policy rather than for policy development (Wilkinson et al., 2004). While the Commission seems to have improved the way it conducts its IA, particularly with regard to the robustness of the analysis, recent evaluations suggest that the process is still conducted too late in the policy process to help with policy development and that environmental concerns such as climate change tend to be crowded out by economic issues (Turnpenny et al., 2008).

Looking specifically at IAs related to the development of the Climate and Energy Package, Russel et al. (2008) observe that the setting of targets for the Climate and Energy Package appeared to be driven by systematic modeling processes within the IA. However, much of the influence of the modeling concerned tweaking the predetermined broad policy position, rather than systematically driving policy development. The importance of analysis was seen by some in the Commission to lie more in 'defending the policy' in negotiations with other DGs, member states, stakeholders and within the Council of Ministers (ibid.). Where the integration of environmental issues was considered, links to the wider sectors and high-level policy objectives (for example SD) were evident but in an ad hoc manner.

Consultation is a formalized part of the EU policy-making processes and is now part of the IA process. It is done primarily in the form of an official public consultation where the public and stakeholders can send in written responses to Commission proposals. Generally, consultation in the Commission has been observed to be fairly transparent and broad in accordance with the Commission's *Minimum Standards of Consultation* (European Commission, 2002). However, as Turnpenny et al. (2008) observe, some groups have tended to have privileged access to Commission policymakers outside the official consultation process. A similar pattern has been observed with the development of the Commission's 2007 Climate and Energy Package. In addition to formal official consultations, there were a number of other forms of stakeholder engagement, including four stakeholder forums established by DG Transport and Energy to discuss future energy policy (but not necessarily climate change), more informal discussions with selected stakeholders, and discussions with member states. In the main, official consultation processes included a wide variety of actors from many parts of society. Other types of stakeholder engagement appeared to be more exclusive. For example, the aforementioned stakeholder forums on energy policy were distinctly under-represented in terms of scientists and non-governmental organizations (Vasileiadou, 2008, pp. 88–100). Moreover, informal dialogue also occurred with selected industry representatives and trade associations (Russel et al., 2009). While stakeholder input was broadly regarded to have some policy impact, it was mainly concerned with consultation on predetermined policy directions rather than with deliberation and reflection (ibid.).

2.3.5 Policy Instruments

The Commission's first choice of instrument to tackle climate change was an EU carbon tax, proposed in 1992. However, this failed to gain support from member states and was eventually withdrawn in 2002. This setback left the Commission searching for other instruments to intervene in the energy sector. The more acceptable solution was found in the EU Emissions Trading Scheme (ETS), proposed in October 2001 (European Commission, 2001b) and adopted in 2003 (Directive 2003/87/EC). After teething problems in the first 'learning-by-doing' trading period 2005–07, most notably the crash of the carbon price after the over-allocation of allowances, the ETS Directive was revised as part of the 2008 Climate and Renewable Energy Package to give the Commission greater control over carbon allocation.[5]

The 'command and control' type approach to climate change mitigation (as opposed to market-based instruments for instance) is evident in that the binding and non-binding targets have also been operated at the EU level traditional legislation, albeit with the use of more flexible Directives (at least in how they are effected) rather than Regulations.[6] The most obvious examples are the burden-sharing agreements drawn up to coordinate the contribution of each member state to the EU's overall climate targets. The first such Burden Sharing Agreement was made in 1998 to help the EU reach its 8 percent reduction under Kyoto (see above). More recently, the Climate and Renewable Energy Package contained the Decision on Effort Sharing (406/2009/EC) which stipulated binding individual GHG reduction targets for member states in non-ETS sectors. Together with the ETS, these measures are intended to facilitate the EU's efforts to reach its 20 percent GHG reduction target by 2020.

The EU has also used a traditional regulatory approach, in the form of Directives, to encourage member states to increase the share of RES (including biofuels) in their energy mix (see Chapter 3 by Knudsen). Furthermore, non-binding targets set out in earlier Directives, such as the RES Directive (2001/77/EC) and a Directive on the promotion of biofuels (2003/30/EC), have been replaced with more ambitious binding targets, despite the original targets not having been met. In this way, the RES Directive (2009/28/EC) adopted as part of the Climate and Renewable Energy package contains a binding target of 20 percent for the RES' share of energy consumption in the EU by 2020 as well as a 10 percent binding target for the use of biofuels for transport fuels.

Binding quantitative targets have not yet been applied so vigorously in the field of energy efficiency. Legislation in the area (for example the energy performance in buildings Directive 2002/91/EC and eco-design requirements for energy-using products and Directive 2006/32/EC) has tended to be rather specific and has not always kept up with technological developments. Most significantly, the Climate and Renewable Energy Package only contained a non-binding 20 percent energy efficiency target in contrast to the binding targets for GHG reductions, RES and biofuels. According to Henningsen (2008, p. 24), 'the current Commission has not performed well on energy efficiency' and no longer seems to be the priority it was. The Commission has subsequently published a bundle of proposals designed to better implement EU energy efficiency commitments in November 2008, but this did not reinforce the 20 percent energy efficiency target by making it binding.

Voluntary Agreements (VAs) have also been widely used to integrate climate change into the EU's use of energy. However, these have mainly been used for specific and relatively small-scale initiatives, especially in energy efficiency – for example the GreenLight Programme (for non-residential electricity consumers to install energy-efficient lighting technologies). While some of these VAs at the EU level are considered successful by the Commission, in many cases it is too early to tell if any significant emissions savings will be made. However, a recent review of VAs to tackle climate change warned against an over-reliance on VAs because of their limited effect on emission reductions compared with mandatory regulation or economic instruments (ADAM, 2008). In particular, questions on the effectiveness of VAs have been raised after the failure of the European Automobile Manufacturers' Association Voluntary Agreement to deliver to carbon dioxide targets by car companies that eventually led to a more traditional legislative approach in the form of the controversial passenger cars and CO_2 Directive (443/2009/EC) (Farmer, 2011).

2.3.6 Monitoring and Learning

Monitoring and learning are essential parts of EPI. Monitoring and learning can generate information on how integration structures and processes are performing, how resources are being allocated and how these efforts are being reflected in terms of policies and environmental impacts. The Cardiff Process was an important cross-sector mechanism aiming to promote learning across the nine sectors involved. However, the resulting strategies (including that for the energy sector) were regarded as one-off policy statements by the council formations, thus limiting their use for ongoing monitoring and learning.

Another potential platform for learning through systematic monitoring and review at the cross-sectoral level through the EU SDS has also been missed. A review of the EU SDS as part of the Lisbon process did include three environmental structural indicators, all of which relate to climate change issues either directly or indirectly (namely GHG emissions, energy intensity, and volume of transport). However, these indicators do not measure the *process* of integration of climate change into energy policy in the EU – only the *outcomes* of integration. While monitoring these outcomes is vitally important – especially GHG emissions when monitoring progress towards specific international and internal targets – these measures are blunt instruments in terms of learning how well policy integration is occurring.

On the other hand, the evolution of the numerous internal policy instruments demonstrates a degree of policy learning at the sectoral level on the effectiveness of specific policy instruments that have been put in place. For example, some of the changes to the ETS agreed in the 2008 Climate and Renewable Energy Package have attempted to rectify the over allocation of allowances seen in the first phase of the scheme. Similarly, the failed non-binding targets in the 2001 RES Directive have been replaced by the stricter and, most importantly, legally binding targets of the new RES Directive.

2.4   DISCUSSION

When reflecting on the progress on integration presented above we have found it useful to differentiate (as the EEA framework does) between those EPI (or climate change integration) activities which are cross-sectoral, such as the Cardiff Process and the SDS, and those EPI activities which are sector-specific, such as the 2006 Green Paper on Energy (European Commission, 2006) and the Climate and Renewable Energy Package. This approach helps to differentiate integration which may be occurring within the sector owing to cross-sector EPI measures and integration directly related to activities within the energy sector.

In general, while cross-sectoral EPI initiatives are potentially important for the integration of climate change into energy policy, they have failed to deliver significant results. For example, the Cardiff Process and the SDS resulted in important opportunities for progress in a number of the EPI categories evaluated in the framework: namely political commitment, administrative culture and practice, and monitoring and learning. However, while these two high-level initiatives illustrated political support for EPI, they did not indicate a high level or sustained level of *political leadership* for EPI. The Cardiff Process has been at the mercy of the interest (or lack of it) of successive EU Presidencies and the SDS has not enjoyed anything like the high level of interest shown towards the Lisbon Strategy for Growth and Jobs. In the absence of this political leadership, these initiatives have not been sufficiently embedded or implemented at a sectoral level.

On the other hand, sector-specific initiatives appear to have been more successful in promoting the integration of climate and energy issues at the EU level. For example, climate change was one of the three policy objectives in the 2006 Energy Green Paper. The inclusion of climate change issues in this high-level energy strategy document marked the beginning of a 'new energy landscape' where the interdependence of environmental impacts of energy use was acknowledged and then acted upon in subsequent high-profile packages of targets and measures. Similarly, while the Cardiff Process and the SDS failed to result in any sustained political leadership for EPI in the energy sector, the political support for the integration of climate change issues across EU policy sectors has gathered strength in recent years. For example, heads of state and governments rather than energy and environment ministers agreed the March 2007 binding targets as well as the 2008 Climate and Energy Package. As our analysis shows, this high-level commitment has been promoted by the large number of internal and external drivers supporting climate change integration.

Sectoral policy instruments have also been the most prominent mechanisms within the EEA framework to contribute to the integration of climate and energy policies, at least in terms of the sheer number of policy instruments. A cross-spectrum of instruments has been used, as would be expected for EPI, which predicts a wide use of policy instruments and not just a reliance on traditional command-and-control regulation. The EU's flagship emissions reduction instrument in the sector is the ETS (a market-based instrument). While early teething problems have been evident, it is believed that it will deliver significant emission reductions in the future (EEA, 2009). However, there is still evidence of a strong reliance by the Commission on traditional, more hierarchical policy instruments; even market-based instruments, such as the ETS, have needed Directives or Regulations to lay down their rules and procedures. In addition, early attempts to encourage RES though non-binding targets for member states did not prove successful. It is also clear that many of the less-traditional instruments such as VAs have not had a significant impact. On the other hand, it appears that lessons have been learnt from the past two decades of policy instrument design and implementation. Revisions of important instruments such as the RES Directives and the ETS Directive in the Climate and Renewable Energy Package incorporated significant improvements in design. It remains to be seen however if these changes will lead to significant improvements in implementation.

There are, though, some remaining gaps in the progress in this category of the evaluation framework, that is policy instruments. For example, energy efficiency is now believed to be the weakest area of EU climate policy, and it is notable that this is the only remaining area where an EU-wide target (that is to increase energy efficiency by 20 percent) is non-binding (Henningsen, 2008). In addition, the Commission's choice of policy instruments is still limited by the requirement for unanimity in the Council in matters of a fiscal nature (that is an energy/carbon tax) and the preservation in the Lisbon Treaty of 'energy sovereignty' (that is the right to choice in energy sources) (art. 176a (3), TFEU).

2.5   CONCLUSIONS

The EEA's evaluation framework has helped us to compile an ordered and slightly nuanced picture of progress in the integration of climate change and energy issues within the framework of the European energy policy (that is an issue fundamental to European energy policy in the future, but until now one scarcely studied in depth). It has allowed us to see that any progress made is due mainly to sector-specific integration initiatives as well as the strong supporting context for integration. Generic EPI initiatives have contributed very little to this progress. Perhaps this finding should not be surprising when we consider what is already known about the numerous difficulties in implementing EPI (for example Lenschow 2002; Jordan and Lenschow, 2008). Indeed, in a state-of-the-art review of the EPI literature, Jordan and Lenschow (2010, p. 21) warn us that 'the sobering truth is that "learning" or a "change of awareness" seems to take place in response to political crises (for example, accelerating climate change) rather than the combined impact of different EPI instruments'.

The framework has also allowed us to identify a number of weak integration areas. For example, the EU's IA and consultation processes have not yet led to the embedding of integrated policy design and analysis in the sector. However, these mechanisms will offer significant opportunity in future if efforts are made to root the culture and objectives of their implementation in the administrative practices and processes of the energy sector. In addition, the framework has pointed to some strong areas of integration, such as political commitment and policy instruments, while also pointing to some gaps and trends within these categories. For example, the continued high reliance on traditional command-and-control policy instruments is not what would be anticipated for EPI. This suggests that while academics conceive of the climate change policy problem as one of policy integration, the EU may be reverting back to a more traditional regulatory approach to how it addresses the problem in practice.

By contrast, this framework does very little to explain why policy integration is occurring in each category of the framework. Other EPI evaluation frameworks may therefore be more useful if more theoretically underpinned explanations of integration are required. In addition, while focusing entirely on the process of integration can be illuminating, policy outcomes can also be revealing. For example, a report published by the EEA in 2009 concluded that all but one (Austria) of the EU-15 will meet their Kyoto Protocol targets for 2012 (EEA 2009). While this tells us nothing about how these targets will have been achieved, it does indicate that positive progress is being made. However, in the same report the EEA also claim that on the basis of current policies within member states the EU as a whole is only on target to reduce its GHG emissions by 14 percent of 1990 levels by 2020. Therefore, there is significantly further to go within member states in implementing the EU's current climate and energy targets within the framework of the emergent European energy policy.

NOTES

1. The authors would like to thank two anonymous referees for their comments on an earlier, though rather different, version of the ideas set out in this chapter.
2. This target was to be increased to a 30 percent reduction in GHG emission if a suitable agreement was reached with other industrialized countries as a result of the Copenhagen COP of the UNFCCC in December 2009. However, since such an international agreement has not been agreed and despite the support of a number of member states, the target remains at 20 percent.
3. However, public opinion appears to have become less favorable recently in the wake of the economic crisis (European Commission, 2009) and in light of media focus on the accuracy and legitimacy of climate science (*The Economist*, 2010).
4. In the end, however, the EU was apparently marginalized in the main discussions at Copenhagen in December 2009 and the most significant negotiations mainly took place between Brazil, China, India, South Africa and the US.
5. The resulting Directive was formally adopted in April 2009 as Directive 2009/29/EC.
6. A Regulation is directly applicable law in member states and is mostly used for rather precise purposes. A Directive is binding as to the results to be achieved, but leaves the member states the choice of form and methods (Farmer, 2011).

REFERENCES

ADAM (2008), *An Appraisal of EU Climate Policies: Deliverable for the Adaptation and Mitigation Strategies: Supporting European Climate Policy*, project co-funded by the European Commission within the Sixth Framework Programme (2002–2006), Amsterdam: IVM.

Collier, Ute (1994), *Energy and Environment in the European Union: The Challenge of Integration*, Aldershot: Avebury.

Collier, Ute (2002), 'EU energy policy in a changing climate,' in Andrea Lenschow (ed.), *Environmental Policy Integration, Greening Sectoral Policies in Europe*, London: Earthscan Publications.

Council of the European Union (2006), *Renewed EU Sustainable Development Strategy*, 10117/06, Brussels, 9 June.

ENDS Daily (2009a), 'MEPs alarmed by plans for new DG energy and climate,' 12 May.

ENDS Daily (2009b), 'Green groups fear weakening of DG environment,' 22 December.

ENDS Report (2009), 'Mandate of new EU Energy Department emerges,' 27 April.

European Commission (1992), *A Community Strategy to Limit Carbon Dioxide Emissions and Improve Energy Efficiency*, COM (92) 246, Brussels, 1 June.

European Commission (2001a), *A Sustainable Europe for a Better World: A*

European Union Strategy for Sustainable Development, COM(2001) 264, Brussels, 15 May.

European Commission (2001b), *Proposal for a Directive of the European Parliament and the Council Establishing a Framework for Greenhouse Gas Emissions Trading Within the European Community and Amending Council Directive 96/61/EC*, COM (2001) 581, Brussels, 23 October.

European Commission (2002), *Towards a Reinforced Culture of Consultation and Dialogue: General Principles and Minimum Standards for Consultation of Interested Parties by the Commission*, COM(2002) 704, Brussels, 11 December.

European Commission (2006), *Green Paper: A European Strategy for Sustainable, Competitive and Secure Energy*, COM(2006) 105, Brussels, 8 March.

European Commission (2007), 'Commission proposes an integrated energy and climate change package to cut emissions for the 21st century', European Commission press release IP/07/29, Brussels, 10/01/2007.

European Commission (2008a), *Attitudes of European Citizens Towards the Environment*, Eurobarometer special report, 295/Wave 68, Brussels, 2 March.

European Commission (2009), *European's Attitudes Towards Climate Change*, Eurobarometer special report, 313/Wave 71, Brussels, 1 July.

European Commission (2010), *Energy 2020: A Strategy for Competitive, Sustainable and Secure Energy*, COM(2010) 639. Brussels, 10 November.

European Environment Agency (EEA) (2005), 'Environmental policy integration in Europe', EEA technical report no. 2/2005, Copenhagen.

EEA (2009), 'Greenhouse gas emission trends and projections in Europe 2009: tracking progress towards Kyoto targets', EEA report no. 9/2009, Copenhagen.

Farmer, A. (ed.) (2011), *Manual of European Environmental Policy*, London: Taylor & Francis.

Fergusson, M., C. Coffey, D. Wilkinson and D. Baldock (2001), *The Effectiveness of Council of the European Union Integration Strategies and Options for Carrying Forward the Cardiff Process*, London: Institute for European Environmental Policy.

Haug, C. and A. Jordan (2010), 'Burden sharing: distributing burdens or burden sharing efforts?', in Andrew Jordan, Dave Huitema, Harro van Asselt, Tim Rayner and Frans Berkhout (eds), *Climate Change Policy in the European Union: Confronting the Dilemmas of Mitigation and Adaptation?*, Cambridge: Cambridge University Press, pp. 83–102.

Henningsen, J. (2008), 'EU energy and climate policy – two years on'. European Policy Centre issue paper **55**, September, Brussels.

Hertin, J., and Berkout F. (2003), 'Analysing institutional strategies for environmental policy integration: the case of EU enterprise policy', *Journal of Environmental Policy and Planning*, **5** (1), 39–56.

Institute for European Environmental Policy (IEEP) (2009), *Action Taken to Address Climate and Energy Issues Across EU Member States and Prospects for Implementation of the Climate and Renewable Energy Package: A Review for the European Climate Foundation*, London.

Jordan, A. and A. Lenschow (eds) (2008), *Innovation in Environmental Policy? Integrating the Environment for Sustainability*, Cheltenham, UK and Northampton, MA, USA: Edward Elgar Publishing.

Jordan, A., A. Schout and M. Unfried, (2008), 'The European Union', in A. Jordan (ed.), *Innovation in Environmental Policy? Integrating the Environment for Sustainability*, Cheltenham, UK and Northampton, MA, USA: Edward Elgar Publishing, pp. 159–79.

Jordan, A., and A. Lenschow (2010), 'Environmental policy integration: a state of the art review,' *Environmental Policy and Governance*, **20** (3) 147–58.

Jordan, A., D. Huitema, H. van Asselt, T. Rayner and F Berkhout (eds) (2010), *Climate Change Policy in the European Union: Confronting the Dilemmas of Mitigation and Adaptation?*, Manchester: Manchester University Press.

Lafferty, W.M. and E. Hovden (2003), 'Environmental policy integration: towards an analytical framework', *Environmental Politics*, **12** (3), 1–22.

Lenschow, A. (2002), 'New regulatory approaches in "greening" EU policies', *European Law Journal*, **8** (1), 19–37.

Nilsson, M. and A. Persson (2003), 'Framework for analysing environmental policy integration', *Journal of Environmental Policy and Planning*, **5** (4), 333–59.

Oberthür, S. and M. Pallemaerts (2010), 'The EU's internal and external climate change policies: a historical overview', in S. Oberthür and M. Pallemaerts (eds), *The New Climate Policies of the European Union*, Brussels: VUB, pp. 27–63.

Pallemaerts, M M Herodes and C. Adelle (2007), 'Does the EU sustainable development strategy contribute to environmental policy integration?', EPIGOV working paper no. 9, January.

Pallemaerts, M. (2008), 'Climate change, natural gas and the rebirth of EU energy policy', paper presented at Monash University EU Centre, 28 November, Prato, Italy.

Russel, D., A. Haxeltine, D. Huitema, M. Nilsson, J. Hinkle and T. Rayner (2008), 'Climate change appraisal in the EU: current trends and future challenges' in Mike Hulme and Henry Neufeldt (eds), *Making Climate Change Work for Us: European Perspectives on Adaptation and Mitigation Strategies*, Cambridge: Cambridge University Press, pp. 19–44.

The Economist (2010), 'Greener than thou: the politics of the environment', 13 February, pp. 32–3.

Turnpenny, J., M. Nilsson, D. Russel, A. Jordan, J. Hertin and B. Nykvist,(2008), 'Why is integrating policy assessment so hard? A comparative analysis of the institutional capacities and constraints', *Journal of Environmental Planning and Management*, **51**, 759–75.

Vasileiadou, E. (2008), 'Collaborative policy-making? Assessing stakeholder consultations in the European energy policy', ADAM Deliverable D1.2b; accessed at www.adamproject.eu.

Wilkinson, D., M. Fergusson, C. Bowyer, J. Brown, A. Ladefoged, C. Monkhouse and A. Zdanowicz (2004), *Sustainable Development in the European's Commission's Integrated Impact Assessments for 2003*, London: Institute for European Environmental Policy.

World Commission on Environment and Development (WCED) (1987), *Our Common Future*, Oxford: Oxford University Press.

3. Renewable energy and environmental policy integration: renewable fuel for the European energy policy?

Jørgen K. Knudsen

3.1 INTRODUCTION

The Brundtland Report in 1987 pointed to the need for amending the political–administrative systems within which sectoral policies, such as energy, are formulated and implemented, in order to achieve sustainable development (SD) (WCED, 1987, p. 313). Most crucially, the report pointed to the importance of a stronger integration of environmental concerns into sectoral decision-making (ibid.). This focus has been associated with the concept of 'environmental policy integration' (EPI). The EU is considered as a frontrunner in issues pertaining to EPI at a global level. In recent years, there has been an accelerated focus on climate change (see Chapter 2 by Adelle et al.). These developments are most clearly represented by the EU's Climate and Energy Package adopted in 2008, which establishes a triple-twenty percent target for greenhouse gas (GHG) emission reductions, increased use of renewable energy sources (RES) and increased energy efficiency, all to be achieved by 2020 (European Commission, 2008a). Although the increased emphasis on climate change implies a more limited focus than the broader SD agenda with which EPI is related (see Chapter 2 by Adelle et al.), nearly 20 years of experience in developing and implementing EPI mechanisms have provided important lessons with direct relevance to climate change policies as well.

EPI in the EU is supported by the art. 11 of the Treaty on the Functioning of the European Union (TFEU) (ex-art. 6 of the EC Treaty) which requires that: 'Environmental protection requirements must be integrated into the definition and implementation of the Community policies and activities … in particular with a view to promoting sustainable development' (art. 11, TFEU). Despite the relatively 'soft law' nature of the article, this constitutional principle implies a substantial responsibility for the governing procedures of the different policy sectors. There remains, however, considerable disagreement as to how EPI in general, and art. 11 TFEU (ex-art. 6) in particular, are to be interpreted (Pallemaerts, 2006; Williams, 2007; Jordan et al., 2008, pp. 159–60). It is therefore important to provide further assessments of what EPI entails in practice in specific EU settings, such as the energy policy sector. On this background the present chapter will discuss how EPI is reflected in the promotion of RES in the EU. Moreover, it tackles the question of to what extent EPI can stimulate a stronger EU RES policy, and – eventually – a more sustainable European energy policy.

The case of RES touches upon two important characteristics of EPI. First, there is a horizontal, cross-sectoral dimension implying that environmental concerns are formulated and implemented across various policy sectors. In the context of the European energy policy, this highlights the extent and nature of the coordination and potential integration between different subdomains: in particular, security of supply, market development, energy usage and efficiency, and research and innovation. Second, EPI must be implemented across levels of governance: that is, vertically (from the EU to national and regional–local levels). As far as the second aspect is concerned, the process of identifying effective measures 'from below' may also lead to a stronger sense of responsibility among the sector and its key stakeholders (Persson, 2007, p. 43). Here, the vertical dimension of EPI will be illustrated by a brief comparative assessment of the four Nordic countries, Denmark, Finland, Norway and Sweden, discussing how and to what extent relevant EU strategies and policies have represented drivers in this regard. As traditional front-runners, the status in these countries may be considered as a critical test of the connection between EU RES policies and EPI. The EU is here assumed to require both the horizontal and vertical dimensions in order to ensure a stronger follow-up of EPI, and the fulfillment of the 2020 targets.

This chapter proceeds as follows. Section 3.2 outlines the challenges that EPI represents for European governance. Section 3.3 looks at EPI and renewable energy in the European energy policy; within it, Subsection 3.3.1 discusses how EPI has been related to RES in the EU, while Subsection 3.3.2 provides an assessment of how EPI and RES are connected and followed up at the national level. Section 3.4 provides a summarizing discussion of the potential of EPI for contributing to a stronger common EU RES policy. Conclusions are finally drawn in Section 3.5.

3.2 ENVIRONMENTAL POLICY INTEGRATION: THE CHALLENGE FOR EUROPEAN GOVERNANCE

EPI has been perceived as a particular challenge to public governance and has been associated with communicative, organizational and procedural processes and tools (Lafferty 2004b; Persson 2007; Jordan and Lenschow, 2008b). In addition to more academically based research, a number of EPI-relevant studies with a more practical, political–administrative approach (OECD, 2001a, 2001b, 2002a, 2002b; EE, 2005a, 2005b) have also been published over the last decade and a half. However, a clear consensus as to what EPI implies (or should imply) has yet to emerge, not least in relation to specific sectors (Knudsen, 2009b). This lack of clarity is related to the conceptual basis, the theoretical foundation, the analytical scope and, most particularly, the priority that should be accorded to environmental concerns. Hence there is a need to further clarify EPI with insights from specific sectors using a comparative approach.[1]

A major aspect of the conceptual discussion on EPI is its relationship to SD. In particular, two core ideas have been referred to in this connection (Lafferty and Knudsen, 2007): (1) the widely recognized SD goal of balancing the interests/concerns/priorities of the so-called 'three pillars': the economic, social and environmental dimensions of societal developments; and (2) the crucial OECD notion of 'decoupling' the drivers of 'business as usual' from negative environmental impacts. Concerning the first of these ideas, Lafferty and Hovden (2003, p. 9) have defined EPI as implying

> [t]he incorporation of environmental objectives into all stages of policy making in non-governmental policy sectors, with a specific recognition of this goal as a guiding principle for the planning and execution of policy.

The application of this 'guiding principle' should furthermore be

> [a]ccompanied by an attempt to aggregate presumed environmental consequences into an overall evaluation of policy, and a commitment to minimize contradictions between environmental and sectoral policies by giving principled priority to the former over the latter.

The essential requirement of this understanding of EPI is that it should function as a 'first-order principle'. Crucially, the concept should guarantee that every effort is made to assess the impacts of short-, medium- and long-term sectoral policies on the life-sustaining capacities of the affected ecosystems; *and* to clearly limit, or otherwise qualify in advance, those impacts that represent unacceptable risks of degradation. However, this definition does not *always* imply outcomes in favor of the environmental dimension of SD. What is important is that the environmental aspect should be accorded 'principled priority' in trade-offs between the different concerns. The outcome of such trade-offs must then be based on democratically decided guidelines (Lafferty and Knudsen, 2007). This perspective on EPI also resonates with judicial interpretations of art. 11 TFEU (ex-art. 6) (cf. Williams, 2007). Although the article's wording is in imperative terms, it cannot be regarded as laying down a standard according to which environmental concerns are always assumed to be the prevalent interest (ibid.). Yet, according to this interpretation, the article requires that environmental concerns are always at the very least taken into account (ibid.).

The second core idea stipulated by the Lafferty/Hovden definition is related to 'decoupling'. This concept, as first and most prominently put forth by the OECD, proclaims that the dominant economic practices of existing Western societies can be shown to be negative for the environment and that therefore efforts must be made to 'decouple' such practices from their negative environmental impacts (OECD, 2001a, p. 13). Building further on the notion of decoupling, 're-coupling' has been viewed as the process of defining and implementing new, more sustainable means of production and consumption; that is to say, an enhancement of 'green innovation' (Lafferty and Ruud, 2006). Re-coupling also resonates with another crucial premise of the Brundtland Report: the idea that continued economic growth is necessary, provided that the quality of growth changes (WCED, 1987, p. 52).

It is, however, also important to address the procedural aspect of EPI. In this regard Lafferty (2004a: 205–8) proposes a 'benchmark approach' developed on the basis of specific mechanisms as documented by the OECD (2002a). The benchmarks stress the importance of designing and operating mechanisms that ensure both a *horizontal* (governmental) coordination of EPI and a sector-based (ministerial level) *vertical* follow-up. Clear political–administrative responsibilities and institutional mandates, as well as strategies, related action-plans and budgetary provisions are among the key mechanisms profiled in this context. EPI mechanisms should hence be considered as parts of an interactive whole (serving the promotion of SD). The coordination and overall integration of horizontal and vertical mechanisms thus become crucial.

As clearly indicated by art. 11 TFEU (ex-art. 6) and other strategic efforts, the EU has taken several concrete steps to formalize the principles discussed above into operational and procedural terms (as will be further elaborated in Section 3.3). What is generally lacking in current EPI research are, however, empirical studies of how a trans-sectoral approach to EPI interacts with a more 'vertical', sector-specific approach (Knudsen, 2009b). EPI, as related to SD, constitutes a concept stemming from the global level, but adopted and implemented at the EU, national and regional–local levels. Furthermore, SD and EPI are overall references for ambitious EU policy targets. Studying how EPI is implemented and transferred across different levels of governance stands out therefore as a crucially important research task.

In general terms multilevel governance is an extensively employed but debated concept, with numerous contributions emphasizing different patterns of interaction and causal mechanisms (Hooghe and Marks, 2003; Pierre and

Peters, 2005, pp. 80–100). It has been generally recognized that multilevel governance is also a major challenge for EPI, but beyond such recognition there are few overviews of empirical studies (EEA, 2005a, p. 46; Homeyer and Knoblauch, 2008; European Research Area, 2009). Nevertheless, some recent works have attempted to explore EPI within specific federal–state contexts (see European Research Area, 2009; Hornbeek, 2008; Jordan et al., 2008; Knudsen, 2010; Wurzel, 2008). Other contributions have emphasized the need to increase the overall institutional and administrative capacity for coordination, both vertically across levels and horizontally within national and EU-level administrations, in order to fully accommodate EU ambitions for 'coherence' within different sectoral policy areas (Jordan and Schout, 2008).

For the most part, research on multilevel governance in the broader sense has also been particularly focused on the EU, specifically concentrating on the transition to a less state-centered, more complex regional polity (Bache and Flinders, 2004, pp. 195–200). In this regard, the emergence of new policy networks and the growing challenge for governments to coordinate both within and across levels of governance has been emphasized as a major challenge for EPI, not least in an EU context (Jordan and Schout, 2008). Building on this challenge of complexity, EPI studies have also focused on the importance of 'policy learning' and gradual, institutional capacity-building as an important way of inducing a stronger bottom-up integration of environmental concerns (Nilsson and Eckerberg, 2007).

In this regard, the challenge of *implementing* EPI standards and related targets is also increasingly addressed in recent research. Jordan and Lenschow (2008a, pp. 330–5) point to the importance of including perspectives on policy analysis in EPI research, and to clearer distinctions between the different phases of policy-making processes, from agenda-setting to evaluation and revision. They maintain that different types of EPI instruments (symbolic, organizational and procedural governing mechanisms) should be related to and studied according to their function within a policy cycle perspective (ibid.). Finally, as highlighted by the research field on policy analysis and policy implementation, different sets of contextual factors are important for understanding how policy projects and programs, including specific policy instruments, are followed up and fulfilled (Knudsen, 2009b).

3.3   EPI AND RENEWABLE ENERGY IN THE EUROPEAN ENERGY POLICY

From the 1990s emerged an intertwined focus on the principal and procedural aspects of EPI within the EU. In particular, the EU Commission made efforts to put EPI into operational practice, albeit aimed mainly at internal procedures

(Wilkinson, 1997; see also Chapter 2 by Adelle et al.). Since these first efforts were considered to produce only mixed results, the 1998 EU Cardiff summit formulated a strategy that more explicitly addressed EPI in the decision-making processes, particularly with the aim of increasing the responsibilities of both the Council and the European Parliament (Lenschow 2002). Even more significantly, however, EPI was specifically incorporated as EU law by art. 11 TFEU (ex-art. 6), as referred to above. The Cardiff Process may also be considered as a 'prelude' to the EU Strategy for Sustainable Development (SDS) (Pallemaerts 2006: 25). The SDS, adopted in 2001, may be considered as a potentially strong horizontal EPI mechanism (see also Chapter 2 by Adelle et al.). The EU SDS is also part of the wider Lisbon strategy for competitiveness. SD is thus a major concern in the EU's overall policy vision and strategy, and is to be considered *as a basic principle* when sectoral policies are formulated (Tanasescu, 2006). Guidelines on how to conduct an eventual trade-off between different concerns of SD, which are differently emphasized by the two strategies, are not stipulated however.

Given the EU's presumed role as an EPI front-runner (with specific reference to art. 11 TFEU (ex-art. 6), one would expect the EU to be relatively good at integrating environmental thinking into the work of all of its policy sectors (Jordan et al. 2008, p. 159). Yet it has been argued that a particular challenge for the EU is the polity's historical legacy and rationale for governance: that is, economic growth and market development (Bomberg, 2004). Lundqvist (2004a, p. 330), on the other hand, maintains that a more 'coherent' approach to SD governance by the EU is possible, providing that one considers the positive resources inherent in the Union's multilevel pluralistic structure. Lundqvist (2004a) also stresses, however, that several institutional features of the EU work against a stronger priority for SD – most notably the lack of a strong and consistent political leadership. Analyses like these clearly document the challenges and tensions underlying the EU's EPI ambitions. This is recognizable not least in the energy sector, where there are strong tensions between the economic drivers and the ambitions of reinforcing the environmentally benign potentials of the sector. This latter aspect may again be related to the horizontal character of EPI.

Nevertheless, the EU Directive on the promotion of renewable electricity (RES-E), adopted in 2001, did include references to all SD concerns, and environmental protection even stands out as the primary motivation:

> The Community recognizes … that their exploitation [of renewable energy sources] contributes to environmental protection and sustainable development. In addition this can also create local employment, have a positive impact on social cohesion, contribute to security of supply and make it possible to meet the Kyoto targets more quickly. It is therefore necessary to ensure that this potential is better exploited within the framework of the internal market. (*Official Journal, 2001*)

The RES-E directive was evaluated in 2005 and 2006, revealing that the overall indicative target would not be fulfilled, not least because of inadequate national follow-up (European Commission, 2005, 2007). Furthermore, the Commission concluded that such fulfilment was not conceivable with a common EU-wide promotional scheme for RES-E, as initially proposed (ibid.). In January 2008 the EU Commission put forth a number of proposals for more ambitious climate and energy policies. Included in the Climate and Energy Package was a proposal for a revised Directive on RES, replacing the RES-E Directive but extending the scope to heating/cooling and renewable fuels for transport (European Commission, 2008b). The RES Directive was finally adopted in December 2008 (see Chapter 1 by Solorio Sandoval and Morata).

The RES Directive's key objective is to ensure that 20 percent of all energy used by 2020 is from RES, compared with the 2005 level. Whereas the member states are differently committed and are free to stimulate electricity and heating, they must all respectively achieve a 10 per cent share of renewable fuels for transport (*Official Journal*, 2009). Importantly, the new RES Directive both contains more ambitious and *binding* national targets, and omits the former ambitions of a common, standardized promotional scheme for the EU as a whole (ibid.). The member states are encouraged meanwhile to cooperate on joint RES projects, as well as engage in common support schemes, such as, for example, common tradable RES certificate schemes (see Chapter 4 by Busch and Jörgens). Stronger requirements concerning the phasing of new RES production, not least through facilitating grid access, are also underlined. The member states are more forcefully required to take the necessary steps to develop and adopt a transmission and distribution infrastructure ('shall' instead of 'should' as in the RES-E directive) (ibid.). The member states were also required to adopt national action plans before 30 June 2010, in order to clarify how they will fulfil the national targets (to be approved by the Commission). By reinforcing both the RES target and providing a target for energy efficiency (both strategically related to GHG abatement), one may argue that the EU has provided a clear focus on decoupling through its adoption of the Climate and Energy Package. Given the more ambitious and binding national targets, the new RES Directive will also represent a more demanding challenge for national policy objectives and strategies.

The re-coupling potential is furthermore demonstrated by the related efforts of reinforcing energy innovation and technology development. These activities are particularly related to the EU Strategic Energy Technology (SET) Plan and the European Institute of Innovation and Technology (EIT). The final version of the SET Plan was adopted in October 2009 and includes industrial initiatives, energy efficiency ('Smart Cities') and the establishment of a European Energy Research Alliance (EERA). The SET Plan is considered to be the technology pillar of the EU climate and energy policy (European

Commission, 2009). The EIT, for its part, is set to become the flagship for excellence in European innovation. Sustainable energy constitutes one of its three priorities (EIT, 2010).

3.3.1 Horizontal EPI and RES: Tensions and Integration Potentials

As emphasized above, the new RES Directive was launched through the Climate and Energy Package in 2008 and climate mitigation is, therefore, a succinct rationale behind the directive. As argued above, there is a strategic linkage between the Climate and Energy Package, the RES Directive and EPI efforts. A critical question, however, concerns the robustness of this linkage when it comes to other related energy policy concerns. Moreover, legal prescriptions do not operate in a void. It is therefore important to focus on other means of implementation as well, not least through communication and networks. Such factors are employed increasingly within the EU, involving different categories of public and non-public actors and stakeholders at different levels (Knill and Lenschow, 2005). The EU has for some years aimed to reinforce both formal and informal networks as an alternative mode of governance, based on the limitations experienced with traditional, hierarchical regulation (Schout and Jordan, 2005). In particular, various networks serve to advise the Commission, coordinate national enforcement and promote information exchange among national regulators (Eberlein and Newman, 2008).

In the case of the EU's work on SD, there have been features of a 'steering network' involving scientific experts, think tanks, NGOs and industry groups (Bomberg, 2009). This network has in particular been activated through the European Consultative Forum on the Environment and Sustainable Development, an independent advisory body (Bosselmann, 2006). There is also a European SD Network, composed of public administrators with responsibilities for the national SD strategies (Steurer, 2008). While these networks do not have any formal decision-making authority and generally have limited political leverage, they provide the EU institutions with important inputs on both further policy development and implementation. In addition, in the more specific area of renewable energy, there has also been a strong 'upwards' communication of national experiences. Having adopted feed-in tariff schemes to stimulate RES-E production, for example, some countries have promoted these actively as the best regulatory approach to RES-E in the case of potential common EU policies (Rowlands, 2005).

Economic arguments and the potential for innovation and industrial development have, moreover, figured as a key motivation for the RES directive itself, and the Danish and German examples of expanding industries related to renewable energy, in particular, have been profiled as prominent examples. On the other hand, recent and current economic setbacks have substantially affected negotiations on the new EU RES Directive. Several member states have then demonstrated considerable recalcitrance *vis-à-vis* the proposed, demanding national targets, fearing that higher energy prices would hamper national industrial competitiveness. An additional question is also whether relevant stakeholders in the EU have been trying to promote, or possibly limit, the importance of environmental concerns. The following brief assessment is mainly based on stakeholders' reactions and positions *vis-à-vis* the Commission's initial proposal for the RES Directive, as put forward in January 2008.

As indicated above, a critical feature of the Commission's proposal was the absence of any ambitions of a common EU support scheme for promoting renewable energy, which had been a key objective of the former RES-E Directive. As an overall observation, clearly mixed signals were coming from the branch organizations around funding mechanisms and instrumentation. On the one hand, Eurelectric, the principal organization for electricity producers, was a very active proponent of a common, EU-standardized support scheme in the form of tradable certificates (Eurelectric, 2008). On the other hand, the more technology-specific branch organizations largely defended the existing nationally based and often fixed support systems (EREF, 2008; EWEA, 2008). One organization was however also concerned about how the Commission was to combine the targets for more renewable energy with the targets for emission reductions of CO_2 (EWEA, 2008). In this regard, the European Wind Energy Association (EWEA) called for a separate setting of targets for CO_2 reductions and RES respectively, in order to define a realistic contribution to CO_2 reductions from the RES sector, as compared with other sectors (ibid., p. 10). Whereas the core focus of the co-decision process[2] of the RES Directive was the debate on biofuels and the related sustainability criteria (ENDS 2008), the European Parliament also proposed stronger reporting requirements and interim targets (ibid.). Hence, two levels of EPI-relevant thinking can be primarily discerned in relation to the RES Directive: CO_2/GHG emissions vs. RES; and the SD potential of the RES contribution, as reflected by the debate on biofuels. The latter case stood out as the most prominent and controversial issue, at least in the public debate.

3.3.2   EPI and Renewable Energy in the EU Member States

EPI mechanisms and policies promoting renewable energy, and more specifically renewable electricity (RES-E), have been implemented and connected to different extents and in different ways in the Nordic countries of Denmark, Finland, Norway and Sweden (Knudsen, 2009a).[3] The four countries are all committed to combating climate change through the Kyoto Protocol, and RES-E constitutes an important area for fulfilling their obligations to reduce

GHG emissions. In addition, these countries also share a common, general wholesale electricity market, NordPool. This market structure, the world's first cross-national electricity market, clearly influences the economic framework for promoting RES in the Nordic region (Knudsen et al., 2008). In this regard, Denmark and Sweden demonstrate the strongest cases of a linkage between an EPI framework and RES-E promotion (Knudsen, 2009a). They are also the most successful in providing new RES-E production capacity. In Sweden a sector-encompassing program for SD, initiated in the mid-1990s, has been connected with a comprehensive energy-policy program, which focuses on a switch from nuclear and fossil-based generation to a reinforced stimulation of RES-E (Lundqvist, 2004b; Nilsson and Eckerberg, 2007; Chen and Johnson, 2008). In Denmark a specific political–institutional dynamic between energy and climate change has played a vital role, especially during the 1990s. Integrated energy- and climate-policy strategies here constitute a framework for an array of differentiated economic and regulatory instruments aimed directly at stimulating the phase-in of RES-E production (Hvelplund, 2005; Karnøe and Buchorn, 2008). The promotion of RES-E has thus been considered directly instrumental *vis-à-vis* the fulfillment of national climate change mitigation targets. The Danish RES-E promotion has also been coordinated with energy efficiency programs, turning Denmark into one of the world's most energy-efficient economies (IEA, 2006).

Yet at first glance, EU policies have so far not represented substantial drivers for the relevant national strategies in the Nordic countries. The national indicative targets provided by the EU RES-E Directive are roughly similar to and/or supplemented by national targets set prior to and/or independently of the directive (Chen and Johnson, 2008; Karnøe and Buchkhorn, 2008; Kivimaa 2008; Knudsen et al., 2008). The EU's reinforced ambitions, as expressed by the triple-twenty targets for 2020, will, however, imply a more demanding national follow-up in coming years. Danish and Swedish RES-E initiatives reflect EPI standards more substantially than is the case with Norway. This is due primarily to the anchoring of RES-E initiatives within more consistent policy frameworks that address energy production and usage, with decoupling as a core perspective. Furthermore, Danish RES-E initiatives also imply a stronger and more innovative re-coupling potential than in the case of the other two countries (Knudsen, 2009a).

As far as more general EPI mechanisms are concerned, Denmark and Sweden also illustrate how EPI can constitute a framework with the potential of facilitating the promotion of RES-E. This is demonstrated by the more consistent procedural and institutional linkages between the strategic level and related follow-up mechanisms in the two countries, although in different ways. The Danish approach is more sector-specific and includes a stronger interaction with stakeholders in bottom-up processes, while the Swedish approach is characterized by a more sector-encompassing strategy within a relatively centralized bureaucratic framework (Knudsen 2009a). A particularly interesting feature to emerge is the manner by which a successful implementation of wind power in Denmark has both stimulated and legitimized further development of a more integrated political-strategic framework for energy and climate. Good policy performance 'on the ground' has, in other words, contributed to a general reinforcement of EPI standards throughout the energy system.

In short, contextual differences among the Scandinavian states have provided different bases for the promotion and integration of RES-E into existing energy systems (Knudsen, 2009a). The cases also demonstrate that strong EPI performance depends on solidly anchored and enduring political commitments. Nevertheless, the analysis of the Nordic countries demonstrates that the impact of the EU on national EPI progress is ambiguous. The EU policy processes and legal acts have thus far not required any reinforced integration by national authorities in the Nordic region. On the other hand, one can say that the most prevalent policy instruments with relevance for climate and energy, the EU Emission Trading System (ETS) and the RES Directive, represent challenges in terms of national implementation. If the follow-up of these directives is coordinated, they may also provide a potential for stimulating a more integrated national climate and energy strategy.

3.4   DISCUSSION: CAN EPI INDUCE STRONGER EU RES PROMOTION AND A MORE SUSTAINABLE EUROPEAN ENERGY POLICY?

Whereas the EU has succeeded in formulating ambitious policy targets, clearly anchored in an overall vision for sustainable development, it is difficult to discern a consistent, systematic linkage between an overall strategic level and specific follow-up measures at a sectoral level. Building on former and current EU strategies, there is an overall and principal 'EPI-thinking' ('software'; cf. Jordan, 2002) in place, albeit lacking a sufficiently strong political-institutional anchoring and mandate. Thus, there are few effective operational tools ('hardware'; cf. Jordan, 2002) to provide a more consistent follow-up within the various policy sectors, not least across levels. These challenges are reflected in the processes of implementing the RES-E and RES Directives.

The EU targets related to GHG emission reductions in 2020 and beyond currently represent the most relevant cross-cutting objective. However, if this objective really is to become the principal driver for further sectoral policy development, the emitting sectors' commitments must be clarified. Currently, the Climate and Energy Package's objectives for renewable energy, energy efficiency and the emission trading system may be seen as relevant clarifications in this regard. But to what extent are these integrated into the EU's overall energy policy thinking and the emergent European energy policy?

To more substantially bind the energy sector and the member states, the 2020 targets must be seen in connection with the prevalent interests of the sector. These are not least related to three overarching concerns that have traditionally determined energy policy development, at both EU and national levels: that is, environment, competitiveness and security-of-supply. These concerns may be considered conflicting and partly contradictory: for example, more European coal instead of Russian natural gas for security-of-supply reasons is not a viable way of fulfilling the climate mitigation objective, unless facilities for carbon capture and storage (CCS) are more widely applied (see Chapter 5 by Fischer for CCS and Chapter 8 by Herranz Surrallés and Natorski for further discussion on energy security). On the other hand, a reinforced and more stringent focus on GHG emission reductions may also entail unintended societal and environmental side effects, as was succinctly illustrated by the debate on the sustainability criteria for biofuels, in relation to the RES Directive in 2008.

The outcome of an eventual trade-off between different sets of environmental concerns (for example climate change mitigation vs. biodiversity) depends, moreover, on the overall normative balance of the process applied: most specifically, on how social and economic concerns are taken into consideration. This will, in turn, depend on whether decision-makers employ a medium- or a long-term perspective and, furthermore, whether they perceive relevant changes within a local, national or global context (cf. Lafferty and Langhelle, 1999, p. 7). In order to clarify priorities, the EU could therefore focus more substantially on how to make relevant trade-offs and decide what perspective and priorities to apply in specific instances.

In this regard, in order to reflect EPI and the strategy for SD more forcefully, a stronger focus on and prioritizing of *decoupling* should emerge. Concretely, one could more forcefully address the potential of coordinating the RES promotion with measures for energy efficiency and more sustainable energy usage. A robust linkage between these two subdomains is currently lacking. Furthermore, there are no substantial mechanisms for stimulating a coherent approach at the national level, by requiring common action plans and reporting mechanisms for RES and energy efficiency, for example. Currently, there are no clear requirements in the relevant EU legal acts that could lead to a more coordinated and coherent treatment at both EU and national levels (that is an overriding task for the European energy policy).

Another positive impetus to strengthen both EPI and the promotion of RES is represented by the increased EU prioritization of energy research, innovation and technology development. This focus may also induce a *re-coupling* of the energy sector. Clear indications of an increased commitment are the establishment of the European Institute of Innovation and Technology (EIT) and the adoption of the Strategic Energy Technology Plan (SET-Plan). Importantly, these activities are also succinctly related to the ambitions for competitiveness and innovation, as expressed through the EU 2020 Strategy (European Commission, 2010). These activities also provide a possibility for cooperation in the long term, producing stronger synergies between energy and environment, through innovation and research.

However, a reinforced connection between EPI and energy must also be anchored *vis-à-vis* different national policy approaches and contexts. A critical question here is whether this should imply more standardized, common mechanisms and policy instruments: in other words, a stronger top-down steering along a vertical EPI dimension. Such standardization may, however, also (at least implicitly) undermine more context-sensitive policy measures, which can represent more realistic ways of implementing EU policies nationally. The former RES-E Directive was actually criticized for not taking national and regional–local contexts sufficiently into account, thus overestimating the potential of an 'EU standardization' (Lafferty and Ruud, 2008).

This latter aspect is also related to the importance of avoiding 'policy pitfalls' (cf. Mallon, 2006, pp. 5–33). One such pitfall is the tendency to under-define policy objectives owing to a lack of specifications and insufficient room for differentiation in terms of both regional–local circumstances and technological characteristics. Accordingly, there is a risk that objectives are not clarified *vis-à-vis* scope and scale and that they cut across sectors and issues in an unclear manner (ibid.). However, in the case of the new EU RES Directive, this issue was addressed during the decision-making process, whereby the European Parliament introduced a set of interim targets and related reporting mechanisms in order to provide a more realistic basis for the fulfillment of the overall 2020 target. This clearly demonstrates that learning occurs and changes can take place within the process of the European energy policy formation.

3.5   CONCLUSIONS

An underlying premise in this assessment has been the importance of employing a principal understanding of EPI as a fundament for procedural and institutional mechanisms, which can further reinforce the integration of environmental concerns in sectoral policy-making. Building on the EU's experiences with EPI and given the existence of several relevant mechanisms and networks, it is not unthinkable that a reinforcement of EPI could take place. At the same time, it is important to emphasize the challenges of implementing EPI within sectoral domains. Experiences from the decision-making process of the RES Directive indicate that there are very different approaches for following up EPI and that few or no stakeholders currently promote a strong EPI vision *vis-à-vis* the EU institutions. Thus there is a clear need for providing stronger political engagement and attention, as well as improving external communication and incorporating stakeholder perspectives from an early stage. Furthermore, the case of RES also demonstrates the challenges for promoting EPI *from* the EU *towards* the national level. Experiences with the former RES-E Directive demonstrate the importance of a context-sensitive approach and differentiated measures. Moreover, the current RES Directive is not substantially integrated into an overall strategy for decoupling energy production and usage from environmental degradation. This potential can be, and will need to be, reinforced by a stronger coordination between the EU policies for RES and energy efficiency.

A stronger coordination between relevant innovation and technology development activities and the RES Directive may represent a fruitful way of inducing a more coherent energy policy strategy and more robust trajectories towards the 2020 targets. Moreover, a stronger integration between innovation and RES may also represent re-coupling in accordance with EPI standards. In sum, a more coherent strategy along these lines could represent forceful incentives for a more sustainable European energy policy, as well as stimulating a more consistent follow-up of EPI within the EU.

NOTES

1. An important exception to this overall picture is provided by a comparative study of EPI in the agricultural and energy sectors in Sweden (Nilsson and Eckerberg, 2007).
2. That is, the decision-making process through and between the Council and the European Parliament, in particular in matters pertaining to the internal market and the environment – cases that particularly involve energy.
3. Three of the countries are 'full members' of the EU, whereas Norway is not an EU member state, and thus not an integral part of the EU decision-making system. However, since 1994, Norway's relations to the EU have been regulated through the Agreement on the European Economic Area (EEA). The EEA Agreement provides Norway with full access to the EU's internal market. Hence, Norway is also bound by market-related EU policies and legislation, not least in matters pertaining to energy and the environment.

REFERENCES

Bache, I. and M. Flinders (2004), 'Conclusions and implications', in I. Bache and M. Flinders (eds), *Multi-level Governance*, Oxford: Oxford University Press, pp. 195–206.

Bomberg, E. (2004), 'Adapting form to function? From economic to sustainable development governance in the European Union', in W.M. Lafferty (ed.), *Governance for Sustainable Development: The Challenge of Adapting Form to Function*, Cheltenham, UK and Northampton, MA, USA: Edward Elgar, pp. 61–94.

Bomberg, E. (2009), 'Governance for sustainable development: the United States and the European Union compared', in M.A. Schreurs, H. Selin and S.VanDeever (eds), *Transatlantic Environment and Energy Politics: Comparative and International Perspectives*, London: Ashgate, pp. 21–40.

Bosselmann K. (2006), 'Missing the point? The EU's institutional and procedural approach to sustainability', in M. Pallemaerts and A. Azmanova (eds), *The European Union and Sustainable Development*, Brussels: VUB Press, pp. 105–25.

Chen, Y. and F.X. Johnson (2008), 'Sweden: greening the power market in the context of liberalization and nuclear ambivalence', in W.M. Lafferty and A. Ruud (eds), *Promoting Sustainable Electricity in Europe: Challenging the Path Dependency of Dominant Energy Systems*, Cheltenham, UK and Northampton, MA, USA: Edward Elgar, pp. 219–49.

Eberlein, B. and A. Newman (2008), 'Innovating EU governance modes: the rise of incorporated transgovernmental networks', *Governance*, **21** (1), 25–52.

European Institute of Innovation and Technology (EIT) (2010), Official website of the European Institute of Innovation and Technology, accessed June 2011 at http://eit.europa.eu/home.html.

ENDS Europe Daily (2008), 'New EU renewable energy law "finalised"', *ENDS online*, accessed December 2010 at www.endseuropedaily.com/articles.

European Renewable Energies Federation (EREF) (2008), 'The new draft directive on the promotion of renewable energies in Europe until 2020', accessed December 2010 at www.eref-europe.org/htm/press_release.html.

Eurelectric (2008), *Eurelectric Position Paper on the European Commission's Proposal for a New EU Directive on the Promotion of the Use of Energy from Renewable Sources, WG Energy Policy and WG Renewables & Distributed Generation*, Brussels, April.

European Commission (2005), *Communication from the Commission: The Support of Electricity from Renewable Energy Sources*, COM(2005) 627 final, Brussels, 7 December.

European Commission (2006), 'Consolidated version of the treaty establishing the European Community', *Official Journal of the European Union*, 29 December, C 321 E/46.

European Commission (2007), *Communication from the Commission to the Council and European Parliament. Green Paper: Follow-Up Action Report on Progress in Renewable Electricity*, COM(2006) 849 final, Brussels, 10 January.

European Commission (2008a), 'Climate change: Commission welcomes final adoption of Europe's climate and energy package', *Press Release* IP/08/1998, Brussels, 17 December.

European Commission (2008b), *Proposal for a Directive of the European Parliament and of the Council on the Promotion of the Use of Energy from Renewable Sources* COM (2008) 19 Final, Brussels, 23 January.

European Commission (2009), *Communication from the Commission to the European Parliament, the Council, the European Economic and Social Committee and the Committee of the Regions. Investing in the Development of Low Carbon Technologies* (SET-Plan), COM (2009) 519 Final, Brussels, 7 October.

European Commission (2010), 'Communication from the Commission. Europe 2020:

A European Strategy for Smart, Sustainable and Inclusive Growth', COM(2010) 2020, Brussels, 3 March.

European Environment Agency (EEA) (2005a), 'Environmental policy integration in Europe: state of play and an evaluation framework', European Environment Agency Technical report no. 2/2005, Copenhagen.

EEA (2005b), 'Environmental policy integration in Europe: administrative culture and practices', EEA Technical report no. 5/2005, Copenhagen.

European Research Area (2009) *Environmental Policy Integration and Multi-Level Governance (EPIGOV), Finalized Project, European Policy Brief*, Brussels: European Research Area.

EWEA (2008) 'Making 180 GW a reality by 2020: EWEA position on the future EU legislation for renewable energy and its impact on the wind industry', accessed December 2010 at www.ewea.org/index.php?id=182.

Homeyer, I. von and D. Knoblauch (2008) 'Environmental policy integration and multi-level governance: A state-of-the-art report', Ecologic – Institute for International and European Environmental Policy EPIGOV paper no 31, Berlin.

Hooghe, L. and G. Marks (2003), 'Unraveling the central state, but how? Types of multi-level governance', *American Political Science Review*, **97** (2), 233–43.

Hornbeek, J. (2008), 'The United States of America', in A.J. Jordan and A. Lenschow (eds), *Innovation in Environmental Policy? Integrating the Environment for Sustainability,* Cheltenham, UK and Northampton, MA, USA: Edward Elgar, pp. 268–88.

Hvelplund, F. (2005), 'Denmark', in D. Reiche (ed.), *Handbook of Renewable Energies in the European Union*, Frankfurt am Main, Germany: Peter Lang, pp. 83–100.

International Energy Agency (IEA) (2006), *Energy Policies of IEA Countries: Denmark 2006 Review*, Paris: IEA.

Jordan, A. (2002), 'Efficient hardware and light green software: environmental policy integration in the UK', in A. Lenschow (ed.), *Environmental Policy Integration: Greening Sectoral Policies in Europe*, London: Earthscan Publications, pp. 35–56.

Jordan, A.J. and A. Lenschow (2008a), 'Environmental policy integration: an innovation in environmental policy?', in A.J. Jordan and A. Lenschow (eds), *Innovation in Environmental Policy? Integrating the Environment for Sustainability*, Cheltenham, UK and Northampton, MA, USA: Edward Elgar, pp. 313–41.

Jordan, A.J. and A. Lenschow (eds) (2008b), *Innovation in Environmental Policy? Integrating the Environment for Sustainability*, Cheltenham, UK and Northampton, MA, USA: Edward Elgar.

Jordan, A.J. and A. Schout (2008), *The Coordination of the European Union: Exploring the Capacities of Networked Governance*, Oxford: Oxford University Press.

Jordan, A.J., A. Schout and M. Unfried (2008), 'The European Union', in A.J. Jordan and A. Lenschow (eds.), *Innovation in Environmental Policy? Integrating the Environment for Sustainability*, Cheltenham, UK and Northampton, MA, USA: Edward Elgar, pp. 159–79.

Karnøe, P. and A. Buchhorn (2008), 'Denmark: path creation dynamics and winds of change', in W.M. Lafferty and A. Ruud (eds), *Promoting Sustainable Electricity in Europe: Challenging the Path Dependency of Dominant Energy Systems*, Cheltenham, UK and Northampton, MA, USA: Edward Elgar, pp. 73–101.

Kivimaa, P. (2008), 'Finland: big is beautiful: promoting bioenergy in regional-industrial contexts', in W.M. Lafferty and A. Ruud (eds), *Promoting Sustainable Electricity in Europe: Challenging the Path Dependency of Dominant Energy Systems*, Cheltenham, UK and Northampton, MA, USA: Edward Elgar, pp. 159–88.

Knill, C. and A. Lenschow (2005), 'Compliance, communication and competition: patterns of EU environmental policy making and their impact on policy convergence', *European Environment*, **15** (2), pp. 114–28.

Knudsen J.K. (2009a), 'De- and re-coupling energy: environmental policy integration (EPI) and the case of renewable electricity in Scandinavia', SINTEF Energy Research AS technical report TR A6844, Trondheim, Norway.

Knudsen, J.K. (2009b), 'Environmental policy integration: conceptual clarification and comparative analysis of standards and mechanisms', doctorial dissertation, University of Twente, Ensticede, Netherlands, defended 2 December.

Knudsen, J.K., O. M. Larson and A. Rudd (2008), 'Norway: trying to maintain maximum RES-E in a petroleum driven economy', in W.M. Lafferty and A. Ruud (eds), *Promoting Sustainable Electricity in Europe: Challenging the Path Dependency of Dominant Energy Systems*, Cheltenham, UK and Northampton, MA, USA: Edward Elgar, pp. 250–78.

Knudsen, Jørgen K. (2010), 'Integrating environmental concerns in a trans-Atlantic perspective: the case of renewable electricity', *Review of Policy Research*, **27** (2), 127-46.

Lafferty, W.M. (2004a), 'From environmental protection to sustainable development: the challenge of decoupling through sectoral integration', in W.M. Lafferty (ed.), *Governance for Sustainable Development*, Cheltenham, UK and Northampton, MA, USA: Edward Elgar, pp. 91–220.

Lafferty, W.M. (ed.) (2004b), *Governance for Sustainable Development*, Cheltenham, UK and Northampton, MA, USA: Edward Elgar.

Lafferty, W.M. and E. Hovden (2003), 'Environmental policy integration: towards an analytical framework,' *Environmental Politics*, **12** (3), 1–22.

Lafferty, W.M. and J. Knudsen (2007), 'The issue of "balance" and trade-offs in environmental policy integration: how will we know EPI when we see it?', EPIGOV paper no. 11, Ecologic Berlin.

Lafferty, W.M. and O. Langhelle, (1999), 'Sustainable development as concept and norm', in W.M. Lafferty and O. Langhelle (eds), *Towards Sustainable Development: On the Goals of Development – and the Conditions of Sustainability*, London: Macmillan, pp. 1–29.

Lafferty, W.M. and A. Ruud (2006), 'Standards for green innovation: applying a proposed framework to governmental initiatives in Norway', *Evaluation*, **12** (4), 454–73.

Lafferty, W.M. and A. Ruud (eds) (2008), *Promoting Sustainable Electricity in Europe: Challenging the Path Dependency of Dominant Energy Systems*, Cheltenham, UK and Northampton, MA, USA: Edward Elgar.

Lenschow, A. (ed.) (2002), *Environmental Policy Integration: Greening Sectoral Policies in Europe*, London: Earthscan.

Lundqvist, L.J. (2004a), 'Management by objectives and results: a comparison of Dutch, Swedish and EU strategies for realising sustainable development', in W.M. Lafferty (ed.), *Governance for Sustainable Development*, Cheltenham, UK and Northampton, MA, USA: Edward Elgar, pp. 95–127.

Lundqvist, L.J. (2004b), *Sweden and Ecological Governance: Straddling the Fence*, Manchester: Manchester University Press.

Mallon, K. (2006), *Renewable Energy Policy and Politics*, London: Earthscan.

Nilsson, M. and K. Eckerberg (eds) (2007), *Environmental Policy Integration in Practice: Shaping Institutions for Learning*, London: Earthscan.

Organisation for Economic Co-operation and Development (OECD) (2001a), *Policies to Enhance Sustainable Development*, Paris: OECD.

OECD (2001b), *Sustainable Development. Critical Issues*, Paris: OECD.
OECD (2002a), *Governance for Sustainable Development: Five OECD Case Studies*, Paris: OECD.
OECD (2002b), 'Improving policy coherence and integration for sustainable development: a checklist', OECD Policy Brief, PUMA, Paris, accessed December 2010 at http://www.oecd.org/dataoecd/60/1/1947305.pdf.
Official Journal (2001), 'Directive 2001/77/EC of the European Parliament and of the Council of 27 September 2001 on the promotion of electricity produced from renewable energy sources in the internal energy market', *Official Journal of the European Communities*, L 283/33–40, 27 October,
Official Journal (2009), 'Directive 2009/28/EC of the European Parliament and of the Council of 23 April 2009 on the promotion of the use of energy from renewable sources and amending and subsequently repealing Directives 2001/77/EC and 2003/30/EC', in *Official Journal of the European Union*, L 140/16, 5 June.
Pallemaerts, M. (2006), 'The EU and sustainable development: an ambiguous relationship', in M. Pallemaerts and A. Azmanova (eds), *The European Union and Sustainable Development*, Brussels: VUB Press, pp. 19–52.
Persson, Å. (2007), 'Different perspectives on EPI', in M. Nilsson and K. Eckerberg (eds), *Environmental Policy Integration in Practice: Shaping Institutions for Learning*, London: Earthscan Publications, pp. 25–48.
Pierre, J. and B.G. Peters (2005), *Governing Complex Societies, Trajectories and Scenarios*, Basingstoke: Palgrave Macmillan.
Rowlands, I.H. (2005), 'The European directive on renewable electricity: conflicts and compromises.' *Energy Policy*, **33** (5), 965–74.
Schout, A. and A.J. Jordan (2005), 'Co-ordinating European governance: self-organising or centrally steered?', *Public Administration*, **83** (1), 201–20.
Steurer, R. (2008), 'Sustainable development strategies', in A.J. Jordan and A. Lenschow (eds), *Innovation in Environmental Policy? Integrating the Environment for Sustainability*, Cheltenham, UK and Northampton, MA, USA: Edward Elgar, pp. 93–113.
Tanasescu, I. (2006), 'The political process leading to the development of the EU Sustainable Development Strategy', in M. Pallemaerts and A. Azmanova (eds), *The European Union and Sustainable Development*, Brussels: VUB Press, pp. 53–77.
World Commission on Environment and Development (WCED) (1987), *Our Common Future*, Oxford: Oxford University Press.
Wilkinson, D. (1997), 'Towards sustainability in the European Union? Steps within the European Commission to integrate environment into other European Union policy sectors', *Environmental Politics*, 6 (1), 153–73.
Williams, R. (2007), 'The integration of environmental protection requirements into EC development cooperation policy draft', *EPIGOV* research papers. Ecologic–Institute for International and European Environmental Policy, Berlin.
Wurzel, R.K. (2008), 'Germany', in A.J. Jordan and A. Lenschow (eds), *Innovation in Environmental Policy? Integrating the Environment for Sustainability*, Cheltenham, UK and Northampton, MA, USA: Edward Elgar, pp. 180–201.

4. Europeanization through diffusion? Renewable energy policies and alternative sources for European convergence

Per-Olof Busch and Helge Jörgens

4.1 INTRODUCTION

In recent decades, cross-national policy clustering has become a distinctive feature of international and European environmental policy-making. Since the late 1960s, virtually every country in the world has created government institutions for the protection of the environment and adopted basic legislation in the areas of air pollution control, nature or water protection (Busch and Jörgens, 2005). This trend is even more pronounced in the group of European Union (EU) member states. Here, over the last 30 years, an impressive convergence of domestic patterns of environmental policy-making can be observed (Holzinger et al., 2008).

Can a similar degree of policy clustering also be observed with regard to programs aimed at the promotion of renewable energy sources (RES)? And if so, what are the mechanisms that drive the EU-wide convergence of these programs? In order to provide an answer to these questions, this chapter examines the cross-national spread of support schemes for electricity generation from RES sources, namely mandatory feed-in tariffs (FIT) and green certificate systems, in the period from 1988 to 2005.

This chapter explores the main driving forces as well as the barriers of a greater promotion of electricity from RES in the EU member states; it proceeds as follows. Section 4.2 presents three modes of international policy coordination. Section 4.3 then examines the spread of mandatory FIT and green certificate systems in the EU and links it to the three mechanisms of international policy coordination. Section 4.4 presents a discussion on the interactions in the proliferation of RES policies in the EU. Finally, Section 4.5 draws some tentative conclusions on the role of policy diffusion as a Europeanization mechanism. Overall, the chapter shows that diffusion–that is processes of voluntary imitation and learning among governments–has played a major role in the Europeanization of domestic RES policies (that is 'green Europeanization' of energy policy).

4.2 THREE MODES OF POLICY COORDINATION

Cross-national policy clusters either can be the result of independent but similar national reactions to comparable problem pressures or else can result from cross-national policy coordination. From a Europeanization perspective it is the latter – that is the mutual adjustment of domestic policies triggered by political, economic or ecological interdependence – that is most relevant. In this chapter we therefore focus on the possible ways in which interdependence triggers international policy coordination and ultimately leads to the emergence of policy clusters and to policy convergence.

We define policy coordination as the mutual adjustment of the interests, goals and actions of collective actors in the international system (Lindblom, 1965; Keohane, 1984). A closer look at the literature shows that mutual adjustment can occur in three different ways. From an international relations and Europeanization perspective, international policy coordination has been understood as resulting either from multilateral negotiations and supranational decision-making or from the coercive exploitation of asymmetries in military, political or economic power by hegemonic actors in the international system. In other words, scholars have focused primarily on centralized, top-down, hierarchical modes of international policy coordination, while decentralized and non-coercive processes of cross-national policy change have largely been ignored as independent sources of global political order (see Jörgens, 2004). This conceptual void has been filled by scholars of domestic and comparative politics who have increasingly pointed out processes of cross-national imitation and learning – often termed 'policy diffusion' – as a third and independent mechanism of international policy coordination (Simmons and Elkins, 2004; Busch and Jörgens, 2007).

Bringing together these two perspectives, we can distinguish three broad classes of mechanisms through which governments coordinate their policies: (1) cooperation, (2) coercion and (3) diffusion. They differ on a number of dimensions, including their basic mode of operation, the principal motivations of policymakers to consider adopting foreign policy models, the importance of reciprocity in the decision-making process, and national policymakers' leeway to influence the design and content of an externally provided policy or to reject it altogether.

Since this chapter is mostly interested in the international sources of policy clusters, our typology does not include a fourth class of mechanisms, namely, parallel but independent domestic responses to similar policy problems or functional requirements. However, in our empirical analysis this 'null hypothesis' (Simmons and Elkins, 2004, p. 172) will always be taken into account.

4.2.1   Cooperation

The term 'cooperation' describes multilateral and state-centered processes where negotiations among sovereign states and the subsequent formulation of multilateral agreements or supranational law are followed by domestic implementation and compliance. Thus, from a domestic policy perspective, cooperation refers to the conscious modification of internal policies by governments committed to multilateral standards which they have had a hand in drafting (Howlett 2000, p. 308). It is characterized by highly institutionalized and centralized, top-down decision-making procedures in the course of which the cooperating states consent on the international harmonization of their policies. Law-making within the EU constitutes the most prominent case of legally binding intergovernmental cooperation.

Cooperative policy coordination involves various submechanisms of domestic policy change that have received wide scholarly attention in the international relations and Europeanization literature, including negotiation, harmonization, legalization and compliance. A characteristic feature of cooperation is its emphasis on reciprocity, which basically means that governments make their pursuit of a common policy goal conditional upon all other involved parties pursuing the same goal.

While nations engage voluntarily in cooperative decision-making, once an agreement is reached and legalized they are more or less strongly obliged to comply with it and to implement it. Thus, at the implementation stage, cooperation involves a significant degree of sacrifice of national autonomy and sovereignty. The principal motivations for states to engage in processes of international cooperation are to address collective, often trans-boundary, problems where unilateral action is judged insufficient, or to harmonize different national regulations in order to reduce barriers to the free movement of people, capital and goods and to avoid trade distortions. Beyond seeking solutions for specific policy problems, international cooperation often aims at a general increase of global capacities to deal with pressing challenges such as environmental degradation, poverty, energy crises, or malfunctions of the international financial system.

4.2.2   Coercion

Coercion occurs when external actors intentionally force nations to adopt policy innovations which they would not have adopted otherwise and do so by exploiting economic or political power asymmetries. As Simmons et al. (2008, pp. 10–11) put it:

> The underlying logic of coercion ... involves power asymmetries that strong actors exploit to impose their preferences for policy change on the weak. ... Essentially, coercion involves the [usually conscious] manipulation of incentives by powerful actors to encourage others to implement policy change.

Coercion as a mode of intergovernmental policy coordination comprises a set of causal mechanisms ranging from the forceful imposition of policies to economic and political conditionality. At a lower level of analysis, forceful imposition encompasses further sub-mechanisms like economic sanctions or military intervention. Similarly, conditionality can be disaggregated into the submechanisms of intergovernmental reinforcement by reward, by punishment or by support.

In instances of coercion, the actors involved differ fundamentally in their principal motivations as well as in their opportunities to shape the content of the adopted policies. The principal motivation for actors that attempt to impose policies is to export their own fundamental values and principles. By contrast, policymakers in nations on which policies are imposed either simply shy away from superior power or cede to its demands because of the expected political or economic benefits which imposing actors offer in exchange for conformity with their demands. These incentives range from access to monetary resources – for example, development loans offered by the World Bank or the International Monetary Fund – to access to important organizations or institutions – such as membership of the EU (Schimmelfennig and Scholz, 2008).

Reciprocity plays an important role in almost all forms of coercion. In conditionality, which is the coercive mechanism used most frequently in the environmental policy field, the dominant actor threatens the withdrawal of benefits or the withholding of rewards if the targeted government does not adopt the desired policy. The targeted government is, in principle, free to reject the adoption of the desired policy. However, in most cases this option remains a theoretical one, as receiving countries are highly dependent economically or politically on the dominant state. Moreover, policymakers in the targeted nations have little or no opportunity to influence the content of the imposed policies. Conditionality, therefore, is a take-it-or-leave-it situation where economic and power asymmetries between the dominant and the targeted states limit the prospects of renegotiating the policy content or the terms of adoption.

In sum, coercion eliminates almost any voluntary element in national decisions to adopt a policy innovation. More often than not, targeted nations cannot afford to defy and resist political or economic coercion, although the option to forgo the incentives or face the consequences of non-conformity with external demands exists at least theoretically.

4.2.3 Diffusion

We define diffusion as a process by which information on policy innovations is communicated in the international system and these policies are then adopted voluntarily and unilaterally by an increasing number of countries over time (Rogers, 2003; Simmons et al., 2008). Diffusion thus refers to an international spread of policy innovations driven by information flows rather than by hierarchical pressure or collective decision-making within international institutions. At the micro level, diffusion processes involve mechanisms of social learning, copying, mimetic emulation, and political or economic competition. An essential feature of policy diffusion is that it occurs in the absence of formal or contractual obligation. Furthermore, diffusion is basically a decentralized and horizontal process (Levi-Faur, 2005). Unlike in the case of multilateral legal treaties and other forms of international cooperation, which are negotiated centrally between governments and subsequently implemented top-down, with diffusion decision-making procedures are decentralized and remain at the national level. The system-level effects of diffusion processes become manifest only through the accumulation of individual cases of imitation or learning with respect to one and the same policy item. In the absence of a centralized regulatory regime with highly visible and explicitly stated aims, international policy diffusion may thus result in a 'regulatory revolution by stealth' (Levi-Faur and Jordana, 2005, p. 8).

Unlike coercion and cooperation, reciprocity plays no constitutive role in diffusion processes. Individual states take over the policies of other states unilaterally, unconditionally and without requiring other states to do same. Sometimes states adjust their policies to those of another country without the latter even noticing it. Due to their voluntary character, national policymakers' influence on the content of the adopted policy, as well as their autonomy to decide whether to adopt a policy, is significantly higher in processes of policy diffusion than in instances of cooperation or coercion. The individual motivations of policymakers to voluntarily emulate other countries' regulatory approaches vary greatly. First of all, policymakers may act in a rational manner by looking across borders for effective solutions to pressing domestic problems. Where domestic actors face great uncertainties about the potential outcomes of different policy choices, rational lesson-drawing becomes less feasible. In these cases, domestic policymakers may prefer to model their policies on those countries that are generally perceived as being successful. In the early stages of a diffusion process, policymakers may also be actively persuaded by other national, international and transnational actors to adopt certain rules or measures (Haas, 1992). During the later stages of diffusion processes, when a regulatory approach has already been adopted by a fair number of countries, other motivations, such as international pressures to conform, the attempt of political elites to enhance the legitimacy of their actions, and/or their desire to enhance their self-esteem within an international society structured by emerging normative standards of appropriate behavior, may become increasingly important (Finnemore and Sikkink, 1998).

In sum, diffusion comprises a variety of mechanisms which are distinct from the mechanisms underlying cooperation and coercion because of their decentralized and largely voluntary character, as well as the high degree of autonomy they leave national policymakers to choose whether to adopt, modify or ignore a policy observed elsewhere.

4.3 PROMOTING ELECTRICITY GENERATION FROM RES IN THE EU: THE PROLIFERATION OF FEED-IN TARIFFS AND GREEN CERTIFICATES

Based on the analytical framework outlined in the previous section, we now analyze the international spread of national support schemes for the generation of electricity from RES sources, namely mandatory feed-in tariffs and green certificate systems. As we will see, this spread is most pronounced in the group of EU member states, but in order to capture the entirety of what has recently been termed the 'transformative power' of the EU (Grabbe, 2006; Börzel and Risse, 2009) – that is, both internal and external Europeanization impacts – we extend our analysis to a total of 43 OECD and central and eastern European countries.[1]

4.3.1 Characteristics of Feed-In Tariffs and Green Certificate Systems

FIT and green certificate systems (or quota obligations) are the two main policy instruments for increasing electricity generation from RES or, in short, for renewable electricity (RES-E) production. To promote RES-E, FIT fix the price to be paid for RES-E, whereas green certificate systems or quota obligations fix the quantity of RES-E to be generated or consumed (IEA, 2008, pp. 92–5). FIT oblige electricity producers, suppliers or consumers to buy RES-E that operators of RES plants feed into the grid, and to pay a fixed price for this electricity. Usually, the fixed price is set in advance for a period of several years and is paid by electricity suppliers to domestic operators of RES plants. Green certificate systems or quota obligations oblige electricity producers, suppliers or consumers to acquire a minimum quantity of green certificates that are issued for the production, supply or consumption of a specified amount of RES-E. The minimum quantity may be defined either as a percentage of electricity production or consumption or as an amount in absolute units. Compliance is monitored and possible non-compliance sanctioned through, for example, fines or denial of access to the electricity grid. In the case of green certificates, these have to be tradable at least in domestic trading schemes. Hence, the minimum quantity of certificates can be acquired either by producing or consuming RES-E or else by buying surplus green certificates on the green certificate market.

4.3.2   Proliferation Patterns

4.3.2.1   Feed-in tariffs
From 1989, when the first FIT for RES-E was introduced in the Netherlands, to 2005, 21 EU member states plus the non-EU countries Switzerland, Norway, Turkey and South Korea decided to promote the production of RES-E with FIT (see Figure 4.1). Overall, the cross-national spread of FIT evolved at a relatively constant rate. Only in three single years did the number of annual introductions lie above the average of the entire proliferation period, namely in 1994 (Greece, Luxembourg and Spain), 1998 (Austria, Estonia and Latvia) and 2005 (Ireland, Slovakia and Turkey).

4.3.2.2   Green certificate systems
In 1998 the first green certificate system was introduced in the Netherlands, alongside the already existing Dutch FIT. By 2005 green certificate systems existed in 11 countries – nine European and two non-European OECD coun-

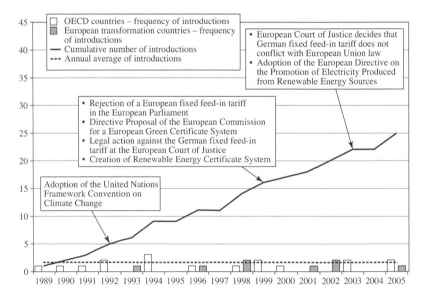

Source: Own data.

Figure 4.1   Cross-national proliferation of feed-in tariffs

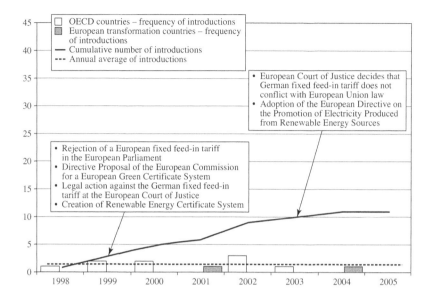

Source: Own data.

Figure 4.2   Cross-national proliferation of green certificate systems

tries (see Figure 4.2). Like the proliferation of FIT, the proliferation of green certificate systems evolved without noticeable accelerations. In four years green certificate systems were introduced in only one country each year (in 1998 in the Netherlands, in 2001 in Poland, in 2003 in Sweden and in 2004 in Romania). In two years they were adopted in two countries, namely Denmark and Italy, in 1999, and in Australia and Austria in 2000. Only once, in 2002, were three green certificate systems introduced within a single year (in Belgium, Japan and the United Kingdom).

4.3.2.3   Interactions of the proliferation of FIT and green certificate systems

A closer look at the data reveals that the proliferation of FIT and of green certificate systems did not occur independently of each other, but that the two processes were strongly interdependent. While from 1989 to 1998 FIT were the preferred instrument to promote the generation of electricity from RES, this changed considerably afterwards. Between 1999 and 2003, FIT were abolished in five European countries, namely, Italy (1999), Denmark (1999), Poland (2001), Belgium (2001) and Sweden (2003), and subsequently replaced by green certificate systems. The Spanish government also considered replacing the FIT with a green certificate system, but eventually refrained from doing so.

As a result, the proliferation of FIT slowed down after 1998 (from one adoption every 0.7 years between 1989 and 1998 to one adoption every 1.4 years between 1999 and 2005), while the proliferation of green certificate systems started in that very year. The net increase in the number of countries in which FIT were implemented amounted to only five between 1999 and 2005. At the same time, the number of green certificate systems in European countries increased by eight between 1999 and 2005.

In the next subsection we identify the driving forces of the spread of FIT and, since 1999, of green certificate systems in the EU and beyond. In particular, we explore whether and to what extent processes of policy diffusion mattered in the proliferation of these instruments. By systematically comparing the proliferation of FIT and green certificate systems we show how the two proliferation processes interacted and explain the slowdown in the proliferation of FIT and the parallel rise of quota systems.

4.3.3   Driving Forces in the International Proliferation of RES-E Policies

A number of observations suggest that diffusion mattered significantly in the international proliferation of FIT and green certificate systems, whereas cooperation and coercion played no role. In many cases governments explicitly referred to similar policies implemented elsewhere when introducing either a FIT or a system of green certificates. In some cases, national governments went as far as to commission empirical studies that compared the application, successes and challenges of FIT and green certificate systems in different countries. On this basis, they were able to identify the advantages and disadvantages of each of the two instruments before deciding which one to opt for in their country.

4.3.3.1   Feed-in tariffs: models and direct policy transfer

Above all, the German regulations on FIT evolved into a widely recognized and imitated model for the introduction of FIT in many European countries and beyond (Bechberger et al., 2003, pp. 7–8). For example, the German laws strongly influenced the adoption and the design of FIT in the Czech Republic. By distributing a translation of the German laws to members of the Czech parliament and government, the Czech renewable energy association set off the public debate about an appropriate instrument for the promotion of RES-E. The debate eventually culminated in the adoption of the Czech FIT in 2001 (personal communication by Martin Bursik, former Czech environmental minister, 6 March 2002), which features major similarities with the German FIT. Likewise, Greece (Ministry of Development, 2004, p. 2), Spain (Bechberger et al., 2003) and Switzerland (Eco-news, 2003) used the German laws as a blueprint for their FIT. In Austria national decision-makers repeatedly brought the German model into the public debate on the introduction of a FIT and demanded that the German example be followed (Nationalrat der Republik Österreich, 1996).

Interestingly also, the German government referred explicitly to foreign experience when it first adopted its FIT in 1991 (Deutscher Bundestag, 1988, p. 35). Again in 1998, when the first regulation on FIT was amended, the German government legitimized and justified its decision with the successful increase of RES-E production in foreign countries where FIT were operating (Deutscher Bundestag, 1998, p. 8).

In two cases, governments commissioned studies that systematically compared foreign experience with instruments for the promotion of RES-E before deciding to adopt FIT. In France, Lionel Jospin, the former French prime minister, asked Yves Cochet, a member of the French parliament, to produce a study evaluating foreign policies for the promotion of RES-E. The study was to compile the necessary information about foreign experience and identify a policy that could be transferred to France (Cochet, 2000, p. 36). It recommended a FIT that was a synthesis of the policies of several EU member states (ibid. pp. 20–3). The recommendation was based on the successes of several European countries in boosting the use of RES sources FIT. Green certificate systems, by contrast, were seen much less enthusiastically, and the report pointed out the difficulties in their implementation and concluded that they were less effective FIT in achieving ambitious goals (ibid., pp. 40–3). The adoption of a FIT in Austria is another case in point. Much as in the French case, the Austrian FIT was based on a commissioned study that analyzed and compared existing FIT in all EU member states, Norway and Switzerland (Cerveny and Resch, 1998).

4.3.3.2 Green certificate systems: failed cooperation and mediated diffusion powered by the European Commission

As in the case of FIT, coercion was absent in the proliferation of green certificate systems. A closer look at the individual domestic adoptions of green certificate systems suggests that again diffusion processes mattered in their international spread. However, while decentralized and bilateral processes of imitation and learning drove the spread of FIT, the spread of green certificate systems was characterized by a more centralized approach, with the European Commission actually trying to harmonize national RES policies. In October 1998 the European Commission presented a draft directive that called for a harmonization of RES policies by introducing a Europe-wide green certificate system and by establishing a European market for the trade of renewable certificates (Hinsch, 1999). The European Commission justified its proposal with fears that different policy instruments or differences in the level of promotion could create barriers to trade within the liberalized European electricity market and cause unfair competition (European Commission, 1998b, pp. 3–5). Ultimately, this attempt to harmonize member states' policies failed as the German government strictly opposed the Commission draft Directive and other EU member states that had already implemented an FIT were at least reluctant to switch to a system of tradable certificates (Lauber, 2005).

After lengthy negotiations a Council Directive on the promotion of electricity produced from RES (2001/77/EC) was adopted in September 2001. However, instead of choosing between FIT and green certificate systems, the directive postponed harmonization to 2012, leaving it to the member states to decide which instrument to opt for. Still, the directive included criteria for assessing RES instruments that were generally biased in favor of green certificate systems. On the basis of these criteria, the different national policies for the promotion of RES policies should be evaluated in 2005 and a model for the EU-wide harmonization of national RES-E policies should eventually be selected. Hence, while the ultimate decision on harmonization was postponed, the European Commission was successful in including assessment criteria that were likely to favor green certificate systems.

Two other observations underscore the favorable attitude of the European Commission toward green certificate systems. First, the majority of RES research projects funded by the European Commission examined the economic and trade implications of a green certificate system, sought to derive policy recommendations on how a European green certificate system should ideally be designed and were aimed at facilitating the exchange of experiences among national policymakers and practitioners. Second, the European Commission granted financial and logistical support to the Danish government during the drafting of its green certificate system (Lauber, 2001, p. 11). Thus, although attempts to legally harmonize national RES policies failed, the ideas promoted by the European Commission found their way into the political and scholarly debate and created favorable conditions for the gradual diffusion of green certificate systems. As harmonization failed, the mechanism by which green certificate systems spread among European countries switched from cooperation to 'mediated' diffusion, that is, diffusion powered by the information-based promotion of this policy model.

The European Commission was however not the only actor that promoted green certificate systems at the international level. When the European Commission declared its intent to harmonize member states' RES policies, the Renewable Energy Certificate System (RECS) was founded. This international organization gathers representatives of national governments and companies from twenty countries (including all member states of the EU) and supports the implementation of green certificate systems in Europe and beyond. RECS has set itself the goal of coordinating existing or future national green certificate systems and establishing an international market for the trade of renewable certificates without waiting for a harmonization by the European

Commission (Bliem, 2001, pp. 99–100). Further underscoring its favorable attitude toward green certificate systems, the European Commission granted financial support to the RECS, in particular for a two-year test of an international RES-E certificate trade from the 2001 until 2002.

The international promotion of green certificate systems evidently mattered in national RES decision-making. In an overall assessment Lauber concludes:

> Parallel to the discussions of RECSs [renewable energy certificate systems] in the preparation of the EU directive, several States prepared such systems at the domestic level, on the assumption that this was the best market approach and with the expectation that a European market for RECs would develop in near future. (Lauber, 2001, p. 8)

For example, the study that informed the British government prior to its decision to introduce green certificate systems explicitly discussed related political developments at the European level and their implications for the British policy choice:

> The extent to which the EU is able to promote their policies within Member States is crucial. From the publication of the White Paper in 1997 to the current debates over the merits of a Directive on Fair Access for Renewables to the Electricity Grid, a fundamental shift has occurred within the European renewable energy policy world ... As the timetable of the Single Market (SEM) moves closer, it has become clear that renewable energy policy is expected to be complementary to the principle of a SEM ... Thus, while the White Paper concentrated on targets and how to get there, the Draft Directives have been explicit in their support for competition as the basis of promoting renewables and of the need for individual Member State renewable energy policies to meet the EU Competition and State Aid requirements. [R]enewables within the European Commission policy, as with renewables in the United Kingdom, are expected to fit with the move towards a competitive single market. (Mitchell and Anderson, 2000, pp. 25–6)

The authors of the study identified the publications in which the European Commission defined its position in favor of green certificate systems as 'key driver' for the renewable policy choices in the United Kingdom and other EU Member States (Mitchell and Anderson, 2000, p. 26).

Similarly, the Dutch government's choice of a green certificate system was influenced by a study that explicitly recommended taking into account the active promotion of that instrument by the European Commission. This recommendation was based on the assumption that by adopting a green certificate system the Netherlands could move ahead of likely European developments and thereby actively shape these processes:

> An internal EU energy market will generate demand for trade in renewable energy. The experience currently being gained with the trade in green labels and ultimately perhaps also with renewable certificates will give the Netherlands a head start within the EU. (van Beek and Benner, 1998, p. 88)

The Danish actors in the RES sector anticipated the European developments, too. They expected that the ongoing liberalization of the internal European electricity market in the mid-term future would further reinforce the European trend in favor of green certificate systems (Ruby, 2001). Consequently, Denmark introduced a green certificate system 'in order to influence the operational rules of the model that it believed would be the future choice for the EU' (Meyer, 2003, p. 604).

Compared with these strong indications of mediated diffusion, direct policy transfer was less apparent during the international proliferation of green certificate systems. Nevertheless, in a few countries governments also drew on systematic comparisons of policies implemented elsewhere. The aforementioned study commissioned by the Dutch government examined and compared RES-E policies across 18 mostly European countries (van Beek and Benner, 1998). In their conclusions the authors recommended the introduction of a green certificate system, even though they also pointed out the merits and successes of feed-in tariffs (van Beek and Benner, 1998, p. 89). Similarly, the British and Australian governments sought to learn from foreign experiences in their decision-making processes by commissioning studies that explored the promises and limitations of different RES instruments (Mitchell and Anderson, 2000; Parliament of Australia, 2000).

4.4   DISCUSSION: INTERACTIONS IN THE PROLIFERATION OF RES-E POLICIES

Overall, our observations support the interpretation that diffusion mattered in the international proliferation of FIT and green certificate systems. By highlighting the European Commission's attempt to adopt a binding requirement for member states to introduce green certificate systems as well as the active promotion of this instrument by various international organizations since 1998, our study also offers a plausible explanation for the slowdown in the international proliferation of FIT in European countries and their replacement by green certificate systems in some European countries. Overall, we have shown these distinct proliferation patterns to result from the operation of three mechanisms of international policy coordination: direct diffusion in the case of FIT and failed cooperation followed by internationally mediated diffusion in the case of green certificate systems.

But how did these mechanisms interact with each other? A closer look at the efforts of the European Commission as well as other international organizations to promote green certificate systems allows for additional insights into the interaction of direct and mediated diffusion and (unsuccessful) cooperation.

Already in the 1990s, the European Commission dismissed FIT as an appropriate model for harmonizing RES-E policies in Europe. In a report that preceded its 1998 draft directive, the European Commission took an unambiguous position: '[T]he move from a fixed tariff approach towards one based on trade and competition is at some stage inevitable' (European Commission, 1998a, p. 17). While green certificate systems were perceived to be compatible with the rules of the internal electricity market, FIT were perceived to restrict competition between energy sources and across countries, and to create barriers to the international trade of electricity (for example European Commission, 1998a, pp. 15–16). Consequently, the draft directive proposed to prohibit FIT. Yet the European Commission's position did not prevail, mainly because of the resistance of German and Spanish renewable energy associations, the German red–green government that had come to power in 1998, and the opposition of the European Parliament to this proposal (Hinsch, 1999, p. 56).

While not resulting in legal harmonization, the position of the European Commission created political uncertainty about the future of FIT. At least until the adoption of directive 2001/77/EC in 2001, it remained uncertain whether the European Commission's position would win general support. This uncertainty about future binding legislation and the resulting fear on the part of EU member states of having chosen the 'wrong instrument' elucidates to some extent the decline in the proliferation of FIT after 1998.

Other events and processes in European institutions added to this uncertainty about the future of FIT in Europe. Most importantly, in 1998 the German energy company Preussen Elektra brought an action against the German FIT at the *Landgericht* (district court) of Kiel, which forwarded this case to the European Court of Justice (ECJ). Preussen Elektra justified its legal action by arguing that the German FIT constituted an inadmissible state subsidy that violated European competition laws and the liberalization of the European electricity market. In March 2001 the ECJ decided that the German FIT was not an inadmissible state subsidy. Nevertheless, the ECJ qualified its decision and emphasized possible implications for international trade by warning 'that those rules were capable, at least potentially, of hindering intra-Community trade' (ECJ 2001). Although the case was eventually rejected, between 1998 and 2001 the pending decision of the ECJ created a legal uncertainty that prevented EU member states from introducing FIT. If the ECJ had come to the conclusion that the German FIT violated European competition and trade law, the then existing FIT would certainly have had to be abolished. Moreover, the European Parliament rejected the demand for introducing a European wide FIT in 1998 for the third time since 1996, thereby underscoring the dismissive attitude of major European institutions toward FIT (European Parliament, 1996; Rothe, 1998).

However, the international promotion of green certificate systems by the European Commission could not have had such a strong impact on EU member states without the emergence of the internal European electricity market. The adoption of the Council Directive concerning common rules for the internal market in electricity (96/92/EC) in 1996 created a new framework for national and international energy policies. As a result, regulatory competencies were increasingly shifted from domestic institutions to the European Commission and other European institutions. This shift in competencies enabled the European Commission to assume an increasingly influential role. The shift thus generally increased the potential effects that the European Commission's favorable attitude toward green certificate systems and its dismissive attitude toward FIT had on domestic decisions about the appropriate renewable electricity support policy.

Against this background, it can be concluded that the mediated diffusion of the green certificate systems in combination with the liberalization of the internal European electricity market had significant side effects on the international proliferation of both instruments (that is contributing to the 'green Europeanization' of energy policy in the EU). The strong promotion of green certificate systems created, on the one hand, favorable conditions for their proliferation. On the other hand, other legal and political developments created increasing uncertainty about the future of FIT and negatively affected the spread of this earlier instrument. The emerging internal electricity market in Europe increased the influence of the positions put forward by the European Commission by introducing criteria for the assessment of RES-E policies that further favored the adoption of green certificate systems.

4.5   CONCLUSIONS

From a Europeanization perspective, the most interesting findings of this case study relate to the interactions between the two parallel proliferation processes (that is as part of the 'green Europeanization' of the energy policy). First of all, it is worth noting that the EU-wide spread of FIT in the 1990s was not driven by legal harmonization – the Europeanization mechanism most prominently emphasized in the Europeanization and international relations literature – but by loosely coordinated instances of bilateral imitation and learning. This finding substantiates our claim that decentralized and voluntary mechanisms of policy coordination can have effects that are very similar to those of centralized policy-making.

Second, the case study shows that supranational attempts to legally harmonize domestic policies can have the intended effect even if they ultimately fail. Again, this effect results from a largely voluntary and unilateral adaptation of domestic policies to internationally communicated policy models and international policy discourses. Diffusion, thus, can be both an independent source of cross-national policy clustering and a significant side effect of failed cooperation. In both cases, international policy clustering and convergence occurs in the absence of successful international cooperation or coercion. It shows that especially in highly institutionalized contexts like the EU, policy diffusion can be a valid mechanism of international policy coordination.

Third, and with regard to the distinction between direct and mediated diffusion, our analysis suggests that if two policy innovations that pursue identical goals proliferate simultaneously then the innovation that is predominantly driven by mediated diffusion may affect and supersede the spread of the alternative policy innovation that is driven mainly by direct policy transfer. In the particular case of instruments for promoting RES-E, the analysis suggests that mediated diffusion is not only a strong mechanism of proliferation but may also have significant side effects on the spread of other, competing instruments. Such side effects can be expected in particular if the international actor that communicates and promotes the policy innovation has some regulatory powers in the related policy area. In such cases, national decision-makers may anticipate a possible harmonization by this actor and adopt the policy that is favored by that actor before harmonization actually becomes effective. Moreover, the analysis revealed that diffusion-driven proliferation processes may also be affected by the degree of compatibility between the policy and existing norms, such as competition and free trade.

To sum up, based on these empirical findings, this chapter supports the view that diffusion as a distinct Europeanization mechanism should be paid more attention in future research regarding both the Europeanization of energy policy and the RES policy in the framework of the European energy policy. In particular, scholars as well as policymakers should be more attentive to the way in which legal harmonization might impact upon existing diffusion processes.

NOTE

1. Albania, Australia, *Austria*, Belarus, *Belgium*, Bosnia, *Bulgaria*, Canada, Croatia, *Czech Republic*, *Denmark*, *Germany*, *Estonia*, *Finland*, *France*, *Greece*, *Hungary*, *Ireland*, Iceland, *Italy*, Japan, *Latvia*, *Lithuania*, *Luxembourg*, Macedonia, Moldova, New Zealand, *the Netherlands*, Norway, *Poland*, *Portugal*, *Romania*, Russia, *Slovakia*, *Slovenia*, *Sweden*, Switzerland, *Spain*, South Korea, Turkey, Ukraine, *United Kingdom*, and the United States (EU member states are in italics).

REFERENCES

Bechberger, M., S. Körner, and D.T. Reiche (2003), 'Erfolgsbedingungen von Instrumenten zur Förderung erneuerbarer Energien im Strommarkt', *FFU-Report* 00–06, Environmental Policy Research Centre, Berlin.

van Beek, A. and J.H.B. Benner (1998), *International Benchmark Study on Renewable Energy: Final Report to the Dutch Ministry of Economic Affairs*, Rotterdam: Consultants on Energy and Environment, CEA.

Bliem, M. (2001), *Wirtschaftspolitische Optionen für erneuerbare Energieträger im liberalisierten europäischen Energiemarkt*, Graz, Austria: Institut für Volkswirtschaftslehre und Volkswirtschaftspolitik, Karl-Franzens-Universität.

Börzel, T.A. and T. Risse (2009), 'The Transformative Power of Europe: The European Union and the Diffusion of Ideas', KFG working paper no. 1, Berlin.

Busch, P.O. and H. Jörgens (2005), 'International patterns of environmental policy change and convergence', *European Environment*, **15** (2), 80–101.

Busch, P.O and H. Jörgens (2007), 'Dezentrale Politikkoordination im internationalen System – Ursachen, Mechanismen und Wirkungen der internationalen Diffusion politischer Innovationen', in Katharina Holzinger, Helge Jörgens and Christoph Knill (eds), *Transfer, Diffusion und Konvergenz von Politiken*, Wiesbaden, Germany: VS Verlag, pp. 56–84, published in *Politische Vierteljahresschrift*, Special issue **38**/2007.

Cerveny, M., and G. Resch (1998), *Feed-in Tariffs and Regulations Concerning Renewable Energy Electricity Generation in European Countries*, Vienna: Energieverwertungsagentur.

Cochet, Y. (2000), 'Rapport au Premier Ministre: Stratégie et moyens de développement de l'efficacité énergétique et des sources d'énergie renouvelables en France', Paris.

Court of Justice of the European Communities (2001), 'An obligation to purchase at minimum prices does not constitute state aid merely because it is imposed by statute', press release no. 10/2001, 13 March.

Deutscher Bundestag (1988), 'Antwort der Bundesregierung auf die große Anfrage zur Förderung und Nutzung erneuerbarer Energiequellen in der Bundesrepublik Deutschland', 20 July.

Deutscher Bundestag (1998), 'Gesetz über den Vorrang erneuerbarer Energien (Erneuerbare-Energien-Gesetz, EEG)'.

ECO-NEWS (2003), 'Die Schweiz orientiert sich am deutschen EEG', Förderverein Ökologische Steuerreform 2002, accessed 6 June 2003 at www.foes-ev.de/news11/3artikel9.html.

European Commission (1998a), *Electricity from Renewable Energy Sources and the Internal Electricity Market*, Brussels: European Commission.

European Commission (1998b), *Report to the Council and the European Parliament on Harmonisation Requirements: Directive 96/92/EC Concerning Common Rules for the Internal Market in Electricity*, Brussels: European Commission.

European Parliament (1996), *Resolution on a Community Action Plan for Renewable Energy Sources*, A4–0188/1996, Brussels.

Finnemore, M., and K. Sikkink (1998) 'International norm dynamics and political change', *International Organization* **52** (4), 887–917.

Grabbe, H. (2006), *The EU's Transformative Power: Europeanization Through Conditionality in Central and Eastern Europe*, Basingstoke: Palgrave Macmillan.

Haas, P.M. (1992), 'Introduction: epistemic communities and international policy coordination', *International Organization*, **46** (1), 1–35.

Hinsch, C. (1999), 'Aufgeschoben ist nicht aufgehoben: Europäische Einspeiserichtlinie wird hinter den Kulissen weiter diskutiert', *Neue Energie*, (3), 56–8.

Holzinger, K., C. Knill and B. Arts (eds) (2008), *Environmental Policy Convergence in Europe: The Impact of International Institutions and Trade*, Cambridge: Cambridge University Press.

Howlett, M. (2000), 'Beyond legalism? Policy ideas, implementation styles and emulation-based convergence in Canadian and U.S. environmental policy', *Journal of Public Policy*, **20** (3), 305–29.

International Energy Agency (IEA) (2008), *Deploying Renewables: Principles for Effective Policies*, Paris: IAE.

Jörgens, H. (2004), 'Governance by diffusion – implementing global norms through cross-national imitation and learning', in W.M. Lafferty (ed.), *Governance for Sustainable Development: The Challenge of Adapting Form to Function*, Cheltenham, UK and Northampton, MA, USA: Edward Elgar, pp. 246–83.

Keohane, R.O. (1984), *After Hegemony: Cooperation and Discord in the World Political Economy*, Princeton, NJ: Princeton University Press.

Lauber, V. (2001), 'The different concepts of promoting RES-electricity and their political careers', paper read at the Conference on the Human Dimensions of Global Change: Global Environmental Change and the Nation State, 7–8 December, Berlin.

Lauber, V. (2005), 'European Union policy towards renewable power', in Volkmar Lauber (ed.), *Switching to Renewable Power: A Framework For the 21st Century*, London: Earthscan, pp. 203–16.

Levi-Faur, D. (2005), 'The global diffusion of regulatory capitalism', *Annals of the American Academy of Political and Social Science*, **598**, 12–34.

Levi-Faur, D. and J. Jordana (2005), 'Preface: the making of a new regulatory order', *Annals of the American Academy of Political and Social Science*, **598**, 6–9.

Lindblom, C.E. (1965), *The Intelligence of Democracy: Decision Making Through Mutual Adjustment*, New York: Free Press.

Meyer, N.I. (2003), 'European schemes for promoting renewables in liberalised markets', *Energy Policy*, **31**, 665–76.

Ministry of Development (2004), 'National report regarding penetration level of renewable energy sources in the year 2010.' accessed 23 February at www.ypan.gr/docs/NATIONAL_REPORT_OF_GREECE_ON_DIRECTIVE_2001_77.doc.

Mitchell, C. and T. Anderson, (2000), *The Implications of Tradable Green Certificates for the UK*, London: Department for Business, Innovation and Skill, accessed 17 June 2004 at http://www.berr.gov.uk/files/file15148.pdf.

Nationalrat der Republik Österreich (1996), *Stenographisches Protokoll. 38. Sitzung des Nationalrates der Republik Österreich*, XX Gesetzgebungsperiode, 20 September.

Parliament of Australia (2000), *Renewable Energy (Electricity) Bill 2000 – Renewable Energy (Electricity) (Charge) Bill 2000. Report of the Senate Environment, Communications, Information Technology and the Arts References Committee*, Canberra: Senate Environment, Communications, Information Technology and the Arts References Committee.

Rogers, E.M. (2003), *Diffusion of Innovations*, 5th edn, New York: Free Press.

Rothe, M. (1998), 'Konkreter Vorschlag im Herbst: MdEP Mechthild Rothe zum EU-Weißbuch "Erneuerbare Energien"', *Neue Energie*, pp. 14–15.

Ruby, J. (2001), 'Zweifelhafte Zertifikate: Nach heftigen Kontroversen warten die Dänen weiter auf ihr neues Ökostrom-Gesetz', *Neue Energie*, pp. 74–6.

Schimmelfennig, F. and H. Scholz (2008), 'EU democracy promotion in the European neighbourhood: political conditionality, economic development and transnational exchange', *European Union Politics*, **9** (2),187–215.

Simmons, B.A. and Elkins, Z. (2004), 'The globalization of liberalization: policy diffusion in the international political economy', *American Political Science Review*, **98** (1), 171–89.

Simmons, B.A., F. Dobbin and G. Garrett (2008), 'Introduction: the diffusion of liberalization', in Beth A. Simmons, Frank Dobbin and Geoffrey Garrett (eds), *The Global Diffusion of Markets and Democracy*, Cambridge: Cambridge University Press, pp. 1–63.

5. Carbon capture and storage: the Europeanization of a technology in Europe's energy policy?

Severin Fischer[1]

5.1 INTRODUCTION

Within a comparatively short time, carbon capture and storage (CCS) has become a topic of enthusiastic and heated discussion among scientists, policy-makers and non-governmental organizations (NGOs) in the European Union (EU) and its member states. While little is in fact known about the practical use of this technology and the system surrounding it, most of the actors have already taken a normative decision on its further deployment. In general, the idea behind using CCS is surprisingly simple: by capturing the harmful greenhouse gases (GHG) before or during the fuel combustion process, transporting them to a storage site and then storing the emissions underground, either in empty natural-gas fields or in saline geological layers, the high-carbon combustion technologies of today can become part of the low-carbon-technologies and clean development options of tomorrow. While no large-scale CCS demonstration project has been finalized in the EU to date, its integration into national and European energy policies is already an impressive achievement in itself.

This success story was driven by a few strategic considerations: in 2006, around 81 percent of European energy consumption derived from carbon-intensive fossil fuels, such as hard coal, lignite, oil or natural gas (Eurostat, 2009). Meanwhile, the EU will be asked to reduce its 1990 emissions level by 80 to 95 percent by 2050 in order to remain within a global 2 °C scenario, according to the Intergovernmental Panel on Climate Change (IPCC) recommendations (IPCC, 2007). By comparing both figures, the challenge on the climate front becomes apparent. When we look at the global situation, the need for new technological solutions to reduce greenhouse gas emissions appears even more urgent: in a business-as-usual scenario, energy sector CO_2 emissions will rise in the range of 130 percent by 2050 compared with 2005 (IEA, 2008). Additionally, the majority of new energy infrastructure investments in developing and emerging economies will be related to the use of hard coal or lignite. Therefore, finding low-carbon solutions will be of utmost importance for the future.

Despite the need to radically cut emissions, there is another aspect to be borne in mind in considering CCS as a technical solution. For most countries inside and outside the EU, solid fuels are not only a cheap energy source; they also offer a high degree of energy security. In Europe, this is an important factor for Poland and other coal-based central and eastern European countries, fearful of a higher dependency on Russian natural gas as a direct consequence of a low-carbon development strategy. Similarly, outside the EU, large economies like China see no alternatives to relying on domestic fossil resources, mainly solid fuels, to satisfy the massively growing energy needs of their societies. Looking at the climate and security challenges, it becomes clear why such high expectations are focused on CCS. Nevertheless, the rudimentary level of technical experience and unidentified environmental concerns pose a serious threat to the prolonged success story of CCS. This demonstrates the ambivalent nature of the CCS debate today. In this context, it would be especially interesting to analyze the policy-making process launched a couple of years ago and look at how advocates of CCS managed to enter the arena of EU policy-making and how they acted in this environment (promoting the 'green Europeanization' of CCS policies in the EU).

The appearance of CCS in European energy policy and the Europeanization of CCS policies is the topic of the following pages. Section 5.2 starts with the agenda-setting stage regarding CCS in the EU. Next, Section 5.3 deals with questions surrounding regulation and the development of financial incentives for the use of CCS technologies. Section 5.4 outlines the penetration of CCS into the European energy policy agenda. Section 5.5 then looks at the consequences of the EU CCS policy. Finally, Section 5.6 approaches to the CCS future in the core of the emergent European energy policy.

5.2 CCS IN THE EUROPEAN ENERGY POLICY: THE AGENDA SETTING PHASE

Capturing carbon dioxide from industrial activities is not a recently mooted idea, but actually a rather well-known technique. Capturing carbon has a long tradition (IEA, 2009, p. 8), especially in upstream oil and gas production activities. It was not by accident that resource-rich countries like Norway started promoting CCS in the first place: with a competitive advantage in technology use, they realized that using CCS for emission mitigation could create a completely new market and generate business opportunities for domestic companies and technologies. Other countries soon joined the CCS roadmap. In the EU, CCS entered high-level political discussions for the first time in 2005, during negotiations about the second phase of the European Climate Change Programme (ECCP II). A special working group was set up to identify challenges and opportunities for enhancing CCS and for using it as a new climate policy instrument. At an early stage of this process, the European Commission realized the political opportunities offered by this situation: if the EU could be the promoter and driving force behind the integration of CCS into Europe's climate strategy, the Commission would also have a leading role to play (that is at the same time that the Commission was launching the European energy policy; see Chapter 1 by Solorio Sandoval and Morata).

With the decision on the EU Energy Action Plan (2007–2009) (European Council, 2007), the European Council followed the Commission's recommendations, published in an energy policy Green Paper one year before (European Commission, 2006). The Action Plan identifies the deployment of CCS as a principal challenge in the European Energy Technology Policy. Heads of state and governments asked the Commission to improve knowledge about CCS, to promote the deployment of 12 demonstration plants until 2015 and to develop the technology towards full and cost-effective market integration in 2020.

The decision to put such a strong emphasis on CCS was not unanimous among the member states. Southern European EU members in particular were not all in favor of concentrating on a specific technology that could not be used in most regions around the Mediterranean Sea, because of unsuitable geological formations and the relatively high likeliness of earthquakes. At the same time, the expectations of smaller and less economically developed member states were rather low, assuming that the centralized CCS structure and the strategy's limitation to 12 demonstration plants would not benefit their interests. Last but not least, the French position on CCS was rather reserved owing to the competition with nuclear energy as *the* low-carbon technology in Europe's energy mix. In the end it was a coalition between the European Commission's Energy Directorate-General, industry representatives and strong CCS advocates from among the member states, such as the United Kingdom and the Netherlands, with some support from Germany and Poland, that pushed the topic onto Europe's energy agenda. With this mandate, the Commission started to prepare legislation on CCS in 2007. It concentrated on two crucial aspects: the regulation of local and global risks related to the use of CCS and the establishment of investment security and favorable conditions for integrating CCS into the European energy markets.

5.3   ADDRESSING THE CHALLENGES FOR CCS AND THE POLICY-MAKING PROCESS

Lack of experience in the use of CCS technologies constituted a fundamental problem for establishing a legal framework from the start. It raised the question as to how policymakers should regulate potentially negative impacts from the application of a mainly unknown technology and at the same time offer incentives to invest in large-scale demonstration projects. In a communication from January 2008, the European Commission elaborated further on the challenges it had to face in addressing both aspects (European Commission, 2008). Three central questions had to be answered: how far the use of CCS should be regulated at the EU level, compared with national legislation; whether there should be one comprehensive legal framework for all three steps involved in the CCS technology system (capture, transport and storage); and whether support schemes for CCS should be established at the national level or whether it would be possible to fund CCS from the EU budget.

The Commission decided to consider these questions in the context of the Climate and Energy Package, published in January 2008 as part of the overall climate policy concept that was supposed to be finalized before the start of the Copenhagen negotiations in December 2009 (see Chapter 1 by Solorio Sandoval and Morata; Chapter 2 by Adelle at al.). It also gave an indication of how the Commission intended to deal with the topic: approaching CCS from the climate change perspective and setting up legislation under the environment chapter of the treaties were meant to give the concept a sounder basis, rather than arguing on the grounds of energy policy considerations (that is promoting the 'green Europeanization' of energy policy).

5.3.1   Regulating the Use of CCS in the EU

The environmental risks connected to CCS can be analyzed along two general lines: on the one hand, the global risks relating to the release of captured GHG, either during transportation of CO_2 or caused by leakages in the storage sites, had to be addressed; on the other hand, local environmental impacts and security concerns seemed crucial. This included water management, the protection of flora and fauna, and protection from possible seismic activities following the injection of gases into geological formations. Thus, it was necessary to identify clearly the shared responsibilities of the operators of installations, pipeline systems or storage sites and the duties of the competent state authority. Without clear provisions, the danger of delayed investments due to unresolved legal questions would have seriously damaged the competitive position of companies on the global technologies market (Zakkour, 2007a).

The European Commission decided to pursue a comparatively cautious approach in drafting a directive for CCS use. All three steps in the CCS chain were addressed separately, and at each stage it was asked how far existing legislation could already provide a basis for regulating their use. The Commission reached the conclusion that existing legislation could be applied to two of the steps: the capture of carbon emissions inside an installation and transport to the storage site. For the first issue, the industrial emissions Directive (Directive 96/61/EC) seemed suitable. For the second issue, the Regulation for the secure transport of natural gas could apply (Regulation 2005/1775/EC). Only the last step, the storage of emissions, required a completely new set of rules because of its unique requirements. Therefore, the focus of the Directive was on creating a framework for the storage of GHG.

To this end, some specific issues concerning the rules and procedures for storing CO_2 had to be resolved. Among other things, the institutional responsibility for storage permissions, the liability for storage sites and financial implications required legal clarification. Also, minor issues concerning the CO_2 stream, access to storage sites and administrative implications had to be tackled. It was clear to the Commission that not all questions could be left to the member states, owing to the danger of triggering a race to the bottom on environmental standards in the community. On the other hand, subsidiarity and proportionality of EU action seemed relevant in this context, especially for questioning whether local environmental implications could best be addressed by the member states.

From the outset of the negotiations, it was clear that the Commission would not gain any real decision-making power as to where the use of CCS could be enforced, or in which member states it would be applied. Nevertheless, the Commission tried to ensure the introduction of strict rules for the approval of storage sites and technical issues when using CCS, including a European registry. The Commission also pushed for its own involvement in overseeing the reporting and monitoring duties of CCS power plant and storage site operators. Despite its interest in information, most responsibilities for long-term security of underground storage sites and other safety provisions were left to member state authorities. Additionally, most criteria for the transfer of surveillance responsibilities were rather weak and subject to the political decisions of national governments.

During the negotiations on the Directive, some member states and the European Parliament turned out to be more enthusiastic about setting up specific qualitative and quantitative aspects of governance modalities for CCS installations than the Commission had initially proposed. This resulted in the inclusion of specified schemes for the consistency of the gas stream (especially with regard to acid substances), the introduction of a 20-year surveillance obligation for member states' authorities after closing a storage site, and more-detailed provisions for payments towards a security deposit, to name just a few examples. Yet, the responsibilities remained largely with the national authorities.

Intensive debates were held on the possibility of including a so-called 'Schwarzenegger clause' in the Directive. The European Commission wanted to introduce a provision that would have obliged all combustion plants with a capacity of more than 300 megawatts (MW) to provide spatial and technological opportunities for a possible retrofitting with CCS technology in a medium-term perspective. The Environment Committee of the European Parliament wanted to go even further and introduce emissions performance standards for power plants with a capacity of more than 300 MW, which would have made CCS practically compulsory from that date on. According to the final first reading agreement, the operator of a combustion plant now has to verify the existence of possible storage sites, the possibility of building a CO_2 transport infrastructure and the technical and economic potential for CCS improvements. At the end of the day, however, the provision is not forcing operators of industrial installations to use CCS technologies and does not involve any emissions standards at all.

Since April 2009, the EU has had a single legal framework for the application of CCS technology, which leaves most decisions to the member states (Directive 2009/31/EC). Still, the EU has developed common CCS standards, thereby offering investment security and preventing a race to the bottom on environmental provisions among member states.

5.3.2 Setting Incentives for Investment in CCS Installations

The decision to support the commercialization of CCS technologies through financial incentives had many opponents in the EU. Following the arguments of many NGOs and some member state governments, direct CCS funding not only would question 'technology neutrality' as a fundamental principle in European policy-making but, even worse, would support investment in a technology that would, if ever applied, have only a bridging function without constituting a long-lasting sustainable solution to environmental needs. Many policymakers, on the other hand, argued that without the support of private investment through public incentives, CCS would never become economically viable (Zakkour, 2007b).

At the moment, the benefits of hindering GHG emissions from entering the atmosphere do not outweigh the costs of building an installation with CCS. The reason for this can be found on different levels. First, there is no real price for emitting GHG. While the EU established an emissions trading scheme in 2005, it covers only parts of the European economy. Additionally, under 2008 legislation, CCS installations would, although gases are stored underground, be obliged to buy certificates for the range of produced emissions. Therefore, taking CCS installations out of the system and putting a high price on carbon would favor investment in CCS technologies. Second, the positive impacts on energy security are not represented in market prices. Despite their harmful environmental effects, domestic resources, such as hard coal or lignite, have an advantage over oil and gas, which are traded on volatile global markets. This has so far not been fully incorporated into investment decisions. Third, Europe's future technology export potential and leadership role is not included in the general market analysis. This is also a macroeconomic challenge for policymakers. Fourth and finally, the positive externalities of CCS for global climate policy are not obvious from merely looking at the present status of technology development: this should receive even more attention, considering the growth of coal-based electricity markets in many emerging economies. The opportunity to develop a low-carbon technology option will be missed under the investment provisions of today's international climate policies. Because of the long-term time frame of infrastructure decisions, missing this chance could have expensive lock-in effects in nearly unchangeable fossil energy structures (IEA, 2009). Contrary to all these arguments, CCS is merely recognized for its negative impacts, such as a drop in energy efficiency of sometimes more than 10 percent.

Taking all these different factors into account, the need to create public incentives for private investment in CCS demonstration plants becomes clear. The European Commission therefore perceived several measures as being applicable:

- Exclusion of CCS from emissions trading.
- Mandatory use of CCS in new installations.
- Direct public financial support to private investments.

While excluding CCS installations from emissions trading would create long-term incentives for the use of CCS technologies – CCS would become competitive when the costs of carbon permits equal the costs of investing in CCS – both provisions (mandatory use and direct subsidies) would integrate the technology into the market much faster. Nevertheless, direct subsidies in particular would violate Europe's aforementioned technology neutrality.

When drafting CCS legislation, the European Commission seemed to be in favor of using option one, but unlikely to mandate the introduction of CCS or to create additional funds for subsidizing its commercialization. In the end, it was the European Parliament's Environment Committee and some member states that brought both topics back onto the agenda. The so-called 'Schwarzenegger clause', mandating the use of CCS in large-scale installations, won a majority in the Environment Committee of the European

Parliament but was dropped in the final inter-institutional agreement. Yet the exclusion of CCS installations from emissions trading, as well as financial assistance from the 'New Entrants Reserve' of the EU Emissions Trading System (ETS), were confirmed in the final negotiations. According to this agreement, revenues from the auctioning of 300 million ETS certificates will be reserved for investments in CCS installations and large-scale renewable energy sources (RES) projects. Depending on the market price of the certificates, this could lend significant support to CCS in the future.

Following the decision on spending the revenues from the New Entrants Reserve, some policymakers in Brussels discovered direct funding to be a practicable way to show presence in energy technology development. In 2009, only a few months after the agreement on the Climate and Energy Package, the 'European Economic Recovery Plan' was launched. The Commission proposed a package of 5 billion euros for infrastructure investment during the crisis and its aftermath. Again, CCS projects would receive a large share of the investment program. Finally, after an agreement had been reached between the European Council and Parliament under the co-decision procedure, 1.05 billion euros were dedicated to seven CCS projects in a geographically and technologically balanced way (Regulation 663/2009/EC). Nevertheless, one important precondition was formulated: companies would have to compete with each other for funding, and funding would be available only to installations that started operating in the next years. This decision marked not only the beginning of competition among companies to finalize projects in time; it also initiated a race among governments to create an investment-friendly environment and set up legal frameworks to provide investment security, in order to attract more CCS project funding for their country from the EU.

As a last and recent step, the European Commission presented a reviewed 'Strategic Energy Technology Plan' (SET-Plan) at the end of 2009, containing strategic priorities and investment needs for the promotion and market launch of certain technologies (European Commission, 2009). CCS projects would receive the largest amount of all the budget items were the SET-Plan to be accepted by the European institutions: 13 billion euros by 2020. The decision on strategic priorities and financial provisions will be an area for further discussions in the years to come.

5.4   MOVING CCS ONTO THE ENERGY AGENDA

As a consequence of legal restrictions in earlier EC Treaties and member states' reluctance to cede to the European energy policy, the EU's performance in this policy field has been rather weak in recent years. Since 2007, the situation has changed and many new projects have appeared on Europe's energy agenda. The establishment of CCS legislation and its growing importance, according to European Council conclusions and financial provisions, leads us to draw several conclusions about the role of CCS in the European energy policy.

From an institutional point of view, the legal background of CCS legislation is an important aspect to consider when analyzing the policy-making process. For environmental reasons (reducing GHG emissions) and on an environmental legal basis (the environment chapter in the treaties), CCS entered the stage of European energy policy. At first glance, CCS is still mainly an environmental policy tool, but looking deeper into the debate it becomes more and more obvious that CCS not only offers new options for the design of energy policies but also emerges as a promising energy policy. Bearing in mind that many EU member states have coal-based economies, CCS could be used as a policy tool to provide energy security, while at the same time ensuring compliance with environmental aims. In economic terms, this technology could cushion the burden of a fast transition to a low-carbon economy in the absence of technological alternatives to RES and the extended use of low-carbon natural gas.

The evolution of CCS from a minor environmental instrument in the tool-box of mitigation options to an integral part of the newly established energy agenda may also be traced by looking at the institutions responsible for nego-tiating CCS regulation. Although the first steps in setting up CCS legislation were negotiated exclusively among environmental policy actors, such as the European Commission DG Environment, the Environment Committee in the European Parliament and the Environment Ministers Council, the design of the energy program in the Economic Recovery Plan, as well as future funding in the Strategic Energy Technology Plan, will be dominated by actors from the energy policy community. From the drafting of legislation in the former DG TREN (now DG ENER) to the negotiation of legislation between the ITRE Committee of the European Parliament and the Energy Ministers Council, as a policy tool CCS has arrived at the centre of European energy policy.

5.5   DISCUSSION: EUROPEANIZING CCS?

From today's perspective, there can be no doubt that CCS is a European issue and that the EU is the main actor in the process of commercializing the tech-nology for industry and electricity production. Although this seems to be quite reasonable from today's point of view, such was not the case some years ago. Why did CCS move onto the European agenda and not just remain an emis-sions mitigation attempt by those member states that wanted to bring the tech-nology to commercialization and integrate it into the energy markets?

There is definitely more than just one answer to this question. A couple of member states played a decisive role in establishing CCS on the European energy agenda in order to receive European funding and develop a wider market for the technology. Front-runners in this regard were the United Kingdom and the Netherlands.

Owing to their privileged geological situation (depleted gas fields) and the need to restructure national energy policies, both member states started to consider CCS as a strategic option quite early on. Together with these two member states, Norway, as a non-EU member but an important player in European energy policy, invested significantly in bringing CCS to the European market, although not without disinterest: Norway had already been using the technology in upstream business for many years and sought to transfer its technological capacities to Continental Europe. This small coalition, together with some active members of the European Parliament, convinced the Commission to take CCS seriously and start developing a strategy to promote it at the EU level. After slow progress in the 1990s and early 2000s, the possibilities provided by CCS technologies entered the national discourse of other member states, such as Germany and in Poland. Convincing both governments was an important task for the CCS coalition because both countries, as heavy consumers of solid fossil fuels, would be in a position to become influential promoters of a CCS strategy in the EU.

In the first few months of drafting the CCS legislation, the European Commission had to answer the question about how much 'Europe' should be involved in regulation on the one hand and in technology support on the other. The decision to step back from most of the regulatory questions and leave them to the member states was already in the first stage of the policy-making process that the Commission proposed. For Commission officials it seemed more important to set up legislation in the form of rather general guidelines, in order to create a reliable legal investment environment. The Commission seemed largely satisfied with this limited influence on safeguards. Yet, for the member states, this offered the opportunity to shift responsibility for the need to develop CCS legislation to the EU level, because of the legal obligation to transfer EU legislation (even though only guidelines from the directive) into national law. Looking at the growing civil resistance to CCS in some member states, from the perspective of national governments this was a necessary step to initiating any CCS legislation at all.

On taking a look at the financial provisions for supporting CCS investments, the interaction between the European and national levels, on the one hand, and between the institutions themselves on the other, seems even more interesting. While the arrangement to exclude CCS installations from the ETS had to be organized EU-wide anyway (owing to the European nature of the system), the setting up of financial instruments to support CCS in the EU was a completely new issue for EU policy-making. Several member states introduced this idea during the negotiations on the ETS directive and used it as a bargaining tool. The idea was to reserve some funding from the ETS revenues for CCS, in order to overcome the heavy burden on some member states' electricity markets. After the decision to fund CCS projects via the New Entrants Reserve in the ETS, the Commission started to consider European financing from other sources as well. When it turned out that funds from the European Economic Recovery Plan could be invested in energy projects, the Commission was very quick in stating that CCS would need additional support. Accordingly, companies were expected to urge governments to create favorable investment conditions through national legislation. This ensures that the introduction of CCS technologies can be accomplished much faster than with any other mechanism. It puts pressure not only on companies to finalize projects but also on national governments and legislators to consider it a national priority to come in first in the CCS race. A first glance at the maturity of different CCS projects in Europe supports this theory: not only by providing access to financing, but also by requiring projects to be prepared at an early point in time, the Commission created a technology race between different actors which brought the commercialization of CCS an important step forward.

5.6   CONCLUSIONS

The role of CCS in the future of the European energy policy is still not clear. It will depend on three different issues: the role that the mitigation of GHG emissions plays in the coming years; how fast the development of demonstration plants for CCS is going to proceed; and finally, whether CCS technologies will prove to be a reliable instrument for reducing emissions with a high degree of security for the local and the global environment. The answers to these questions will determine the future of CCS, not only in Europe but worldwide. Despite those general considerations, the policy approach and the choice of instruments are still in flux. The future of CCS in Europe's energy strategy will depend heavily on the success or failure of the present programs and, of course, on the development of public opinion. If civil society is not included in the drafting of future strategies then CCS might fall victim to public resistance.

Despite these limitations, CCS also offers significant opportunities in the long run. While the complete decarbonization of Europe's electricity sector will already be difficult to achieve without CCS, reducing global greenhouse gas emissions and adapting Indian, Chinese or South African development plans to IPCC recommendations would seem to be nearly impossible without the use of CCS technologies. Thinking a few decades ahead, CCS could be used to clean industrial processes and serve as a net sink for carbon emissions by storing emissions from biomass heating or electricity production. This perspective should also be considered when evaluating CCS policies (IEA, 2009). The processes of integrating CCS into EU policies and disseminating knowledge about the technology and the supporting instruments have just begun. Without massive progress in the coming years, it will be difficult to argue that CCS can make any sort of breakthrough, delayed or otherwise. Its success is also closely linked to the implementation of the European energy strategy. Failing to get CCS technology ready by 2020 will undermine the credibility of future European projects in strategic technology planning.

NOTE

1. The author is grateful to Julian Schwartzkopff for his comments and contributions during the process of writing this chapter.

REFERENCES

European Commission (2006), *Green Paper: A European Strategy for Sustainable, Competitive and Secure Energy'*, COM(2006) 105, Brussels, 8 March.
European Commission (2008), *Communication from the Commission to the European Parliament, the Council, the European Economic and Social Committee and the Committee of Regions: Supporting Early Demonstration of Sustainable Power Generation from Fossil Fuels*, COM(2008) 13, Brussels, 23 January.
European Commission (2009), *Communication from the Commission to the European Parliament, the Council, the European Economic and Social Committee and the Committee of Regions: Investing in the Development of Low Carbon Technologies (SET-Plan)* COM(2009) 519, Brussels, 7 October.
European Council (2007), *European Council Presidency Conclusions, 8/9 March 2007*, 7224/1/07 REV1, Brussels, 2 May.
Eurostat (2009), 'EU Energy and Transport in Figures', *Statistical Pocketbook 2009*, Luxembourg: Eurostat.
Intergovernmental Panel on Climate Change (IPCC) (2007), *Fourth Assessment Report: Climate Change 2007*, Geneva: IPPC.
IEA (2008), *World Energy Outlook 2008*, Paris: IEA.
International Energy Agency (IEA) (2009), *Technology Roadmap: Carbon Capture and Storage*, Paris: IEA.
Zakkour, P. (2007a), *Choices for Regulating CO_2 Capture and Storage in the EU*, European Commission discussion paper, ERM, Amsterdam – London – Katowice.
Zakkour, P. (2007b), 'Incentivising CO_2 capture and storage in the European Union', European Commission discussion paper, ERM, Amsterdam – London – Katowice.

6. Redrawing the 'green Europeanization' of energy policy

Israel Solorio Sandoval and Esther Zapater[1]

6.1 INTRODUCTION

So far the Europeanization of energy policy has occupied a limited place in the European integration literature. Paradoxically, although energy policy provided an early impetus for European integration (see Lucas, 1977; Matláry, 1997), this policy has remained largely state-centered and the integration process has not been capable of laying the foundations for a full-fledged and coherent Common Energy Policy. Instead, energy policy has been considered one of the weakest areas of integration (see Chapter 1 by Solorio Sandoval and Morata). However for the sake of energy policy's salience in the EU, current developments mainly at the institutional level have been giving more prominence to this policy within the integration process. As the EU commissioner for energy, Günther Oettinger, recently pointed out, there are several indications that 'the Europeanization of energy policy has already started' (Oettinger, 2010), even though the understanding of this process is still weak.

Against this backdrop it is fundamental to acknowledge that energy policy has invariably been considered a very unusual case of policy-making at the European level, owing especially to the pronounced conflicts between the development of common policies on the one hand and divergent national policies on the other (Andersen, 2000). This was the main reason for the ban imposed on the EU in this area before the Lisbon Treaty broke down the barriers that hindered Brussels' action. Nevertheless, despite being recognized only recently as a formal EU policy area, it has been under Brussels's influence for several years and in the 1990s in particular the Commission forged links between energy issues and its formal areas of competence, such as external relations, the environment and the internal market (Matláry, 1997). Interestingly this dynamic led to the de facto construction of a very limited and sector-based energy policy at the European level. Yet the combination of a wide range of energy-related policies was far from being considered an EU policy in itself.

In recent years the emergence of pressing issues such as climate change and energy security at the top of the EU's political agenda has made the development of a comprehensive EU energy policy even more indispensable (European Commission, 2006, 2007). While the EU had a significant record of trying to respond to these challenges by moving towards a sustainable, secure and competitive energy future (Damro et al., 2008; Piebalgs, 2009; Buchan, 2009; Oberthür and Pallemaerts, 2010; Solorio Sandoval, 2011), there was also the remaining issue of coordinating overall action in this policy field. Thus the 2007 action plan 'An Energy Policy for Europe' arose not only as the official birth of the European energy policy but also as 'a springboard for further action' (European Council, 2007, p. 13). Perhaps more significant is the fact that the Lisbon Treaty energy chapter emerged with the task of giving the new European energy policy a real transversal character and no longer a sector-based one. The Treaty of Lisbon has certainly put energy back at the heart of European activity.

The aim of this chapter is to draw an all-embracing picture of the Europeanization of energy policy with a special emphasis on its 'green dimension', that is the component derived from the environmental agenda. In particular this chapter explores (1) the relative importance of the *green driver* against the other elements of the energy *trinity* and (2) the emerging governance patterns of this process in the framework of the emergent European energy policy. The chapter begins by presenting the main analytical tools used to understand the Europeanization of energy policy. Next, it analyzes the overall green contribution to the energy governance of Europeanization compared with the other components of the European energy policy and it reviews the nature of this process. In a later section, it studies the perspectives of change for energy policy. Finally the concluding section summarizes the debates about the energy governance of Europeanization, the development of the European energy policy and further challenges to be faced in this policy field.

6.2   'GREEN EUROPEANIZATION' OF ENERGY POLICY: UNDERSTANDING THE GOVERNANCE CHANGES

'Much of Europe has become *institutionalized* in the sociological sense that its existence and functioning across broad issue areas became unproblematic, taken for granted' (Caporaso, 2007, p. 25). With these words, James Caporaso explained the institutionalization that developed in Europe from the 1980s onwards and opened the door to the Europeanization 'boom' in EU studies. But although this argument is perfectly applicable to several policy areas of European integration (for example notably environmental policy), it is hardly suitable for energy policy, a historically conflictive area for Brussels's participation (Andersen, 2000). As a result the study on the Europeanization of energy policy has been largely neglected and this policy area has been persistently excluded from the main Europeanization handbooks.

To top it all, research on energy policy Europeanization distinguishes itself from other policy fields since this process has been mainly driven by competences in related areas (that is a case of 'indirect Europeanization'). At first sight there is an additional obstacle to understanding the overall change concerning energy governance in the EU, but Europeanization, as a process involving the gradual erosion of national sovereignty (Risse et al., 2001, p. 2), progressively modified energy policy until it was considered a 'shared competence' between the EU and its member states. How can we capture this process? To answer this question this chapter follows the definition of Europeanization by Risse et al. (2001), who describe it as the 'emergence and the development at the European level of different structures of governance' (Risse et al., 2001, p. 2). Our aim here is to analyze how the EU governance system has been uploading many policy-making activities regarding energy in Brussels, while relying on national administrative actors for implementation (Knill and Lenschow 2005). Therefore we undertake *political institutionalization* (a process that involves developing formal and informal rules, procedures, norms and practices governing politics at the EU level; Risse et al., 2001, p. 2) as the parameter guiding our research on the Europeanization of energy governance.

All that said, for the purpose of this contribution it is crucial to underpin the analytical framework in order to appreciate the emergent patterns of governance. Consequently this research relies on Knill and Lenschow's (2003) categorization of the modes of regulation in EU governance to supplement our understanding of the impact of 'green Europeanization' in energy governance. It enables a two-level analysis that adequately captures the range of EU patterns of governance. In general terms the *type of regulation* level considers the distribution of responsibilities across regulatory centers (such as the EU, national executives or non-state actors) and the level of discretion they grant to decentralized actors in the implementation process; while the *steering mechanism* level implies the different mechanisms of policy adaptation at the national level (Knill and Lenschow, 2003, pp. 2–3).

In view of this framework, the *type of regulation* level distinguishes between four patterns of action: (1) 'the *substantive and procedural regulatory standards* fit the image of the EU regulatory state'; (2) 'the *new instruments* are a mixed bag of regulatory tools [and] what they have in common is a more indirect approach towards achieving behavioral change'; (3) 'the self-regulatory model is based on private actors devising concrete regulatory standards in the shadow of the state'; (4) and the *open method of coordination* (OMC) refers to when 'certain policy benchmarks are set for the Union, national responses are formulated independently without the threat of formal sanctions and the EU merely provides a context for enabling cooperation and learning among national policymakers' (Knill and Lenschow, 2003, p. 3). On the other hand the *steering mechanisms* level distinguishes three general mechanisms through which regulators might seek to affect the behavior of the regulated: (1) 'they may be coerced to comply with the regulation'; (2) 'they may be "tempted" to change their behavior due to incentive effects of the regulation'; and (3) 'they may learn, that is redefine their interests on the basis of new knowledge gathered due to the regulatory context and subsequently adapt their behavior' (ibid., p. 4).

As a matter of fact the application of this double-level analysis can be helpful for mapping out the predominant mechanisms in practice within energy policy that relate to its green dimension. Thus it is a necessary step in order to recognize the 'potential for national institutional change and cross-national convergence' (Knill and Lenschow, 2005). The task in the subsequent sections will be to test the effectiveness of this analytical toolkit against the empirical developments in this policy field.

6.3   ASSESSING THE GREEN DIMENSION OF THE EUROPEAN ENERGY POLICY

Following the adopted definition on Europeanization, this section's main undertaking is to measure the political institutionalization of energy policy by means of the related competences. In this sense and given the unusual nature of Europeanization in this policy area, the EU now has a considerable body of legislation to draw from when executing the European energy policy. Against this backdrop it would be enlightening to bear in mind the wider energy policy picture as a useful exercise in determining the relative contribution of each of the drivers of the political institutionalization of EU energy policy. Nonetheless, analyzing the record of EU legislation in energy policy can be a very deceptive exercise. For example, simple research in EUR-Lex on the current legislation in force in this policy area reveals the surprising figure of 437 acts (last accessed August 2011); that by far outstrips the image of energy as a weak policy at the European level. However, when looked at in more detail, it might be disappointing to observe that 184 of them are nuclear energy acts under the Euratom umbrella. Furthermore, a considerable amount of the overall figure is related to acts focused on the coal industry (96) and especially its promotion (70). To be clear, these figures are barely related to the emergent European energy policy, but are instead linked to the CECCA and Euroatom legacies.

In-depth research of the EUR-Lex database could undoubtedly reveal more energy-related legislation. However this practice entails the risk of inflating the data of legislative acts that are actually important for European energy policy development. Therefore it is essential to define a systematized procedure for coping with the Europeanization of energy policy governance. For that reason, since here we are actually interested in the development of the formal and informal rules, procedures, norms and practices that govern the EU energy policy today, this chapter is based on the 'summaries of EU legislation' as the database to be explored in order to map out the political institutionalization. The advantages of the selected database are first that it presents up-to-date coverage of current EU legislation on a range of themes and second that it excludes legal decisions of only temporary interest, such as decisions on grants. Therefore even if it does not present the entire picture of energy policy institutionalization, this database is rather useful for gaining an overall picture of the EU instruments currently in practice in European energy policy. Table 6.1 presents a systematized vision of our findings regarding the EU energy-related legislation until December 2010. For the sake of clarity this analysis does not take into consideration the Euratom-related legislative acts.

While the EU record on energy policy consists of a wide range of instruments ranging from liberalizing measures through market-based tools (mainly taxes, subsidies and the CO_2 emissions trading scheme) and the development of new energy technologies (especially technologies for energy efficiency and renewable or low-carbon energy) to Community financial instruments, a clear predominance of the green dimension as a driver of the institutionalization of energy policy emerges from the table shown above. This is in line with the analysis presented in Chapter 1 on the EPI development and its persistent rapprochement with energy policy (see also Chapter 2 by Adelle et al.).

Thus the legislative instruments adopted in the framework of the green dimension of the European energy policy are both qualitatively and quantitatively important. On one hand an overall analysis of the existing instruments

Table 6.1   Energy policy institutionalization

Europeanization driver	Instruments
General objectives	5
Green dimension	41
Internal energy market	20
Security of supply and external dimension	13
Energy policy institutionalization	79

Source: Own elaboration, data from summaries of EU legislation (accessed December 2010).

related to energy policy shows that the number of instruments related to the environmental agenda exceeds the other approaches traditionally used for adopting legislative energy policy instruments. On the other hand it appears clear that the adopted legislative instruments have contributed to constructing a more sustainable energy policy model. It is clear that the green dimension has contributed decisively to the institutionalization of the European energy policy. Consequently, as contained within the Lisbon Treaty, the environmental dimension is nowadays a priority for the EU's new energy policy to pursue.

Following on with the analysis of the adopted instruments, it is also important to observe the role of the internal energy market dimension, which has noticeably also been a key driver in the Europeanization of energy governance. This is even more the case if we consider the interplay between both drivers and that the internal energy market is ultimately the principal context in which the green dimension occurs. Moreover this data is consistent with the earlier efforts to liberalize energy markets in Europe. Thus the legislative instruments adopted in the context of the internal energy market contribute to the objectives of liberalization and legal approximation (art. 115, TFEU). Nevertheless it is important to assert, even when this agenda necessarily influences the EU's energy markets, that this does not really help configure the European energy policy's objectives as in the case of the green dimension.

Last but not least another factor to remark is the *poor performance* of the security of supply and external dimension driver. This finding, besides agreeing with Natorski and Herranz's (2008) analysis, also shows that there is a considerable distance between its contribution to the political institutionalization of the European energy policy in comparison with the formerly analyzed drivers (see also Chapter 8 by Herranz-Surrallés and Natorski). In this context it is essential to take into consideration the fact that the legislative instruments have a double origin in this case: (1) as a consequence of the internationalization of certain energy-related standards that arose from the core of international organizations such as the International Energy Agency, and (2) the legislative acts focused on the implementation of the Trans-European networks

In short, the green dimension and the internal energy markets are certainly consolidated as the main drivers of the Europeanization of energy governance. However the significance of 'green Europeanization' for the internal energy market is still blurred. Hence it becomes necessary to clarify this exercise with a more qualitative analysis. Figure 6.1 presents an analysis of the institutionalization of energy policy, taking into consideration the distinction between preparatory legislative acts (that is the Commission's Communications) and current legislation (that is Decisions, Directives, Regulations).

The picture is clearly different. This variation is because there are many preparatory legislative acts or 'soft law' instruments on the green dimension of

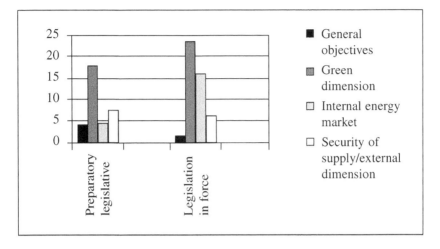

Source: Own elaboration, data from EUR-Lex and summaries of EU legislation (accessed December 2010).

Figure 6.1   Analysis of the institutionalization of energy policy

energy policy, which inflates the data concerning its political institutionalization. This is due to the fact that 'the Commission is increasingly using non-legislative or 'soft law' such as Green Papers and Communications as tools of policy making' (Braun, 2009, p. 430). Table 6.2 reflects this reality within the green dimension of energy policy. Therefore when analyzing data concerning legislation currently in force there is only a slight variation between both (16 acts concerning the internal energy market as against 23 acts concerning the green dimension of energy policy).

The adoption of legislative instruments derived from the green dimension has implied a strategic progress for the European energy policy. In this sense the adoption of Green Papers and strategic communications closely linked to the European fight against climate change has been an essential driver for the definition and consolidation of energy policy at the European level. In other words, the green dimension of energy policy has definitely contributed to the strategic global planning of European energy policy against the fragmentation generated from internal energy market rules and trans-European networks (mainly because of the technical and specific character of this source of legislation).

Overall we can conclude that a basic characteristic of 'green Europeanization' has been its capacity to activate the debate at the EU level on the need for a coherent EU energy policy and its ability to facilitate consensus between the member states and the EU institutions around energy issues.

Table 6.2 Green dimension institutionalization: key measures

Formal legislative acts

1 Council Directive 92/42/EEC of 21 May 1992 on efficiency requirements for new hot-water boilers fired with liquid or gaseous fuels

2 Council Directive 92/75/EEC of 22 September 1992 on the indication by labelling and standard product information of the consumption of energy and other resources by household appliances

3 European Parliament and Council Directive 2000/55/EC of 18 September 2000 on energy efficiency requirements for ballasts for fluorescent lighting

4 Directive 2001/77/EC of the European Parliament and of the Council of 27 September 2001 on the promotion of electricity from renewable energy sources in the internal electricity market

5 Commission Decision 2001/546/EC, of 11 July 2001 setting up a consultative committee to be known as the 'European Energy and Transport Forum'

6 Directive 2002/91/EC of the European Parliament and of the Council of 16 December 2002 on the energy performance of buildings

7 Directive 2003/30/EC of the European Parliament and of the Council of 8 May 2003 on the promotion of the use of biofuels or other renewable fuels for transport.

8 Commission Directive 2003/66/EC of 3 July 2003 amending Directive 94/2/EC implementing Council Directive 92/75/EEC with regard to energy labelling of household electric refrigerators, freezers and their combinations

9 Directive 2003/87/EC of the European Parliament and of the Council of 13 October 2003 establishing a scheme for greenhouse gas emission allowance trading within the Community and amending Council Directive 96/61/EC

10 Council Directive 2003/96/EC of 27 October 2003 restructuring the Community framework for the taxation of energy products and electricity

11 Directive 2004/8/EC of the European Parliament and of the Council of 11 February 2004 on the promotion of cogeneration based on a useful heat demand in the internal energy market and amending Directive 92/42/EEC.

12 Directive 2006/32/EC of the European Parliament and of the Council of 5 April 2006 on energy end-use efficiency and energy services and repealing Council Directive 93/76/EEC.

13 Decision 1639/2006/EC of the European Parliament and of the Council of 24 October 2006 establishing a Competitiveness and Innovation Framework Program (2007–2013).

14 Council Decision 2006/1005/EC of 18 December 2006 concerning the conclusion of the Agreement between the Government of the United States of America and the European Community on the coordination of energy-efficiency labelling programmes for office equipment

15 Directive 2008/101/EC to include aviation into the EU Emissions Trading Scheme (ETS) published in the *Official Journal* on 13 January 2009.

16 Decision No 406/2009/EC of the European Parliament and of the Council of 23 April 2009 on the effort of member states to reduce their greenhouse gas emissions to meet the Community's greenhouse gas emission reduction commitments up to 2020.

17 Directive 2009/28/EC of the European Parliament and of the Council of 23 April 2009 on the promotion of the use of energy from renewable sources and amending and subsequently repealing Directives 2001/77/EC and 2003/30/EC

Formal legislative acts

18   Directive 2009/29/EC of the European Parliament and of the Council of 23 April 2009 amending Directive 2003/87/EC so as to improve and extend the greenhouse gas emission allowance trading scheme of the Community

19   Directive 2009/31/EC on the geological storage of CO2 entered into force establishing a legal framework for the environmentally safe geological storage of CO2 to contribute to the fight against climate change.

20   Directive 2009/33/EC of the European Parliament and of the Council of 23 April 2009 on the promotion of clean and energy-efficient road transport vehicles

21   Directive 2009/125/EC of the European Parliament and of the Council of 21 October 2009 establishing a framework for the setting of ecodesign requirements for energy-using products

22   Regulation (EC) No 595/2009 of the European Parliament and of the Council of 18 June 2009 on type-approval of motor vehicles and engines with respect to emissions from heavy duty vehicles (Euro VI) and on access to vehicle repair and maintenance information and amending Regulation (EC) No 715/2007 and Directive 2007/46/EC and repealing Directives 80/1269/EEC, 2005/55/EC and 2005/78/EC

23   Regulation (EC) No 1222/2009 of the European Parliament and of the Council of 25 November 2009 on the labelling of tyres with respect to fuel efficiency and other essential parameters

Soft Law or Non legislative Acts

1   Communication from the Commission of 14 October 1998: Strengthening environmental integration within Community energy policy

2   Commission Communication of 15 May 2001 'A Sustainable Europe for a Better World: A European Union Strategy for Sustainable Development' (Commission proposal to the Gothenburg European Council)

3   Commission Green Paper, 22 June 2005, *Energy Efficiency – or Doing More With Less*

4   Communication from the Commission of 7 December 2005 – Biomass Action Plan

5   Commission Communication of 13 December 2005 on the review of the Sustainable Development Strategy – A platform for action

6   Commission Communication of 8 February 2006 entitled *An EU Strategy for Biofuels*

7   Communication from the Commission to the Council and the European Parliament of 6 October 2006: *Mobilising Public and Private Finance Towards Global Access to Climate-Friendly, Affordable and Secure Energy Services: The Global Energy Efficiency and Renewable Energy Fund*

8   Communication from the Commission of 19 October 2006 entitled: *Action Plan for Energy Efficiency: Realising the Potential*

9   Communication from the Commission, of 10 January 2007, entitled: *Limiting Global Climate Change to 2 Degrees Celsius – The Way Ahead for 2020 and Beyond*

10   Commission Communication of 10 January 2007: *Sustainable Power Generation from Fossil Fuels: Aiming for Near-Zero Emissions from Coal After 2020*

Table 6.2   Continued

Soft Law or Non legislative Acts

11   Commission Communication of 10 January 2007: *Renewable Energy Road Map. Renewable Energies in the 21st Century: Building a More Sustainable Future*

12   Communication from the Commission of 13 November 2008: *Energy Efficiency: Delivering the 20% Target*

13   Commission Green Paper of 28 March 2007 on market-based instruments for environment and related policy purposes

14   Communication from the Commission to the European Parliament, the Council, the European Economic and Social Committee and the Committee of the Regions of 23 January 2008 entitled: *Supporting Early Demonstration of Sustainable Power Generation from Fossil Fuels*

15   Communication from the Commission to the European Parliament, the Council, the European Economic and Social Committee and the Committee of the Regions of 13 November 2008: *Offshore Wind Energy: Action Needed to Deliver on the Energy Policy Objectives for 2020 and Beyond*

16   Communication from the Commission to the European Parliament, the Council, the European Economic and Social Committee and the Committee of the Regions of 12 March 2009 on mobilising Information and Communication Technologies (ICTs) to facilitate the transition to an energy-efficient, low-carbon economy

17   Communication from the Commission to the European Parliament, the Council, the European Economic and Social Committee and the Committee of the Regions - Investing in the Development of Low Carbon Technologies (SET-Plan)

18   Communication from the Commission to the European Parliament, the Council and the European Economic and Social Committee of 28 April 2010: *A European Strategy on Clean and Energy Efficient Vehicles*

Source: EUR-Lex and Summaries of Legislation (accessed December 2010).

Hence in a complex terrain such as energy policy and with a limited capacity to exert hierarchical authority, the Commission has reconciled itself to 'the position of a strategic node in EU network governance' in order to facilitate agreements (Braun, 2009, p. 431). To pursue this task the Commission has relied on soft law instruments with the effect of giving an overall structure to the European energy policy.

Until now we have been able to capture the significance of energy governance as the 'green driver' in the Europeanization of energy policy. However it is still uncertain what are the main patterns of governance of this process. In the following sections these issues will be dealt with in order to better reflect the 'green Europeanization' of energy governance.

6.4   'GREEN EUROPEANIZATION': THE EMERGENT PATTERNS OF GOVERNANCE

Now that we have examined the relative contribution of the 'green Europeanization' of energy policy, the next step consists of analyzing its emergent patterns of governance. Hence its importance relies on an understanding of the EU regulatory force deployed when the so-called *third industrial revolution* (Pielbags, 2009) was promoted. Before presenting our findings, it is worth noting that this outline corresponds with the analytical objective of clarifying the 'green Europeanization' of the energy governance. However the empirical reality is even more complex. Table 6.3 merely represents an exercise to simplify the modes of governance of 'green Europeanization'.

As can be seen, there is a wide range of governance patterns involved in the 'green Europeanization' of national energy policies. However, and not surprisingly, the new environmental instruments are the predominant type of

Table 6.3   Steering mechanisms and types of regulation

	Regulatory standards	**New instruments**	**Self-regulation**	**OMC**
Coercion	Legally binding (2)	Framework and (5)	Shadow of standards hierarchy (3)	Reporting and procedural rules monitoring (2)
Incentive structures	–	Changes of procedural and/ or material opportunities (3)	Private actors influence regulatory standards (4)	Peer pressure (2)
Learning	–	–	Communication in private networks (1)	Best practice models (1)
	Hierarchy model: power of coercion	**Public-delegation model: traditional subsidiarity**	**Private delegation model**	**Radical subsidiarity model: public-learning approach**

The number inside each box corresponds to the legislative acts that can be situated within the predominant patterns of EU governance in our analysis.

Source: Own classification, based in Knill and Lenschow 2003.

regulation. Thus as a mode to overcome the member states' reluctance on the EU regulatory performance in energy policy, flexible instruments with a mixed bag of regulatory tools have emerged in order to promote national change. This result exposes the delicate distribution of responsibilities between the EU and its member states in the green dimension of energy policy. In this sense it seems the EU will continue using these new modes of governance to become more involved in emerging policy areas such as energy policy (Braun, 2009).

With regard to the steering mechanisms, Table 6.3 also shows the variety of Europeanization mechanisms used for the green dimension of energy policy. Furthermore it draws attention to the fact that, in a more in-depth analysis, most of the instruments are characterized by a mixture of Europeanization mechanisms as a way to counterbalance the EU regulatory limits on energy policy (Solorio Sandoval, 2011). Hence, in order to promote national change, the EU has been increasingly committed to developing a wide range of instruments for adapting institutions, for transforming domestic opportunity structures, and for altering the beliefs and expectations of domestic actors (Knill and Lehmkuhl, 2002).

Certainly it is possible to extract much more information from Table 6.3. However with our limited goal of mapping out the 'green Europeanization' of energy policy, it is just worth mentioning the two main limitations of this process when promoting change at the domestic level. First, it requires the consistent national commitment in most cases. Hence the attainment of the energy trinity, even when it is an increasingly regulated area at the EU level, relies fundamentally on the member states. Second, the nature of this process is problematic for the convergence between the forms of adaptation at the national level. Although it establishes common goals, it does not necessarily facilitate the homogenization of national energy policies. Such a result could have direct implications for the purpose of laying down the basis for the establishment of a common global energy policy. To sum up, if this is an experimental exercise in mapping out the emerging patterns of governance in the 'green Europeanization' of energy governance, we must bear in mind the highlighted implications and limits of this process to avoid a gap between the capabilities and the expectations of the European energy policy.

6.5   WINDS OF CHANGE FOR ENERGY?

Today there are certainly two particular features that forecast winds of change for energy policy in the near future: the Lisbon Treaty Energy provision and the EU's medium- and long-term strategies in this field.

First, the Lisbon Treaty entailed a significant novelty for energy policy: its inclusion in the EU formal competences. Thus energy governance was strengthened with the establishment of a catalogue of exclusive and shared competences between the EU and its member states, whereas the TFEU recognizes energy within the last category together with other related areas such as the internal market, the environment or transport policy (art. 4, TFEU). Furthermore it is clear at first glance that the Lisbon Treaty and its art. 194 on energy provide a new legal basis upon which to develop the EU energy policy. Thus this new chapter closes the circle in the relationship between Europeanization and political integration, as this case exposes the way in which member states pooled a certain level of sovereignty into energy policy only after the EU institutions had begun influencing this policy area through institutional flexibility (a phenomenon that clearly needs further investigation). In fact the inclusion of the energy chapter simply implied the recognition of the work that the EU has been undertaking throughout all these years by means of other policies (environment, internal market and external relations). However the Lisbon treaty is expected to bring some changes to this scenario because the EU ultimately has an explicit energy competence. It is thus worth remarking that the Lisbon Treaty offers a clear new legal basis for pursuing EU ambitions regarding the energy trinity and for boosting policy coherence in this field.

Regarding its decision-making process, the new energy article has been accompanied by the ordinary legislative procedure (art. 194.2, TFEU). Therefore, after years of having to revert to related competences or to the flexibility clause in order to develop energy legislation, the pure existence of this procedure as the ordinary decision-making system for energy is positive for the development of European energy policy. Nevertheless, the renewed legal framework was accompanied by a relevant counterbalance for the EU's regulatory capacity. Accordingly an exception in art. 194 stipulates that the adopted measures 'shall not affect a Member State's right to determine the conditions for exploiting its energy resources, its choice between different energy sources and the general structure of its energy supply' (art. 194.2, TFEU). Certainly the member states' reservations place limitations on the EU's energy activities and limit the degree of sovereignty pooled from the member states. However it is worth remarking that the current institutional set-up now permits more improvements than ever in the coordination of national energy policies and among the different EU policies concerning energy.

In second place, it is worth remarking that a very particular characteristic of the European energy policy is its *flexibility*. Hence, after the 2007 Action Plan approval the Council called on the Commission to implement the elements contained in the Action Plan and to put forward an updated Strategic Review to serve as a basis for the new Action Plan (European Council, 2007). In its Second Strategic Review, the Commission remarked that the 'EU's *new energy and environment policy* agreed by the European Council in March 2007 establishes a forward-looking political agenda to achieve the Community's core energy objectives of sustainability, competitiveness and security of supply' (European Commission, 2008; emphasis added). Nevertheless the EU found several obstacles to adopting a new Action Plan. As a replacement, the European Commission has begun pushing for medium- and long-term strategies for the European energy policy. These are fully represented by the Energy 2020 strategy and the 2050 Roadmap for moving towards a competitive low-carbon economy (European Commission, 2010, 2011).

How should this change be understood within the overall strategy for the European energy policy? In the words of EU Commissioner for Energy Günther Oettinger, 'the Energy 2020 strategy aims at identifying the policy decisions needed to reach [the] 2020 objectives and open the way to the 2050 perspective'. In other words if the Energy 2020 strategy is more a short- and medium-term plan that substitutes the emptiness left by the Action Plan (2007–2009) 'An energy policy for Europe' (which was intended to be milestone in the creation of an energy policy for Europe and renewed by 2010), the 2050 Roadmap brings about the long-term scheme needed in order to better pursue the energy and climate policy goals for the EU.

6.6   CONCLUSIONS

This chapter has highlighted the fundamental role of the *green contribution* to the Europeanization of energy governance, where the environmental path replaced for years the competence limit of the EU in the energy field. Thus there are three fundamental features that needed to be pointed out in this conclusive section. First, there is clearly a direct relationship between the development of the environmental policy and the Europeanization of energy governance (in line with what is suggested in Chapter 1). Second, this chapter has exposed the fundamental contribution of the green dimension to the overall institutionalization of the European energy policy (in qualitative and quantitative terms). Hence it is a fundamental feature of the EU energy policy that definitely requires further attention from the literature on this subject. Finally, the formal energy competence certainly facilitates the increased *policy coherence* necessary for reducing the trade-offs between the related policies. It is hence a path towards reaching an ideal-case scenario in which *win–win* solutions are developed within the emergent European energy policy.

As an early attempt to map out this process there are clearly further challenges for future research on the EU energy policy that this chapter has only partially covered. First of all the green driver has clearly not been the only key pushing forward Brussels's energy-related activities, and the influence of energy security and competitiveness must also be taken into consideration. It is particularly necessary to shed more light on the interplay between the internal market and the green driver as a facilitator of the Europeanization of energy governance. Second, the above-presented simplification on the emergent patterns of governance has a lot more of 'squeezable' information regarding the emergent EU energy policy. Therefore it is a question that requires significantly more dedication. And finally this chapter has clearly traced a relationship between the Europeanization of energy policy and political integration. It is therefore a phenomenon that requires further study based on neofunctionalism theory in order to be better understood.

NOTES

1. This chapter is based on an earlier, although different, paper published at the JCER. Israel Solorio Sandoval is especially grateful to the JCER editors and the two anonymous reviewers for their encouraging comments.

REFERENCES

Andersen, S. (2000), 'EU energy policy: interest interaction and supranational authority', *Arena Working Papers*, **00** (5), accessed 18 November 2010 at www.sv.uio.no/arena/english/research/publications/arena-publications/workingpapers/.

Braun, J.F. (2009), 'Multiple sources of pressure for change: the Barroso Commission and energy policy for an enlarged EU', *Journal of Contemporary European Research*, **5** (3), 428–51.

Buchan, D. (2009), *Energy and Climate Change: Europe at the Crossroads*, Oxford: Oxford University Press.

Caporaso, James (2007), 'The three worlds of regional integration theory', in P. Graziano and V. Vink (eds), *Europeanization: New Research Agendas*, New York: Palgrave Macmillan, pp. 23–34.

Council of the European Union (2007), '*Action Plan (2007–2009): An Energy Policy for Europe*', Presidency Conclusions, Brussels, 8–9 March 2007, accessed 18 November 2010 at http://register.consilium.europa.eu/pdf/en/07/st07/st07224-re01.en07. pdf,

Damro, C., I. Hardie and D. MacKenzie (2008), 'The EU and climate change policy: law, politics and prominence at different levels', *Journal of Contemporary European Research*, **4** (3), pp. 179–92.

European Commission (2006), *Green Paper: A European strategy for Sustainable, Competitive and Secure Energy*, 8 March, Brussels accessed 18 November 2010 November accessed November 18 2010 2010 at http://eur-lex.europa.eu/smartapi/cgi/sga_doc?smartapi!celexplus!prod!DocNumber&lg=en&type_doc=COMfinal&an_doc=2006&nu_doc=105.

European Commission (2007), *Communication from the Commission to the European Council and the European Parliament of 10 January 2007: An Energy Policy for Europe*, accessed 18 November 2010 at http://eur-lex.europa.eu/smartapi/cgi/sga_doc?smartapi!celexplus!prod!DocNumber&lg=en&type_doc=COMfinal&an_doc=2007&nu_doc=1.

European Commission (2008), *Communication from the Commission to the European Parliament, the Council, the European Economic and Social Committee and the Committee of the Regions – Second Strategic Energy Review: An EU Energy Security and Solidarity Action Plan*, accessed November 18 2010 at http://eur-lex.europa.eu/LexUriServ/LexUriServ.do?uri=CELEX:52008DC0781:EN:HTML:NOT.

European Commission (2010), *Communication from the Commission to the European Parliament, the Council, the European Economic and Social Committee and the Committee of the Regions – Energy 2020: A Strategy for Competitive, Sustainable and Secure Energy*, COM(2010) 639, Brussels.

European Commission (2011), *Background Paper: Energy Roadmap 2050 – State of Play*, Brussels, 3 May.

Knill, C. and D. Lehmkuhl (2002) 'The national impact of the European Union regulatory Policy: three Europeanization mechanisms', *European Journal of Political Research*, **41** (2), 255–80.

Knill, C. and A. Lenschow (2003), 'Modes of regulation in the governance of the European Union: towards a comprehensive evaluation', *European Integration online Papers* (EIOP), **7** (1), accessed 18 November 2010 at http://eiop.or.at/eiop/texte/2003–001a.htm.

Knill, C. and A. Lenschow (2005), 'Compliance, competition, and communication: different approaches of European governance and their Impact on national institutions', *Journal of Common Market Studies*, **43** (3), 583–606.

Lucas, N.J.D. (1977), *Energy and the European Communities*, London: Europa.

Matláry, J. (1997), *Energy Policy in the European Union*, New York: St Martin's Press.

Natorski, M. and A. Herranz-Surrallés (2008) 'Securitizing moves to nowhere? The framing of the European Union's energy policy', *Journal of Contemporary European Research*, **4** (2), 71–89.

Oberthür, S. and M. Pallemaerts (2010), 'The EU's internal and external climate policies: an historical overview', in S. Oberthür and M. Pallemaerts (eds), *The New Climate Policies of the European Union: Internal Legislation and Climate Diplomacy*, Brussels: VUB Press.

Oettinger, G. (2010), 'Europeanization of energy policy', speech of Commissioner Oettinger at the dinner debate with the European Energy Forum, 19 October Strasbourg, accessed 18 November at http://europa.eu/rapid/pressReleasesAction.do?reference=SPEECH/10/573&format=HTML&aged=0&language=EN.

Piebalgs, A. (2009), 'How the European Union is preparing the third industrial revolution with an innovative energy policy', EUI working papers RSCAS 2009/11.

Risse, T., M. Green Cowles and J. Caporaso (2001), 'Europeanization and domestic change: introduction', in T. Risse, M. Green Cowles and J. Caporaso (eds), *Transforming Europe: Europeanization and Domestic Change*, Ithaca, NY: Cornell University Press, pp. 1–20.

Solorio Sandoval, I. (2011), 'Bridging the gap between environmental policy integration and the EU's energy policy: mapping out the "green Europeanisation" of energy governance', *Journal of Contemporary European Research*, **7** (3), 396–415.

PART II

The external dimension of the European energy policy

7. A differential approach to energy policy? Explaining the prevalence of market-based energy policy instruments in central and eastern Europe

Michael Dobbins and Jale Tosun

7.1 INTRODUCTION

The accession of ten post-socialist countries[1] to the European Union (EU) has induced a lively academic debate regarding its implications for the European environmental decision-making capacity. Some analysts have argued that the eastern enlargement could negatively impact both on the environmental decision-making capacity of the EU and on the level of environmental protection, and could reverse previously made progress (see Holzinger and Knoepfel, 2000; von Homeyer et al., 2000; Baker, 2001; Wilkinson et al., 2004). This potential setback is generally explained by the traditionally low level of protection in central and eastern Europe (CEE) as well as the purportedly weak administrative capacity of the new EU members (Holzinger and Knoepfel, 2000; Jehlička and Tickle, 2004). Additional aggravating factors are the historical legacies of energy-intensive communist patterns of production, industrial pollution and the weakness of environmental associations and consumer interests (Soveroski, 2000; Skjaerseth and Wettestad, 2007).

On the other hand, optimists point to the new opportunities created by EU enlargement, for example the creation of a pan-European environmental and energy strategy, the joint development of innovative steering instruments together with environmental policy forerunners and the capacity of the EU system to trigger reforms (von Homeyer, 2001). To be sure, there is a novel research perspective – the research on the external governance of the EU – which even claims that the EU positively affects the (environmental) policies of third countries that are not even accession candidates (see Lavenex, 2004; Lavenex and Uçarer, 2004; Lavenex and Schimmelfennig, 2009).

The overarching finding of the empirical analyses of environmental policy change in the CEE countries is that the prospect of EU accession induced an overall tightening of protection standards (see Andonova, 2004; Carmin and VanDeveer, 2005; Knill et al., 2008). In this context, most studies emphasize the relevance of *acquis* conditionality (Schimmelfennig and Sedelmeier, 2004) for these positive developments, that is the necessity for applicant countries to adjust their policies to the *acquis communautaire*. However, how are these dynamics reflected in the instruments related to energy policy?

Against this background it is noteworthy that little attention has been paid to the persistent differences in the regulatory approaches taken by the CEE countries and the EU-15. This is somewhat surprising since the CEE countries had a very specific environmental regulatory regime in place during socialism (see Knill and Lenschow, 2000). In fact, well before the beginning of the economic transition in the late 1980s and in strong contrast to western countries, most CEE countries had market-based instruments in place.[2] In light of this regulatory legacy, this chapter analyzes how frequently market-based instruments are still applied by the CEE countries and how the new member states' regulatory approach differs from those of the EU-15. For the overarching interest of this book, this analysis is significant since CEE countries have hardly been affected by the process of Europeanization (that is certain limits of the EU as an exporter of its 'green-energy' model). As a result, we can observe relatively independent national policy responses to the growing problems of supply, demand and sustainable utilization of energy (see Knill and Liefferink, 2007).

This chapter aims to describe systematic differences across both groups of countries rather than explaining them. In light of the limited knowledge on energy policy-making in the CEE, this undertaking is worthwhile since it offers an ideal basis for future research efforts. Section 7.2 gives an overview of the main changes in CEE energy policy due to the adoption of the *acquis communautaire*. Section 7.3 presents the argument that market-based energy policy instruments should be more prominent in the CEE countries than in the EU-15 owing to the diverging opportunity structures for the industrial and energy policy actors as well as the regulatory legacies of these countries. Section 7.4 outlines the operationalization of our dependent variable, that is the use of environmental taxes on energy-related pollution. Section 7.5 presents the results of our analysis and discusses whether market-based instruments must necessarily lead to a more sustainable use of energy. Finally Section 7.6 summarizes our main findings and presents a brief conclusion.

7.2 THE EUROPEANIZATION OF CEE ENERGY POLICY

The EU is a key actor on the international energy market as the largest importer and second-largest consumer in the world. This situation calls for various measures on which the European Commission in 2000 launched a wide debate (the Green Paper *Towards a European Strategy for the Security of Energy Supply*). And perhaps even more importantly, energy dependence is together with climate change one of the main reasons for the launching of the European energy policy in 2007 (see Chapter 1 by Solorio Sandoval and Morata). Measures in the energy sector should aim at a more stable flow of energy, ultimately underpinning the EU's efforts at energy security. Consequently, the EU has impacted the energy policy arrangements of the CEE countries through the so-called energy *acquis* which constitutes the body of all energy-related EU law, Regulations and policies (chapter 14 of the accession negotiations). Implementing the *acquis* requires not only adequate legislation but also well-functioning institutions (for example a regulatory body as required in the electricity and gas directives, a nuclear safety authority etc.).

During the accession negotiations, the applicant countries had to comply with a number of energy-related EU laws, ranging from technical issues such as quality of gasoline and diesel fuel to large structural issues such as liberalization of the gas and electricity markets.[3] The following measures are the most important domestic policy changes induced by the accession negotiations (see Balmaceda, 2002: p. 18):

- The sulfur content of diesel fuel had to be reduced to 0.05 percent.
- Heating oil with high sulfur content had to be removed from the market.
- Permissions for the research, exploitation and development of hydrocarbons had to be adjudicated in a transparent way.
- The candidate countries had to comply with European Coal and Steel Union regulations, including a reduction of the use of coal, especially its most inefficient and environmentally dangerous types.
- The candidate countries had to adopt Council Directives 68/414/EEC, which forced them to maintain minimum stocks of crude oil and/or petroleum.
- In a similar vein, they had to comply with Council Directives 90/547/EEC and 91/296/EEC on the transit of electricity through transmission grids and the transit of natural gas through grids, respectively.
- The CEE countries had to comply with the EU requirements related to the EURATOM agreement.
- They had to open their internal electricity and gas markets.

Despite the large number of energy policy requirements, the subject of market-based energy policy instruments was not addressed by the energy *acquis* in the early 2000s. In 2007, the Commission Green Paper *On Market-Based Instruments for Environment and Related Policy Purpose* recognized the relevance of market-based instruments and launched a discussion on advancing their use in the EU. In light of the fact that our analysis examines the use of market-based energy policy instruments only until 2004, we can still justify our claim that the EU member states' regulatory approaches represent independent policy responses. Accordingly, we should observe considerable variation in the use of market-based instruments across the EU-15 and the new member states as well as within the two country groups.

7.3 EXPLAINING ENERGY POLICY CHOICES IN THE CEE COUNTRIES

There are numerous instruments for achieving more sustainable energy usage. We can generally distinguish between interventionist regulatory instruments (that is command and control), cooperative instruments (for example commitments and agreements), persuasive instruments (for example information, education, public appeals), procedural instruments (for example auditing programs) and market-based instruments (for example ecological taxes) (see Knill and Liefferink, 2007; Böcher and Töller, 2007). In light of this multitude of instruments, why should a government of a post-socialist transition economy opt for market-based instruments?

The assumption underlying our argument is that the new EU member states – analogous to the EU-15 – are rational actors. They will choose energy policy instruments which maximize their perceived benefits. In line with this assumption, we argue that market-based solutions are bound to be the most attractive and economically expedient instrument for CEE owing to their particular circumstances and because of the incentive structures they create for the most relevant policy actors. To make our argument more plausible, we must first elaborate on the so-called 'pollution haven hypothesis' (see Copeland and Taylor, 2004).

The pollution haven hypothesis refers to the structure effects of trade. It is based on the Heckscher–Ohlin model, which presumes that regions will export goods that use locally abundant factors as inputs. Against this background, the pollution haven hypothesis posits that jurisdictions with weak environmental regulations, that is low-regulating countries, attract polluting industries relocating from jurisdictions with strong environmental regulations, that is high-regulating countries. The underlying reasoning is that environmental regulations raise the cost of key inputs to goods with pollution-intensive production and reduce jurisdictions' comparative advantage in those goods. Hence, the regulatory discrepancies are expected to motivate pollution-intensive industries to migrate from high-regulating countries to low-regulating countries (Ferrantino, 1997, p. 48).

Along these lines, the EU-15 can be regarded as rich in capital, while the CEE countries offer lower costs of labor and production. Since businesses can escape from higher production and labor costs and transfer their production activities to a country with lower manufacturing costs, a shift in industrial production facilities towards CEE has taken place (see Spatareanu, 2007). This has led to massive increases in production in CEE. In addition, the open markets and increasing prosperity have resulted in massive increases in consumption. Despite the increasing energy efficiency due to the market-based usage of resources, industrial and agricultural production and increasing consumption place a considerable burden on the energy sources. In this context, Andonova et al. (2007) argue that both the demand side and the supply side of politics can produce a negative relationship between enhanced exposure to competition and environmental and energy policy. On the demand side, import-competing firms may lose market shares to cheaper imports owing to more stringent environmental policies, which should intensify the opposition to more costly command and control measures. On the supply side, governments must build coalitions for facilitating structural changes since they cannot afford to alienate key industrial interests.

We contend here that the CEE countries find themselves in the cross-fire between what appear to be contradictory goals of EU cohesion and environmental and energy policy. On the one hand, the EU calls for an ecological approach to various areas of life in CEE, while at the same time it provides massive support to the expansion of the traffic and energy infrastructure. A very substantial part of the EU cohesion fund (Konečný and Medarova-Bergström, 2008) flows directly into the construction of roads and airports and thus automatically into increased car, truck and aviation transport. Thus there appears to be a strong preference for investments in high-pollutant modes of transportation, which are known to be the fastest-growing producers of GHG, but are at the same time regarded as indispensable for economic and infrastructural convergence with western European standards.

The environmental policy problem structure in CEE is therefore characterized by the predominance of producer interests and the contradictory aims of EU cohesion and environmental policies, but also by the lack of administrative capacity and the weak influence of environmental interest associations. Against this background, incentives must be created for environmental and energy policy actors, in order to guarantee the success of community and national environmental measures. The selection of the regulatory instrument can play a particularly important and behavior-transforming role in this regard.

We therefore anticipate an increased usage of market-based instruments in CEE. Instruments such as environmental taxes, financial subsidies and emissions trade, which are linked with very clear incentive structures for affected industries and public administration, can be most effectively integrated into the given circumstances and serve to mitigate the pollutant-intensive developments associated with the economic transformation.

The anticipated dominance of market-based instruments in CEE can be explained by the advantages they create not only for producers but also for national governments and the EU. Since former planned economies are extremely energy-intensive (that is require some 50 percent more energy to produce one GDP unit than the EU-15), market-oriented instruments (in particular environmental taxes and fees) can create impulses to increase energy efficiency. An increase in energy efficiency leads in turn to a decrease in manufacturing costs and thus to an increase in competitiveness of central and eastern European manufacturers in the EU internal market (see Dobbins et al., 2004; Jehlička and Tickle, 2004). It can also be assumed that transformation countries will initially profit from emissions trading. For a large part of the concerned countries, more generous Kyoto standards were negotiated than for the EU-15. And as a result of the introduction of improved technology, emissions have been reduced in CEE. Therefore they are likely to be among the sellers of emissions permits.

Another reason why the selection of market-oriented instruments might constitute a rational strategy for CEE governments is that they increase governmental budgets. Such alternative funding sources are of increasing importance since the special environmental funds to finance the implementation of environmental policy introduced in the CEE countries in the early 1990s are continuously diminishing (Andonova et al., 2007). Hence, governments need other funding sources which enable them to invest in or subsidize renewable energy sources (RES). Although such RES are promoted by the EU, they are broadly neglected by the cohesion funds.

Third, the implementation costs of economic instruments are generally lower and less burdensome for poorer countries. Considering the comparatively weak administrative structures in the CEE countries, market-based instruments seem to provide an attractive solution to the widely acknowledged implementation deficits since they are generally perceived to be 'self-enforcing' (see Tietenberg, 1990). Market-oriented instruments can thus reduce the costs of regulatory environmental policy and create incentives for long-term improvements in environmental performance (Holzinger et al., 2006, p. 403).

Finally, it could be rational for the CEE to continue using those market-based instruments, which were in place but virtually unenforced during state socialism. Emission charges and non-compliance fees in the CEE countries, for instance, originated in the 1970s and early 1980s.[4] Since any kind of policy change can be costly, we argue that preserving the previous portfolio of instruments can be seen as a rational behavior to minimize further costs. This point is even more valid when considering the policy adjustment costs CEE countries face during accession negotiations.

In summary, we contend that the particular incentive structures, the budget-maximizing character of market-based energy policy instruments and their relatively low implementation costs as well as the previous existence of market-based energy policy instruments have induced the CEE countries to apply them more often than the EU-15. Consequently, we can rephrase our argument by stating that CEE countries are more likely to apply market-based energy policy instruments since they expect a higher net benefit from them than do the EU-15.

7.4   OPERATIONALIZATION

Energy policy covers a wide area ranging from energy self-sufficiency to energy consumption and reliable distribution, but politically sensitive issues, such as the dependence on third countries because of the need to import energy, are also an integral part of this policy field. Furthermore, energy policy is concerned with the environmental externalities caused by energy production and consumption. In this context, it is important to note that in its 2010 Communication *Energy 2020* the Commission explicitly recognizes sustainability along with competitiveness and security as key objectives of Community energy policy. The sustainability aspect is of major importance to our research perspective since market-based instruments are employed primarily to internalize negative externalities. To measure the application intensity of market-based instruments, we rely on environmental taxes on substances related to energy sources, that is fuels and their combustion. The introduction of environmental taxes usually involves three complementary approaches: a removal or modification of existing distorting subsidies and tax provisions, a restructuring of existing taxes, and the introduction of new environmental taxes. There are hence remarkable political costs associated with such an undertaking. More basically, environmental taxes pursue the objective of internalizing negative externalities via correct pricing of environmental use. Ideally, the tax rate is set at the level of the external costs, although such costs are hard to assess in practice. The main difficulties in assessing external costs are the lack of market information, the spatial and temporal variation in externalities, and the scientific uncertainties in the relationship between emissions and environmental impacts (European Environmental Agency, 2006, p. 24).

Consequently, we only assess whether environmental taxes are in place rather than comparing tax rates, since that would implicitly require the definition of an ideal tax rate, which we are unwilling to set in an arbitrary way. More precisely, we focus on environmental taxes on carbon dioxide (CO_2), sulfur oxide (SO_2), nitric oxide (NO_x), other air pollutants, fuels, car sales and annual car taxes. These measures are related to the use of energy but they also have important implications for the environment.

It is generally quite challenging to collect reliable data on domestic environmental policy outputs. Fortunately though, the European Environmental Agency (2006) offers a comprehensive overview of the environmental taxes applied by the EU-15 and the new member states by 2004. It hence constitutes the data basis for this analysis. Table 7.1 exhibits the use of market-based instruments in the CEE and the EU-15. With the exception of environmental taxes on CO_2 emissions, the CEE countries broadly apply these instruments. This holds particularly true for environmental taxes on SO_2, NO_2, other air pollutants, fuels, car sales and annual car taxes. Remarkable is, however, the low number of CEE countries with CO_2 taxes in place.

The crosses printed in bold indicate in which of the two country groups a certain environmental tax is comparatively more frequently applied. Hence,

Table 7.1   *Use of environmental taxes in CEE (above) and the EU-15 (below) in 2004*

	CZ	EE	HU	LV	LT	PL	SI	SK	BG	RO	
CO_2		×					×				2
SO_2	×	×	×	×	×	×	×	×			**8**
NO_x	×	×	×	×	×	×	×	×			**8**
Other	×	×	×	×	×		×	×			**7**
Fuels	×	×	×	×	×	×	×	×	×	×	10
Car sales	×	×	×	×	×	×		×	×	×	9
Cars	×	×	×	×	×	×	×	×	×	×	**10**

	A	B	DK	FI	F	D	GR	IR	IT	L	NL	P	E	S	UK	
CO_2			×	×	×		×	×			×			×		**7**
SO_2				×	×			×						×		3
NO_x				×	×			×						×		3
Other																0
Fuels	×	×	×	×	×	×	×	×	×	×	×	×	×	×	×	15
Car sales	×	×	×	×	×	×	×	×	×	×	×	×	×	×	×	**15**
Cars			×		×									×		3

Source: Own illustration based on European Environmental Agency (2006, p. 26).

taxes on CO_2 emissions and car sales are applied more often by the EU-15 than by the new member states. On the other side, however, it is surprising to see that the EU-15 have not defined environmental taxes for other air pollutants originating from the combustion of mineral fuels. One reason for this could be that this issue is covered by the EU emissions trading scheme. In the next section we explore whether the differences between the EU-15 and the CEE countries are significant, that is more than just a sporadic variation in the data.

Before we turn to the analysis though, we would like to draw attention to the development of total environmental tax revenues, first at a general level and then as a share of the gross domestic product (GDP) over time. As Figure 7.1 shows, the relatively dramatic increase in the application of market-based instruments, that is environmental taxes, is evidenced by the income generated from environmental taxes in central and eastern European countries. The

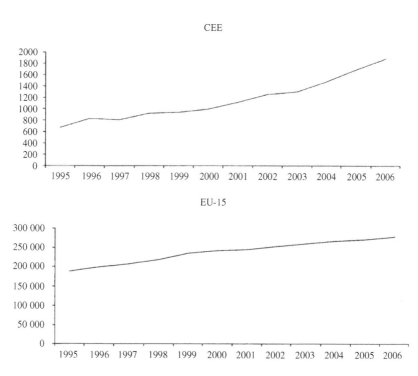

Source: Own illustration based on EUROSTAT (2007).

Figure 7.1   Income from environmental taxes in €m for all new post-socialist member states and EU-15

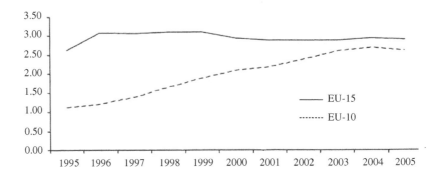

Source: Own illustration based on EUROSTAT (2007).

Figure 7.2   Total environmental tax revenues as a share of GDP 1995–2005

following graphic demonstrates that income from environmental taxes
increased by approximately 280 percent between 1995 and 2006 in central and
Eastern europe, but only by some 48 percent in the EU-15.

However, Figure 7.1 reveals little about the share of environmental taxes as
compared with other GDP revenue. We therefore also analyzed revenue from
environmental taxes as a share of the GDP of the post-socialist countries, as
exhibited by Figure 7.2. The upper curve reflects the development of the environmentally related tax revenues of the EU-15, the lower one the development
for the CEE countries which we refer to as the EU-10 in the figure. The first
major observation is that the revenue level is higher for the EU-15. Yet, since
the 2000s the CEE countries have been approaching the level of the EU-15,
which has been stagnating for the last five years of the observation period.
Taking into account that the income situation is clearly less favorable in the
CEE, this development is remarkable, and signals the comprehensive use of
market-based instruments.

To sum up, there are some notable differences between the use of environmental taxes in the CEE and EU-15. However, in order to make less sugges-
tive statements, in the next section we present some empirical tests for
evaluating our theoretical argument.

7.5   RESULTS AND DISCUSSION

In this section we explore whether the CEE and the EU-15 are significantly
different in their use of environmental taxes. A powerful tool for comparing
group means is a *t*-test. The test is replicated for each and every environmental tax introduced above. However, since there is no variation across both

groups regarding the application of taxes on fuels and car sales, we cannot compute *t*-tests for these two items. Instead, we can contend a priori that there is no significant difference between the country groups with regard to these items. Therefore, we compute only five tests in total. In some cases, the two country groups have an equal variation and in others they have an unequal variation. To determine the equality in variance, we apply Bartlett's test for equal variances. If the test produces a significant test statistic, we employ a *t*-test for independent samples with unequal variances by using Welch's approximation of the degrees of freedom. Table 7.2 presents the results of the *t*-test for the taxes on CO_2, SO_2, NO_x, other pollutants and cars.

A first finding is that the test of equal variation was positive only for environmental taxes on CO_2 emissions, which already hints that the groups display some remarkable differences. Accordingly, the formal *t*-tests showed that the CEE countries differ significantly from the EU-15 in their application of environmental taxes on SO_2, NO_x, other air pollutants and annual car circulation. This implies that of the seven tax items scrutinized here, four were significantly more often applied in the CEE countries, while for the other taxes there was no significant detectable difference. Hence, by and large, the CEE countries are different in their use of environmental taxes on energy-related items.

What are the implications of these findings for the sustainability of energy policies in the CEE? To evaluate this question, we now shift focus to the energy efficiency of the CEE countries. How effective are market-based instruments in reducing the primary energy consumption? Figure 7.3 illustrates the total primary energy consumption in the CEE countries with the average consumption of the EU-15. To facilitate the comparison, the figure also exhibits the average consumption of the CEE countries. Both average values are given by the darker bars. We can see that the average energy consumption, but also individual energy consumption for each of the ten CEE countries, exceeds the EU-15 average. While the energy consumption is relatively low in Slovenia, Latvia and Hungary, the energy needs of Bulgaria exceed the values given for all other CEE countries. High energy consumption is also observable for Estonia, Romania and Slovakia. Yet in direct comparison with Bulgaria their consumption levels are still quite moderate.

Although we cannot make any solid causal statement, we can surely point to the fact that the frequent use of market-based instruments, such as the environmental taxes analyzed in this chapter, must not necessarily lead to a lowering in energy consumption. In fact, there is some empirical work suggesting that the classic command-and-control approach is more effective (see for example Blair, 2008). Nevertheless, we would rather argue that the effectiveness of market-based instruments depends on their design (European Environmental Agency, 2006, p. 6). Hence, market-based instruments work better if:

Table 7.2   t-Test results

CO_2:

Country Group	Mean	Standard Error	N	Difference
EU-15	0.46	0.13	15	0.26
CEE	0.2	0.13	10	

$t = 1.35$, degrees of freedom = 23

SO_2:

Country Group	Mean	Standard Error	N	Difference
EU-15	0.8	0.10	15	−0.6***
CEE	0.2	0.13	10	

$t = -3.51$, Welch's degrees of freedom = 21.12

NO_x:

Country Group	Mean	Standard Error	N	Difference
EU-15	0.8	0.10	15	−0.6***
CEE	0.2	0.13	10	

$t = -3.51$, Welch's degrees of freedom = 21.12

Other:

Country Group	Mean	Standard Error	N	Difference
EU-15	0	0	15	−0.7***
CEE	0.7	0.15	10	

$t = -4.58$, Welch's degrees of freedom = 9

Cars:

Country Group	Mean	Standard Error	N	Difference
EU-15	0.2	0.11	15	−0.8***
CEE	1	0	10	

$t = -7.48$, Welch's degrees of freedom = 14

Source: Own illustration. *** $p < 0.01$, ** $p < 0.05$, * $p < 0.10$.

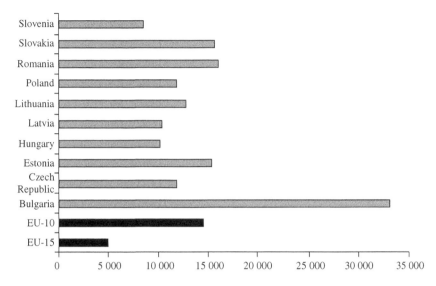

Source: Own illustration based on the US Energy Information Administration's International Energy Statistics.

Figure 7.3   Total primary energy consumption per dollar of GDP

- they are well-designed in themselves and as part of a wider package of instruments;
- the reasons for having them and how revenues will be used are clearly communicated;
- the levels at which 'prices' are set reflect both an incentive to producers and consumers to change behavior and a realistic analysis of affordability.

Therefore we should not regard market-based instruments as a panacea to environmental deterioration and unsustainable energy consumption. Instead, they must be designed in a very careful way. The central shortcoming of the environmental tax system in the CEE is that the rates tend to be low because of concerns about people's ability and willingness to pay (see European Environmental Agency, 2006). For example, despite recent efforts at strengthening the EU-wide use of environmental taxes, Lithuania continues to have a level of environmental taxes slightly below 2 percent of its GDP (Georgescu et al., 2010, p. 1). This is why they fail to correctly internalize the negative externalities caused by the excessive consumption of energy sources (see Sterner 2002, ch. 8). This is reflected clearly by the data from Georgescu et al. (2010, p. 2) regarding the relationship between greenhouse gas emissions and tax levels. The most striking example is Poland, whose GHG emissions are 7.9 percent of total emissions in the EU, while its share of environmental taxes of the total EU environmental taxes is 2.7 percent. Similar observations can be made for Bulgaria, the Czech Republic, Estonia, Hungary, Lithuania, Romania and Slovakia. This implies that there is a disproportional relationship between taxation and actual shares of pollution.

7.6   CONCLUSIONS

In this chapter we have examined the following two research questions: How widely are market-based instruments applied by the CEE countries? Is the regulatory approach of the new member states different from the approach of the EU-15? To address these questions, we focused on the application of environmental taxes related to one particular energy source, that is fuels. Based on our empirical analysis, we can reply to the first question that CEE countries indeed broadly apply environmental taxes. As concerns the difference between the CEE countries and the EU-15, there are some marked differences and on average they dominate the country-group-specific patterns. At the same time, however, there are also similarities in the application of environmental taxes. The difference became most apparent in the cases of taxes on SO_2, NO_x and other air pollutants as well as annual car circulation. Due to this extensive application of environmental taxes, the tax revenues from environmental taxes have been increasing since the year 2000 and are approaching the (stagnating) level of the EU-15. Nevertheless, we also learned that the existence of market-based instruments does not necessarily lead to lower energy consumption. To be sure, the CEE countries still surpass the energy consumed on average by the EU-15. While the level of energy consumption is relatively homogenous in the CEE, Bulgaria clearly represents an outlier with a remarkably high level of energy consumption.

By and large, this chapter represents a first step in analyzing the individual energy policy arrangements of the CEE in the framework of the emergent European energy policy. The main objective of this chapter was to shed light on the fact that the analysis of environmental and energy policy arrangements and their transformation should not only be viewed from the perspective of EU accession and membership (that is 'green Europeanization'). Rather, the CEE countries have their own approaches towards a sustainable energy policy, which we expect to persist despite the most recent developments such as the launching of the European energy policy and the Lisbon Treaty (importantly because of the limits on EU action in this policy field). Unfortunately, however, the insufficient access to data impeded us from conducting a more comprehensive causal analysis. Therefore, we encourage future researchers to revisit this topic and to further our analysis by elaborating a more fine-grained theoretical model and the use of reliable data.

NOTES

1. The ten post-socialist new member states of the EU are Bulgaria, the Czech Republic, Estonia, Hungary, Latvia, Lithuania, Poland, Romania, Slovakia and Slovenia. Cyprus and Malta are left out from this analysis since they are structurally quite different from the previous ten countries.
2. Market-based environmental policy instruments include, above all, tradable emissions permits, environmental taxes, liability instruments, fees, subsidies and deposit systems. They are generally regarded as more 'modern' instruments of environmental policy than the classic command-and-control approach. They have all the efficiency properties of competitive market pricing: they trigger actions among both producers and consumers that allow the achievement of given environmental objectives at the lowest costs. The efficient nature of economic instruments is due to the flexibility given to polluters for devising a cost-effective compliance strategy. Additional advantages of economic instruments are their capacity to integrate environmental concerns with sectoral policy goals and to promote a gradual shift in the allocation of a society's resources required for sustainable development.
3. For further details, see: http://ec.europa.eu/enlargement/archives/enlargement_process/future_prospects/negotiations/eu10_bulgaria_romania/chapters/chap_14_en.htm
4. For an excellent overview of applications of economic instruments in the CEE until 1998, see: http://www.rec.org/REC/Programs/SofiaInitiatives/EcoInstruments/EIReport/chapter4.html

REFERENCES

Andonova, L.B. (2004), *Transnational Politics of the Environment: The European Union and Environmental Policy in Central and Eastern Europe*, Cambridge, MA: MIT Press.

Andonova, L.B., E.D, Mansfield and H.V. Milner (2007), 'International trade and environmental policy in the postcommunist world', *Comparative Political Studies*, **40** (7), 782–807.

Baker, S. (2001), 'The impact of Eastern enlargement on EU environmental governance', paper prepared for presentation at the Environmental Studies Workshop on Environmental Challenges of EU Eastern Enlargement, Robert Schumann Centre – European University Institute, 25–26 May, Florence.

Balmaceda, M. (2002), 'EU energy policy and future European energy markets: consequences for the Central and East European states', University of Mannheim, Germnay, working paper.

Blair, D. J. (2008), 'Trade liberalization, environmental regulation and the limits of reformism: the North American Experience', *Environmental Politics* **17** (5), 693–711.

Böcher, M. and A.E. Töller (2007), 'Instrumentenwahl und Instrumentenwandel in der Umweltpolitik. Ein theoretischer Erklärungsrahmen', in Klaus Jacob, Frank Biermann, Per Olof Busch and Peter Feindt (eds), *Politik und Umwelt*, Wiesbaden, Germany: VS Verlag, pp. 496–521, published in Special Issue **39**/2007 of the *Politische Vierteljahresschrift*.

Carmin, J. and S.D. VanDeveer (eds) (2005), *EU Enlargement and the Environment. Institutional Change and Environmental Policy in Central and Eastern Europe*, Oxford: Routledge.

Copeland, B.R. and S.M. Taylor (2004) 'Trade, growth, and the environment', *Journal of Economic Literature*, **42** (1), 7–71.

Dobbins, M., D. Drüner and G. Schneider (2004), 'Kopenhagener Konsequenzen: Gesetzgebung in der EU vor und nach der Erweiterung', *Zeitschrift für Parlamentsfragen*, **35** (1), 51–67.

European Environmental Agency (2006), *Using the Market for Cost-Effective Environmental Policy – Market-Based Instruments in Europe*, Luxembourg: Office for Official Publications of the European Communities.

Ferrantino, M. (1997) 'International trade, environmental quality and public policy', *The World Economy*, **20** (1), 43–72.

Georgescu, M.A., V. Pendolovska and J.C. Cabeça (2010), 'Distribution of environmental taxes in Europe by tax payers in 2007: In many European countries, households are the main contributors to the energy and transport tax revenue', *Eurostat – Statistics in Focus 67*, Luxembourg, pp. 1–8.

Holzinger, K. and P. Knoepfel (2000), 'The need for flexibility: European environmental policy on the brink of Eastern enlargement', in K. Holzinger and P. Knoepfel (eds), *Environmental Policy in a European Union of Variable Geometry: The Challenge of the Next Enlargement*, Basel, Switzerland: Helbing & Lichtenhagen, pp. 3–35.

Holzinger, K., C. Knill and A. Schäfer (2006), 'Rhetoric or reality? "New Governance" in EU environmental policy', *European Law Journal*, **12** (3), 403–20.

Homeyer, I. von (2001), 'Enlarging EU environmental policy', paper presented at the environmental challenges of Eastern enlargement workshop, Robert Schumann Centre, European University Institute 25–26 May, Florence.

Homeyer, I. von, B. Carius and S. Bär (2000), 'Consequences of Eastern enlargement of the European Union for environmental policy', in M.G. Cowles and M. Smith (eds), *State of the European Union: Risks, Reforms, Resistance and Revival*, Oxford: Oxford University Press.

Jahn, D. and S. Wälti (2007), 'Umweltpolitik und Föderalismus: Zur Klärung eines ambivalenten Zusammenhangs', in Klaus Jacob, Frank Biermann, Per Olof Busch and Peter Feindt (eds), *Politik und Umwelt*, Wiesbaden, Germany: VS Verlag , pp. 262–79, published in Special Issue **39**/2007 of the *Politische Vierteljahresschrift*.

Jehlička, P. and A. Tickle (2004), 'Environmental implications of Eastern enlargement: the end of progressive EU environmental policy?', *Environmental Politics*, **13** (1), 77–95.

Knill, C. and K. Holzinger (2004), 'Marktorientierte Umweltpolitik – ökonomischer Anspruch und politische Wirklichkeit', in Roland Czada and Reinhard Zintl (eds), *Politik und Markt*, Wiesbaden, Germany: VS Verlag, pp. 232–55, published in Special Issue **34**/2004 of the *Politische Vierteljahresschrift*.

Knill, C. and A. Lenschow (2000), 'New environmental policy instruments as a panacea? Their limitations in theory and practice', in K. Holzinger and P. Knoepfel (eds), Environmental Policy in a European Union of Variable Geometry: The Challenge of the Next Enlargement, Basel, Switzerland: Helbing & Lichtenhahn, pp. 317–48.

Knill, C. and D. Liefferink (2007), *Environmental Politics in the European Union*, Manchester: Manchester University Press.

Knill, C., J. Tosun and S. Heichel (2008), 'Balancing competitiveness and conditionality: environmental policy-making in low-regulating countries', *Journal of European Public Policy*, **15** (7), 1019–40.

Konečný, M. and K. Medarova-Bergström (2008), 'Falsche Weichenstellung – EU-Kohäsionspolitik zu Lasten von Klima und Umwelt', *Osteuropa*, **58** (4–5), 189–204.

Lavenex, S. (2004) 'EU external governance in "wider Europe"', *Journal of European Public Policy*, **11** (4), 680–700.

Lavenex, S. and E. Uçarer (2004), 'The external dimension of Europeanisation', *Cooperation and Conflict*, **39** (4), 417–443.

Lavenex, S. and F. Schimmelfennig (2009), 'EU rules beyond EU borders: theorizing external governance in European politics', *Journal of European Public Policy*, **16** (6), 791–812.

Pointvogl, A. (2009), 'Perceptions, realities, concession – what is driving the integration of European energy policies?', *Energy Policy*, **37** (2), 5704–16

Schimmelfennig, F. and U. Sedelmeier (2004) 'Governance by conditionality: EU rule transfer to the candidate countries of Central and Eastern Europe', *Journal of European Public Policy*, **11** (4), 661–79.

Skjærseth, J.B. and J. Wettestad (2007), 'Is EU enlargement bad for environmental policy? Confronting gloomy expectations with evidence', *International Environmental Agreements*, **7** (3), 263–80.

Soveroski, M. (2000) 'European Community enlargement and environmental policy: the impact of growing diversity', in K. Holzinger and P. Knoepfel (eds), *Environmental Policy in a European Union of Variable Geometry: The Challenge of the Next Enlargement*, Basel, Switzerland: Helbing & Lichtenhagen, pp. 111–40.

Spatareanu, M. (2007), 'Searching for the pollution havens: the impact of environmental regulations on foreign direct investment', *Journal of Environment & Development*, **16** (2), 161–82.

Sterner, T. (2002), *Policy Instruments for Environmental and Natural Resource Management*, Washington, DC: RFF Press.

Tietenberg, T.H. (1990), 'Economic instruments for environmental regulation', *Oxford Review of Economic Policy*, **6** (1), 17–33.

Wilkinson, D., C. Monkhouse and D. Baldock (2004), *The Future of EU Environment Policy: Challenges and Opportunities', A Special Report for the All-Party Parliamentary Environment Group*, London: Institute European Environmental Policy.

8. The European energy policy towards eastern neighbors: rebalancing priorities or changing paradigms?

Anna Herranz-Surrallés and Michal Natorski

8.1 INTRODUCTION

As seen in Chapter 1, the objectives of the European energy policy are now commonly depicted as a triangle comprising three policy goals: competitiveness of energy markets, environmental sustainability and security of supply (that is the so-called energy trinity). The European Union (EU) has also progressively attempted to develop an external energy policy based on these three interrelated dimensions. Yet until recently the EU's external activity in the energy policy area was limited to the first two policy goals: that is, promoting the liberalization of energy markets abroad and energy reforms aimed at combating climate change (see Chapter 6 by Solorio Sandoval and Zapater). The lack of specific external policies in the third area, security of supply, is hardly surprising given that prior to the approval of the Lisbon Treaty there was little legal foundation for the EU authorities' involvement in securing external energy supplies. Therefore security of supply, despite having been the trigger for the first measures that the European Communities undertook in the area of energy in late 1960s, remained 'the weakest side of the EU energy policy triangle' (Buchan, 2010, p. 361).

However since the mid 2000s, in the context of tightening world energy markets and the gas supply crises that the EU experienced owing to deteriorating relations between Russia and some Former Soviet Union countries, the EU started to tackle this third aspect of its energy policy. The new consensus on the uncertainties surrounding the EU's future energy supplies was reflected in the Treaty of Lisbon, whose new article on energy policy (art. 194 in the consolidated Treaty on the Functioning of the European Union (TFEU)) assigned security of supply the same priority as energy markets and environmental sustainability. It is in view of these developments that this chapter examines whether and how the EU's concerns with energy security have impacted on the EU's foreign policy practice, assessing in particular whether the aim of security of supply has reinforced or been detrimental to the other areas of the EU's external energy dimension. By so doing the chapter will pay particular attention to whether energy security has boosted or weakened the EU's aim of becoming a 'green-energy' model exporter, as posited in Chapter 1 of this book.

The study focuses on the EU's relations with eastern European countries and the southern Caucasus, a region crucial for the supply and transit of natural gas and, to a lesser extent oil, to the EU. The chapter is structured into four additional sections. Section 8.2 spells out the analytical approach. Sections 8.3 and 8.4 assess the practice of the EU's relations with Eastern neighbors in the bilateral and regional frameworks respectively. The analysis in these two sections is based on a systematic examination of the agreements, reports, declarations and EU external assistance programming documents for the periods 2007–10 and 2011–13. The chapter closes with Section 8.5 providing an appraisal of the empirical findings and a discussion of their implications for the study of the external European energy policy.

8.2   CHANGING PARADIGMS IN THE EXTERNAL EUROPEAN ENERGY POLICY?

With the changes taking place in the energy markets over the last decade, it has become common in academic, political and media contexts to portray the international energy scene as one dominated by a struggle between two energy policy approaches, one market-oriented and the other geopolitical. This divide has been conceptualized elsewhere as a 'markets and institutions' versus a 'regions and empires' approach (Correljé and Van der Linde, 2006). The first paradigm or storyline assumes that the globalization of energy markets and the multilateral arrangements to deal with energy issues, which emerged since the late 1980s in particular, are set to continue. This assumption is based on the idea that energy resources are a commodity that should be open to private investment and traded freely. On the contrary, the second paradigm envisages an international system divided into competing blocks, in which access to energy resources would be an important aspect of the inter-block rivalry. From that perspective, energy is seen as too strategic an asset to be left to market rules and private actors.

However, this characterization of energy developments as a contest between markets and geopolitics seems to be increasingly inadequate for grasping the present context, which is characterized by ever more shades of gray. On the one hand, a dichotomized distinction between energy paradigms may fail to capture that both producing and consuming countries are dependent on markets and geopolitics to a greater or lesser extent. For example, despite the geopolitical aspect of energy, markets are ever more important for oil price discovery, which appears increasingly detached from fundamentals (Fattouh, 2007), and the gas outlook is also changing, with the new possibilities of unconventional gas and important LNG gas markets emerging (De Jong et al., 2010). At the same time, consuming and producing countries are increasingly considering energy security (be it of supply or demand) as one of the priorities of their energy policy, acknowledging its (geo)political character and the need for intervention by public authorities. On the other hand, a picture of markets versus geopolitics is also too one-dimensional, considering the greater worldwide prominence of other energy-related concerns such as combating climate change. In this regard, alongside energy markets and security of supply, environmental sustainability has become another crucial aspect of the energy equation in many countries around the globe. Therefore, more often than not, when analyzing states' energy policies we should expect to find elements of different paradigms coexisting, as part of the political battle between actors for prioritizing different aims. The analytical focus should hence be placed on the interaction between the different dimensions of the energy policy and whether there is equilibrium, synergy or conflict among them.

The external dimension of the emerging European energy policy has mostly been taken as an example of a predominantly market-oriented approach. In this sense the limited external energy policy that the EU started articulating since the early 1990s consisted of promoting the free trade and transit of energy resources, security of energy investments, environmental and safety standards and to certain level the promotion of renewable energy sources (RES). The EU pursued these aims through the Energy Charter Treaty (ECT) signed in 1994 and through several frameworks for energy cooperation and technical assistance, mainly with Former Soviet Union countries (for example the INOGATE program set up in 1996) and southern Mediterranean countries (for example the Euro-Mediterranean Energy Forum established in 1997) (on the Mediterranean dimension of the European external energy policy see Chapter 11 by Escribano-Francés and San Martín González). The ECT included a specific dimension on environment and energy efficiency, most notably the Protocol on Energy Efficiency and Related Environmental Aspects (PEEREA); but, as emphasized elsewhere, environmental obligations within the ECT were conceived as secondary to economic considerations (Bradbrook, 1999, p. 254). This approach to external energy relations was already an incipient attempt at EU 'external governance' (Lavenex, 2004; Lavenex and Schimmelfennig, 2009): namely an attempt by the EU to shape the regulatory space in its neighboring countries – albeit in a loose way, given the lack of development and coherence of the EU's own internal energy policies.

Since mid 2000s, however, in accordance with those accounts envisaging an ascendancy of the 'regions and empires' paradigm, energy security seems to have ranked ever higher on the political agenda of the EU and its member states, with scholars and politicians alike starting to favor the Union's adoption of a more strategic and geopolitical approach to energy policy (see for example Mañé-Estrada, 2006; Umbach, 2010; European Parliament, 2009, 2010). In particular, there have been growing demands to diversify hydrocarbon supplies in order to avoid overdependence on Russia and therefore also to minimize that country's chances to use energy as a political lever *vis-à-vis* the EU. By the same token, increasing calls have been made to develop mechanisms that will allow the EU to speak with one voice and leverage its influence *vis-à-vis* supplier countries (European Commission, 2010a, pp. 23–4) and to also deal with a politically motivated energy supply crisis. Officially the EU energy policy is said to pursue in equal measure the three aims of energy market operation, ensuring energy supplies and promoting environmentally sustainable and low carbon energy resources both within and outside the EU (European Commission, 2006; see also Chapter 1 by Solorio Sandoval and Morata). However pressures to rebalance energy priorities in order to accommodate the security of supply aim could also be an indication of a more paradigmatic shift, if energy security was found to be so prioritized as to systematically override the other energy-related aims.

The extent to which the EU is actually going down the path of this more geopolitical or even securitized energy paradigm and with what consequences is a matter for empirical analysis. To address this question the present chapter examines the EU's relations with countries from eastern Europe and the southern Caucasus taking part in the European Neighbourhood Policy (ENP) and in particular the evolution of priorities in the programing of the EU's financial assistance to those countries. The study assesses both the bilateral and the multilateral dimension of the EU's energy relations with Eastern ENP partners. For the bilateral dimension the countries in focus are Ukraine and Azerbaijan, two countries that play a crucial role in the EU's security of supply for different reasons: Ukraine is the most important transit country for the transport of gas, since roughly 80 percent of current imports from Russia (which in turn account for roughly 40 percent of the EU's gas imports) use the pipelines that cross Ukraine. Meanwhile Azerbaijan has increasingly become the focus of attention as one of the possible gas sources for filling the Nabucco pipeline, a potential main conduit of non-Russian gas in the future. The multilateral dimension focuses on two of the recent EU-sponsored multilateral processes of which energy is a crucial component: first, the Baku Initiative launched in 2004 under the EU's INOGATE program; second the Eastern Partnership launched in 2009.

8.3   THE BILATERAL DIMENSION

8.3.1   External European Energy Policy towards Ukraine: Energy Security as a Catalyst of Energy Reforms

Ukraine is the most important EU partner in the Eastern neighborhood in terms of the extent and institutionalization of its relations in the energy domain. Already at the beginning of the 2000s the EU set its objective of deepening relations in the energy domain by defining the agenda of relations in terms of economic objectives and environmental concerns, emphasizing the need for energy sector reform in Ukraine (Council of the European Union, 2003). The ENP Action Plan with Ukraine also paid special attention to the energy domain, covering issues such as the Ukraine's convergence with general European energy policy objectives and particular principles concerning electricity and gas markets, energy networks, the transit of natural gas, restructuring of solid fuels mines, energy efficiency and the use of RES and cooperation on nuclear safety (Partnership between the European Union and Ukraine, The Cooperation Council 2005, pp. 33–5).

Subsequently the *Memorandum of Understanding (MoU) on Cooperation in the Field of Energy between the EU and Ukraine*, signed on December 2005, framed the cooperation in economic terms, emphasizing that 'the EU and Ukraine share convergent interests and both could benefit from the integration of their respective energy markets', but it was already added that this cooperation should enhance 'the energy security of the European continent' (European Union and Ukraine, 2005, p. 7). The MoU included four specific roadmaps for cooperation: nuclear safety, the integration of electricity and gas markets, security of energy supplies and the transit of hydrocarbons and structural reforms enhancing safety and environmental standards in the coal sector. Furthermore in 2008 the EU and Ukraine agreed on an additional roadmap covering energy efficiency, RES and measures to tackle climate change. These commitments and the progress made in their implementation suggest that the cooperation was evenly encompassed in the different lines of the European energy policy, including economic, environmental and security aspects. Since then Ukraine has made significant progress in the implementation of agreed legal, regulatory and institutional measures in all areas included under the energy cooperation, but the decisive steps in the process of Ukrainian approximation to the EU were made in the exceptional context of the post-2009 gas crisis with Russia.

In 2009 the energy relations between the EU and Ukraine were also strongly framed in security terms. For example in the documents accompanying the joint EU–Ukraine Joint Investment Conference on the modernization of the Ukrainian gas transit system held in March 2009, the representatives of both parties declared that 'the secure flow of energy is fundamental for our economies and our way of life. And energy security has become, along with climate change, one of the key global challenges of the 21st century.' However this highly securitizing tone was used to underline broader economic and market policy objectives, such as achieving 'competitive, transparent and well-functioning energy markets that provide security of demand, security of supply and security of transit, and which are based on a modern, efficient and reliable transportation infrastructure' (Ferrero-Waldner et al., 2009). Indeed the conference confirmed that these security concerns activated instruments to help Ukraine align its regulatory market standards concerning the operation of the gas transmission system with EU Directives (European Commission et al., 2009). As a result the energy relations focused basically on a whole series of normative, regulatory and institutional reforms in different areas of the energy sector, preparing the ground for Ukraine's accession to the Energy Community Treaty in 2011.

This tendency to significantly extend the scope of cooperation in the energy sector has also been reflected in the case of the EU's financial assistance. Until 2006 the EU mainly provided support in the area of nuclear safety, which represented almost all cooperation in the energy domain and 50 percent of all financial assistance funded by the TACIS Programme to Ukraine (more than €300 million). However, while this tendency to grant a considerable amount of assistance to the energy sector continues under the new European Neighbourhood and Partnership Instrument (ENPI), there is a much broader diversification of the sectors benefiting from it. In this regard Ukraine has been granted four projects on a bilateral basis in the energy domain since 2007 (one project in support of energy market integration and three projects supporting energy efficiency and the use of RES in Ukraine), amounting to €184 million. As seen in Table 8.1, during the period 2007–10 the combined amount of budget support and technical assistance in energy efficiency projects was even slightly higher than the amount dedicated to market-related projects.

Last but not least, aside from this direct support, the EU provided around €23 million of additional funds under the Neighbourhood Investment Facility (NIF) in order to mobilize projects with backing from the European Bank for Reconstruction and Development and other International Financial Institutions worth €4.2 billion to support the upgrade and rehabilitation of Ukraine's energy networks, as well as energy efficiency projects intended to support Ukraine's energy security (Table 8.2.).

Therefore, in summary, energy security considerations seem to have been a positive catalyst for widening and deepening cooperation in the other energy domains. The increasing role of energy security considerations in framing the debate about transit networks and infrastructures has allowed a breakthrough

Table 8.1 Bilateral projects funded by the European Neighbourhood and Partnership Instrument (ENPI) 2007–10

Country	Year	Project title	Budget (€)	Framing
Ukraine	2007	Support to the implementation of Ukraine's energy strategy	Budget support (82m) Technical assistance (5m)	Energy market integration; energy security
Ukraine	2008	Support to the implementation of Ukraine's strategy in the area of energy efficiency and renewable sources of energy	Budget support (63m) Technical assistance (7m)	Energy efficiency and RES
Ukraine	2010	Community-Based Approach to Local Development (CBA), Phase II	Participatory activities (17.5m in total)	Energy efficiency
Ukraine	2010	EU 2010 contribution to the Eastern Europe Energy Efficiency and Environment ('5 E's') Partnership Fund	Contribution (10m)	Energy efficiency
Moldova	2010	Energy and biomass project	Technical assistance (14m)	Energy efficiency and RES
Azerbaijan	2007	Energy Reform Support Programme	Budget support (13m); Technical assistance (1m)	Energy security; energy efficiency and RES
Belarus	2007	Support to the Implementation of a Comprehensive Energy Policy for the Republic of Belarus	Technical assistance and pilot projects (5m)	Energy efficiency and RES
Belarus	2010	Support to Belarus in the field of norms and standards related to energy efficiency of consumer goods and industrial products	Technical assistance and pilot projects (9m)	Energy efficiency and RES

Source: Own compilation from ENPI Bilateral Annual Action Programs (2007–10).

138

Table 8.2 Projects funded by the Neighbourhood Investment Facility (NIF) 2008–10

Country	Year	Project's title	Total budget (€)	NIF contribution	Lead institution	Framing
Ukraine	2008	Ukrenergo high voltage transmission networks	301.28m	0.8m for Technical Assistance	EBRD	Energy market and energy efficiency
Ukraine	2008	Technical Assistance Support for Ukrainian municipalities	135m	5 M. for Technical Assistance	EBRD	Energy efficiency (also social and transport policies)
Ukraine	2008	Technical Assistance Framework for Burshtyn Thermal Power Plant Rehabilitation and Efficiency Improvement	250.8m	0.8m. for Technical Assistance	EBRD	Energy efficiency
Ukraine	2008	Energy Efficiency Support for Ukraine*	32.8m	2m for Technical Assistance	EBRD	Energy
Ukraine	2008	Loan Guarantee Programme for Municipal Infrastructure*	100m	10m for Grants	KfW	Energy (also Social and transport)
Georgia	2008	Black Sea Energy Transmission System	220m	8m for Technical Assistance	KfW	Infrastructures
Ukraine	2009	Power Transmission Network Reinforcement	1110m	10m for Technical Assistance	EBRD	Energy security
Ukraine	2009	Hydropower Rehabilitation Project	398.6m	3.6m for Technical Assistance	EBRD	Energy security and energy efficiency

Table 8.2 Continued

Country	Year	Project's title	Total budget (€)	NIF contribution	Lead institution	Framing
Regional	2009	Regional Industrial Energy Efficiency Programme	505,5m	2m for Technical Assistance	EBRD	Environment
Regional	2009	Energy Efficiency Programme for the Corporate sector	302m	2m for Technical Assistance	EBRD	Energy efficiency and RES
Georgia	2010	Enguri Hydro Power Plan Rehabilitation	40m	1m for Technical Assistance and 4m for Grants	EBRD	Energy security, energy efficiency and RES
Ukraine	2010	Naftogas	2000m	2.5m. for Technical Assistance	EBRD	Energy security

* Preliminary approval.

Source: Own compilation from ENPI Interregional Annual Action Programmes (2007–10) and Neighbourhood Investment Facility Annual Reports (2008–09).

to be made both in the implementation of energy market reforms and especially in the introduction of energy efficiency and RES initiatives.

3.2 External European Energy Policy Towards Azerbaijan: Market and Environment in the Shadow of Security of Supply

With Azerbaijan a country participating in the European Neighbourhood Policy, the envisaged energy cooperation between it and the EU followed the general commitments included in the ENP Action Plans, which include the three strands of the EU energy policy triangle: (1) gradual harmonization of Azerbaijani legislation with that of the EU, leading to the convergence of the electricity and gas markets; (2) safety and security of energy supplies and the system of transit to the EU; and (3) development of a comprehensive energy demand management policy (including energy efficiency, climate change and RES) (Partnership between the European Union and Azerbaijan – The Cooperation Council, 2006). However the European energy policy towards Azerbaijan seems to be increasingly prioritizing security of supply over the other aspects.

The special treatment given to Azerbaijan is ostensible in the Memorandum of Understanding on a Strategic Partnership between the European Union and the Republic of Azerbaijan in the Field of Energy, signed in 2006. Unlike the MoU with the Ukraine, this document framed energy relations mainly in the area of security of supply. The parties recognized that they 'share convergent interests and both could benefit from the integration of their respective energy markets, thereby *enhancing the energy security of both sides*' (emphasis added). But more significantly, because of the special concerns over the geopolitical aspects of Azerbaijan's energy security, the parties recalled, in the introduction, 'the importance of ensuring the sovereignty, territorial integrity and inviolability of internationally recognized borders of the States of the region, particularly with a view of elimination of threats and risks in strengthening the European energy security' (European Union and Azerbaijan, 2006, pp. 1–2). This statement, by its veiled reference to Azerbaijan's territorial conflicts with Armenia, as well as to the disputed border with Turkmenistan under the Caspian Sea and the Serdar-Kypaz gas field that lies under the sea bed of this territory, might be seen as a concession to Azerbaijan that indicates the EU's subordination of its foreign policy to energy security.

Especially since 2009, Azerbaijan has been the object of various visits from EU officials with a view to guaranteeing the country's contribution to Nabucco. Although Azerbaijani gas from the Caspian Sea would not suffice to make the project profitable, Azerbaijan's commitment has been deemed instrumental for incentivizing the effective launch of the project. The diplomatic contacts bore fruits in the signing of the Joint Declaration on the

Southern Gas Corridor in January 2011 between the president of Azerbaijan and the president of the European Commission.[1] The joint declaration was a political act to assure both security of supply for the EU and security of demand for Azerbaijan. The statement described the Southern Gas Corridor as strategic for both parties and also hinted at the possibility of extending it beyond Azerbaijan, which would mean Azerbaijan also becoming a transit country for Turkmen gas (Azerbaijan and European Commission, 2011). Yet the sense of strategic competition for Azerbaijani gas is still strong, especially given Russia's parallel offers to Azerbaijan and Turkmenistan to increase its imports from these countries at competitive prices. Azerbaijan still has to decide to whom it will award the contract for the Shah Deniz II gas field. In the words of the spokeswoman for the EU's Energy Commissioner Günther Öttinger, reflecting the EU's strategic stakes in the relations with Azerbaijan, 'for the EU it's decisive that a European project and a European firm gets awarded this contract' (Bloomberg, 2011).

The shift of direction in the EU's approach to energy cooperation with Azerbaijan is conspicuous in the EU's programing documents. Thus the priorities established in the National Indicative Program (NIP) for the period 2007–10 were legislative and economic reforms in the energy sector with a view to improving the competitiveness of the Azerbaijani economy and ultimately alleviating the poverty problem in the country (European Commission 2007, pp. 14–15, 17–18). On this basis the EU granted €13 million of budget support and €1 million of technical assistance for the 'Energy Reform Support Programme'. Conversely the NIP's priority for the 2011–13 period in the domain of energy is the 'strengthening of energy security' (European Commission, 2010b, p. 21–2). Therefore funding should be allocated 'to enhance energy security of the EU and Azerbaijan and the role of Azerbaijan as both an energy producer and transit country' (ibid., p. 21). The aims of market convergence, namely increased energy efficiency and the use of RES, only appear as the last two points in the expected results of the above-mentioned priority of strengthening energy security. Therefore, although it is still early to conclude to what extent this will be a sustained tendency that will determine future funding, the NIP's aims suggest that security of supply has relegated the other two aspects of the energy policy to a secondary position.

The Commission's sponsoring of the Nabucco project has, in fact, caused heated debates around the possible adverse effect of the strategic aim of diversification of supplies with both environmental and market considerations. Environmentalists have expressed concerns and criticism of the EU's allocation of public funds to the Nabucco project, instead of investing in RES and energy efficiency. For example, in its contribution to the European Commission consultation process regarding the external dimension of

European energy policy in 2010, the NGO Bankwatch criticized the fact that the EU's current approach to energy relations with its neighbors has promoted 'opportunities to develop unsustainable and environmentally-unfriendly mega projects' and that 'this has been to the detriment of a focus on the development of renewables that would serve a bigger number of communities within the countries' (CEE Bankwatch Network, 2010). In turn, major gas companies have been very critical of the over-prioritization of security of supply and the political interference of the EU institutions beyond mere flanking political measures. Several companies have also explicitly criticized the creation of the Caspian Development Corporation, a joint project that the Commission launched with the participation of the European Investment Bank and the World Bank for the purpose of incentivizing Caspian countries to choose the EU as a destination for their exports. This block purchasing mechanism, which is an example of an embryonic mechanism through which the EU leverages its position as a single buyer, was dubbed by some gas companies as 'intrusive' (Eurogas, 2009, p. 2) and leading to a 'dangerous politicization of energy' (ibid.; see also E.ON, 2010, p. 4), or 'a negative step that would damage rather than enhance the single European market' (BP, 2010, p. 5).

8.4   THE REGIONAL DIMENSION

8.4.1   INOGATE–Baku Initiative: Energy Security as a Driver of Comprehensive Energy Cooperation

Launched in the mid 1990s, the INOGATE program has been one of the EU's most important instruments for engaging eastern European neighbors in cooperation on energy (see also Chapter 9 by Ciambra). This cooperation framework has undergone a very marked change since the debate on energy security intensified within the EU throughout the second half of the 2000s. More specifically, from a program dedicated to technical assistance in the domain of oil and gas infrastructures, it has become a framework for cooperation in all three domains of energy policy.

The process of upgrading INOGATE towards a more ambitious multilateral regional initiative began with the launch of the Baku Initiative in 2004, in a ministerial conference on energy attended by representatives from the European Commission, the Caspian littoral states (Azerbaijan, Iran, Kazakhstan and the Russian Federation) and their neighboring countries (Armenia, Georgia, Kyrgyzstan, Moldova, Turkey, Ukraine and Uzbekistan). Its adopted conclusions emphasized market and environmental aspects and approached the aim of security of supply in a very technical way, defined as a matter of 'infrastructures' extension, modernization, development, monitoring operations and interconnection' (Baku Initiative, 2004a). On the basis of the Baku agreement, the countries participating in the Initiative institutionalized the cooperation in four working groups: (1) harmonization of legal, regulatory and institutional framework for market liberalization; (2) enhancing the safety and security of energy transportation networks; (3) sustainable energy development; and (4) investment attraction and project facilitation.

In fact, the political character of regional cooperation was explicitly played down by several participating states, exposing strained relations among the countries of the region. Azerbaijan declared that the documents approved during the conference would not be applied with regard to Armenia; Russia and Kazakhstan expressed reservations about the Conclusions and Concept Paper adopted during the conference; and Armenia emphasized that the meeting was of a purely 'technical nature' and that 'no political issues should be included in the conclusions' (Baku Initiative, 2004b). The Russian Federation even distanced itself from cooperating in the Initiative, and at the next conference, held in Astana in 2006, it participated only as an observer.

The 2006 Astana ministerial conference gave a definitive and precise mandate for enhanced energy cooperation in the framework of the Baku Initiative. With the withdrawal of Russia from the INOGATE-Baku Initiative, the process seemed to acquire a more political character and became more biased towards the EU's priorities. The agreed *Road Map* was still based on the four working groups set up in Baku, but the definition of their objectives was slightly different. Most significantly, the aim relating to market convergence specified that this process would be 'on the basis of the EU internal energy market'. Second, the said *Road Map* referred explicitly to energy security, including not only the technical aspects of infrastructures but also the aims of 'addressing the issues of energy exports/imports, supply diversification, energy transit and energy demand' and 'attracting investment towards energy projects of common and regional interest' (Baku Initiative, 2006).

A closer look at the projects financed by INOGATE during the period 1997–2010 clearly reflects the evolution of regional energy cooperation (see Figure 8.1). On the one hand, before 2004 EU funding was allocated to projects on technical aspects relating to the hydrocarbon sector, whereas since 2004 the funding has been evenly distributed among the three energy priorities, including energy markets convergence, enhanced energy security and sustainable energy development. Much as with to the patterns described in the case of Ukraine, increased attention to security of supply has been an important lever for increasing activity and funding in other areas. For example, one of the projects under the priority of sustainable development that was granted higher funding (almost €10 million) was 'Identification and Promotion of Energy Efficiency (EE) Investments', whose objectives were 'reducing energy dependency' and 'improving security of energy supply in the countries

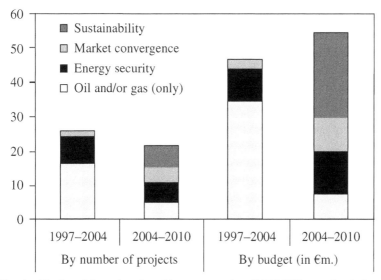

The classification of the projects by subject corresponds to INOGATE's own description of the project thematic domain.

Source: Own elaboration from INOGATE on-line project databases.

Figure 8.1   INOGATE projects 1997–2010 (by number of projects and by (€m.)

concerned by promoting energy efficiency particularly amongst small and medium enterprises (SMEs)' (INOGATE, 2011).

On the other hand, a second important advance has been the progressive introduction of the priority of security of supply in the INOGATE-funded projects. During the period 1997–2004, only a few projects were categorized by INOGATE under the 'energy security' label. Most of them, as Figure 8.1 shows, were simply catalogued as dealing with 'oil' or 'gas', even if in some cases the matter under question related to potential new supply routes. This is an indication that infrastructure projects at the end of the 1990s and early 2000s were regarded mostly in a technical and commercial manner. In fact Russia frequently figured among the beneficiaries of this kind of INOGATE project. Conversely, most projects relating to new infrastructure projects since 2004 have been categorized under the 'energy security' aim, as part of strategic aims to diversify supplies for the EU and exports for the beneficiary countries.

8.4.2   The Eastern Partnership: Security of Supply on the Centre Stage

The Eastern Partnership, launched between the EU and the eastern members taking part in the ENP in 2009, included energy cooperation as one of its four priority areas. The framing of this energy cooperation emphasized particularly the issues of security of supply. Due to the complementary nature of the Eastern Partnership with other EU initiatives concerning the region, this focus on security of supply could constitute the added value of the cooperation. This dominance of the security of supply is apparent in the EU documents, the official statements of participating countries and the working of common bodies established under the Partnership.

According to the EU documents, the security of energy supplies was a primary EU concern when this initiative was launched. The European Commission stressed in its proposals that the Eastern Partnership 'will aim to strengthen the energy security of the EU and of the partners with regard to long-term energy supply and transit'. This priority was clearly related to geopolitical concerns following the Russia–Georgia war in August 2008 and therefore energy security was considered to be threatened by 'the closeness of main hydrocarbon transit pipelines to zones of conflict', especially in the very unstable southern Caucasus (European Commission, 2008, p. 7). The Prague summit declaration included a passage that suggested an overwhelming dominance of energy security concerns in energy relations under the Eastern Partnership framework. In this document the EU and six eastern partners stressed that 'the Eastern Partnership aims to strengthen energy security through cooperation with regard to long-term stable and secure energy supply and transit, including through better regulation, energy efficiency and more use of renewable energy sources' (Council of the European Union, 2009, p. 8).

Beyond these political declarations, the works on security of supply also had practical implications. The Multilateral Platform established in the domain of energy was labeled 'Energy Security'. The European Commission insisted on the security framing of this cooperation, stressing that the Eastern Partnership should aim 'to develop and implement *mutual energy support and security mechanisms*, including early warning mechanisms and joint security actions ... to strengthen contacts on energy security and to enhance energy crisis preparedness' (European Commission, 2008, p. 11, original emphasis). However, the Platform's participants extended this dominant energy security framing when preparing this Platform's work program. In effect the platform's participants agreed on the following four 'core objectives': (1) enhancing framework conditions and solidarity; (2) support for infrastructure development, interconnection and diversification of supply; (3) promoting increased energy efficiency and use of RES; and (4) regulatory framework and approximation of energy policies. According to the plans, activities under the first

Table 8.3 Regional projects funded by the European Neighbourhood and Partnership Instrument (ENPI) 2007–10

Programme	Year	Project title	Budget (€)	Framing
Regional	2007	Support to Energy Market Integration and Sustainable Energy in the NIS (SEMIS)	Technical assistance (6m)	Energy market integration; energy security; energy efficiency and RES
Regional	2007	Strengthening of the INOGATE Technical Secretariat (ITS) in support of the Baku Initiative	Technical assistance (3m)	Other
Regional	2008	Energy Saving Initiative in the Building Sector in the Eastern European and Central Asian countries (ESIB)	Technical assistance (5m)	Energy efficiency and RES and energy security
Regional	2008	Pre-investment project for the implementation of the Trans-Caspian–Black Sea Gas Corridor	Technical assistance (5m)	Energy security, Energy markets integration
Regional	2010	Supporting participation of Eastern Partnership and Central Asian Cities in the Covenant of Mayors	Technical assistance and grants (5m)	Energy efficiency and RES and energy security
Regional	2010	Support to energy security in the Eastern Partnership and Central Asian countries through statistical cooperation;	Technical assistance (4m)	Energy security and energy markets integration
Regional	2010	INOGATE – Strengthening institutional capacity for sustainable energy governance in countries covered by the Eastern Partnership	Technical assistance (4m)	Energy efficiency and RES and energy security

Table 8.3 Continued

Programme	Year	Project title	Budget (€)	Framing
Interregional	2007	Community Budget contribution to the NIF	Grants (total 25m)	Energy efficiency and RES and energy security
Interregional	2008	Community Budget contribution to the NIF	Grants (total 25m)	Energy efficiency and RES and energy security
Interregional	2009	Community Budget contribution to the NIF	Grants (total 25m)	Energy efficiency and RES and energy security
Interregional	2010	European Union Budget contribution to the Neighbourhood Investment Facility (NIF) – commitment for 2010	Grants (total 40m)	Energy efficiency and RES and energy security
Interregional	2010	European Union Budget contribution to the NIF – Additional commitment for 2010	Grants (total 22m)	Energy efficiency and RES and energy security

Source: Own compilation from ENPI Regional East and Interregional Annual Action Programs (2007–10).

148

objective should focus on the preparation and presentation of the security of supply statements,[2] including the comparison of security of supply strategies, establishing the basis for a common early warning system and discussing regional solidarity schemes in order to cope with supply disruptions. Based on this discussion, the Platform's second objective envisaged establishing a list of 'key' interconnection projects 'having a direct and significant impact on security of supply'. The third objective encompassed stakeholders' dialogue in the area of RES and energy efficiency. However it was made clear that 'endogenous sources of renewable energy … significantly contribute to energy security by decreasing external dependency of fossil fuels' (Eastern Partnership, 2009, p. 4). This growing interrelation between energy security and the other priorities is clearly appreciated in the projects funded by the ENPI Regional (Table 8.3), where energy security ranks prominently in all regional projects, although always in combination with other aims, whether energy market reforms or the promotion of energy efficiency and RES.

However with the argument that the Energy Platform would not duplicate but complement the activities of the INOGATE-program – Baku Initiative, security of supply aspects monopolized the debates, considerably limiting any questions related to broader market-institutional or environmental aspects. As the European Commission reported in December 2010 to the ministers of foreign affairs participating in the Eastern Partnership, energy security is 'one of the main activities' due to the awareness and importance continuously attached by Partner countries who 'recognized the need for a regular reporting among Partner Countries … in order to build a robust basis for a constructive dialogue on security of supply issues, including security and solidarity questions' (European Commission 2010c, pp. 10–11). Indeed, during the meeting in October 2010 participants presented the situation of energy supply security in their countries, security of oil supplies (oil interconnections and diversification of supply, safety of offshore oil industry and EU Directive on oil stocks) and discussed some concrete projects connecting Eastern Partnership countries among themselves and with the EU countries. As regards other priorities it was acknowledged in 2010 that the regulatory framework as a fourth priority 'was only indirectly reflected within security of supply statements, when Partner Countries would share information of their existing infrastructure, its use and availability' (European Commission, 2010c, pp. 10–11).

8.5. CONCLUSION

This chapter has examined to what extent recent concerns about energy security have impacted on the European energy policy towards the countries of its eastern neighborhood and in particular the priorities of the EU's assistance. It has enquired specifically whether the aim of security of supply has come to the detriment of the other two dimensions of energy policy (energy market and environmental sustainability) and whether this is an indication of a more underlying change of paradigm in external European energy policy. The cases assessed do indeed show that the priority of security of supply, which until recently did not appear prominently in the EU's external relations, has become a core priority in EU's energy relations with its Eastern neighbors. However the empirical discussion has pointed out that the incorporation of the security of supply has not overtaken other dimensions of the EU's previous policy, but on the contrary has even boosted the EU's promotion of the liberalization of energy markets and environmental sustainability (in particular, energy efficiency measures) in some neighboring countries. In fact the EU seems to have become generally more assertive in its attempts at external Europeanization, formulating more specific demands for regulatory reforms of energy markets, the adoption of standards for energy efficiency and RES, and for measures to prevent and manage energy supply crises in neighboring countries.

For example, in the case of Ukraine the new procedures established for dealing with energy security issues have been accompanied by redoubled efforts to obtain this country's commitment to implement EU market and environmental regulations in the energy domain, and have served as justification for massive EU investments aimed at the rehabilitation of the energy infrastructure while promoting energy efficiency. Also, at the multilateral level, energy security has acted as a trigger for more multifaceted energy cooperation with Eastern neighbors under the INOGATE-Baku Initiative. If previous cooperation focused only on the technical aspects related to infrastructures, it now covers the three strands of the energy triangle on an equal footing. In particular the combination of energy efficiency and energy security was found to be the most common of aims in the EU-financed energy projects, at both bilateral and multilateral levels. Thus the promotion of the EU's 'green-energy' model abroad is now regarded not only as an instrument for combating climate change but also as one that contributes to security of supply, since a more efficient use of energy in producing and transit countries, some of them with extraordinary levels of energy inefficiency, is also seen as contributing to freeing up resources to satisfy the growing world demand for hydrocarbons.

However, one of the particular cases addressed in this chapter, namely the EU's policy towards Azerbaijan) shows the emerging tensions between the aim of security of supply and the other more established strands of the external European energy policy. From a policy focused on extending the Union's regulatory space, the EU has thrown itself into projecting its leverage in order to obtain Azerbaijan's cooperation in the EU's strategic diversification projects. In the well-known terms of Arnold Wolfers, the external European energy policy towards Azerbaijan has shifted from pursuing 'milieu goals' to pursuing 'possession goals'. In this regard the external European energy policy towards Azerbaijan increasingly resembles a more state-like access policy instead of its more traditional external governance or Europeanization approach. As shown in the analysis of the evolution of the EU's funding priorities towards this country, security of supply ranks so high on the agenda that it is overtaking the cooperation in the other two vertexes. The multilateral energy relations under the Eastern Partnership also suggest that security of supply is becoming the strongest pillar of cooperation, the other dimensions being virtually absent. In this case, however, the emphasis on energy security has been justified by avoiding duplications with other regional and bilateral activities and, in fact, the form of cooperation established in energy security has also taken the form of Europeanization, namely by extending the EU's internal *acquis* on security of energy supplies.

More generally, the empirical discussion in this chapter suggests that the inclusion of security of supply in the EU's external relations does not necessarily imply a change of paradigm or that energy policy is being securitized in the classical sense (Buzan et al., 1998) where energy would be approached as a matter of survival and following the 'logics of war' (Ciută 2010). Contrary to the currently *en vogue* reporting of the EU's relations with eastern neighboring countries as a matter of conflict and geostrategic competition, this chapter has argued that the EU's new security of supply priority has just reinforced previous trends in its cooperation on market convergence and environmental sustainability with some of its partners. However, rebalancing priorities by placing security of supply at the top of the hierarchy of aims is not without its consequences. On the one hand it can lead to blunt access-oriented policies void of normative ambitions, as seems increasingly to be the case in the external European energy policy towards countries such as Azerbaijan. But on the other hand it can also have the effect of making EU policy more rigid and non-reflexive in its attempt at external Europeanization, thereby alienating partner countries like Russia who do not wish to adopt the EU model of energy market integration as well as risking the export of the flaws of a still-changing and much-debated European energy policy.

NOTES

1. The Southern Gas Corridor project encompasses the Nabucco gas pipeline, the Trans Adriatic Pipeline (TAP), the ITGI (Turkey–Greece–Italy pipeline), the so-called White Stream (under the Black Sea) and the trans-Caspian link. Already in 2009 a joint declaration of support was signed by the Commission, the Council, the presidents of Azerbaijan, Turkey and Georgia and Egypt's minister of energy. Representatives from Kazakhstan, Turkmenistan, Uzbekistan and Iraq also expressed their support (European Commission, 2009).
2. These documents are compulsory for the members of the Energy Community Treaty; hence Moldova and Ukraine must present them as a consequence of their accession to this organization.

REFERENCES

Azerbaijan and European Commission (2011), *Joint Declaration on the Southern Gas Corridor*, Baku, 13 January.

Baku Initiative (2004a), *Conclusions of the Ministerial Conference on Energy Co-operation Between the EU, the Caspian Littoral States and Their Neighbouring Countries*, Baku, 13 November.

Baku Initiative (2004b), *Conclusions of the Ministerial Conference on Energy Co-operation Between the EU, the Caspian Littoral States and Their Neighbouring Countries, Annex 2 – Statement by Participating Countries*, Baku, 13 November.

Baku Initiative (2006), *Ministerial Declaration on Enhanced Energy Co-operation Between the EU, the Littoral States of the Black and Caspian Seas and their Neighbouring Countries, Annex 1 to the Ministerial Declaration of 30 November 2006, Road Map*, Astana, 30 November.

Bloomberg (2011), 'EU, Azerbaijan sign gas deal to bypass Russia', Brussels, 13 January, accessed 13 March 2011 at www.bloomberg.com/news/2011-01-13/eu-azerbaijan-sign-gas-deal-to-bypass-russia.html.

BP (2010), *BP plc Response to the European Commission DG Energy's Public Consultation on 'Towards a New Energy Strategy for Europe 2011–2020'*.

Bradbrook, Adrian (1999), 'Significance of the Energy Charter Treaty', *Applied Energy*, **64** (1–4), 251–62.

Buchan, David (2010), 'Energy policy: sharp challenges and rising ambitions', in Helen Wallace, Mark Pollack and Alasdair Young (eds), *Policy-Making in the European Union*, 6th edn, Oxford: Oxford University Press, pp. 357–79.

Buzan, Barry, Ole Weaver and Jaap De Wilde (1998), *Security: A New Framework for Analysis*, Boulder, CO: Lynne Rienner.

CEE Bankwatch Network (2010), 'CEE Bankwatch Network contribution to the public consultation process regarding the external dimension of EU energy policy', 7 March.

Ciută, Felix (2010), 'Conceptual notes on energy security: total or banal security?', *Security Dialogue*, **41** (2), 123–44.

Correljé, Aad and Coby van der Linde (2006), 'Energy supply security and geopolitics: a European perspective', *Energy Policy*, **34** (5), 532–43.

Council of the European Union (2003), *Relations with Ukraine – Presidency Work Plan on the Implementation of the Common Strategy of the EU on Ukraine*, 5408/03, Brussels, 17 January.

Council of the European Union (2009), *Joint Declaration of the Prague Eastern Partnership Summit, Prague*, 8435/09, Brussels, 7 May.

De Jong, Dick, Coby van der Linde and Tom Smeenk (2010), 'The evolving role of LNG in the gas market', in Andreas Goldthau and Jan Martin Witte (eds), *Global Energy Governance*, Washington DC: Brookings Institution Press, pp. 221–46.

Eastern Partnership (2009), *Platform 3 – Energy Security. Core objectives and Work Programme 2009–2011*, Brussels, 5 November 2009.

E.ON (2010), 'Public consultation: towards a new energy strategy for Europe 2011–2020', accessed at http://ec.europa.eu/energy/strategies/consultations/2010_07_02_energy_strategy_en-htm.

Eurogas (2009), *Caspian Development Corporation (CDC): Eurogas Preliminary Remarks*, 30 July; accessed at http://ec.europa.eu/energy/strategies/consultations/2010_07_02_energy_strategy_en-htm.

European Commission (2006), *Green Paper: A European Strategy for Sustainable, Competitive and Secure Energy*, COM(2006) 105 final, 8 March, Brussels.

European Commission (2007), *Commission Decision on the Adoption of the Strategy Papers 2007–13 and Indicative Programmes 2007–10 under the European Neighbourhood and Partnership Instrument*, C(2007) 672, 5 March, Brussels.

European Commission (2008), *Communication from the Commission to the European Parliament and the Council – Eastern Partnership*, COM(2008) 823 final, 3 December, Brussels.

European Commission (2009) *The Southern Corridor: EU and Partner Countries Commit to Move Forward*, IP/09/716, 7 May, Brussels.

European Commission (2010a), *State of Play in the EU Energy Policy*, SEC(2010) 1346 final, 10 November, Brussels.

European Commission (2010b) *Azerbaijan: National Indicative Programme 2011–2013*, Brussels.

European Commission (2010c) *Implementation of the Eastern Partnership: Report to the Meeting of Foreign Affairs Ministers*, MD 335/10 REV 2, 13 December, Brussels.

European Commission, European Bank for Reconstruction and Development, European Investment Bank, World Bank and Government of Ukraine (2009), *Joint Declaration: Joint EU–Ukraine International Investment Conference on the Modernisation of Ukraine's Gas Transit System*, 23 March, Brussels.

European Parliament (2009), *Energy Security (Nabucco and Desertec) (Debate)*, Strasbourg, 17 September, accessed 13 March 2011 at www.europarl. europa.eu/sides/getDoc.do?pubRef=-//EP//TEXT+PV+20090917+ITEM-003+ DOC+XML+ V0//EN.

European Parliament (2010), *Security of Gas Supply (Debate)*, Strasbourg, 21 September, accessed 13 March 2011 www.europarl.europa.eu/sides/ getDoc.do?pubRef=//EP//TEXT+CRE+20100921+ITEM-003+DOC+XML+V0// EN.

European Union and Azerbaijan (2006), *Memorandum of Understanding on a Strategic Partnership between the European Union and the Republic of Azerbaijan in the Field of Energy*, 7 November, Brussels.

European Union and Ukraine (2005), *Memorandum of Understanding on Cooperation in the Field of Energy Between the European Union and Ukraine*, December, Kiev.

Fattouh, Bassam (2007), 'OPEC pricing power: the need for a new perspective', in Dieter Helmes (ed.), *The New Energy Paradigm*, Oxford: Oxford University Press, pp. 158–80.

Ferrero-Waldner, Benita, Yulia Tymoshenko and Andris Piebalgs (2009), 'Foreword', in *EU–Ukraine: Partners for Securing Gas to Europe. International Investment Conference on the Modernisation of Ukraine's Gas Transit System. 23 March*, Brussels.

INOGATE (2011), 'Identification and promotion of energy efficiency (EE) invest-ments', accessed 13 March www.inogate.org/index.php?option=com_inogate& view=project&id=14 percent3AIPEEI&Itemid=75&lang=en.

Lavenex, Sandra (2004), 'EU external governance in "wider Europe"', *Journal of European Public Policy*, **11** (4), 680–700.

Lavenex, Sandra and Frank Schimmelfennig (2009), 'EU rules beyond EU borders: theorizing external governance in European politics', *Journal of European Public Policy*, **16** (6), 791–812.

Mañé Estrada, Aurèlia (2006), 'European energy security: towards the creation of a geo-energy space', Energy Policy, 34 (18), 3773–86.

Partnership Between the European Union and Azerbaijan – The Cooperation Council

(2006), *European Neighbourhood Action Plan*, UE-AZ 4603/06, 8 November, Brussels.

Partnership Between the European Union and Ukraine – The Cooperation Council (2005), *European Neighbourhood Action Plan*, UE-UA 1051/05, 14 February Brussels.

Umbach, Frank (2010), 'Global energy security and the implications for the EU', *Energy Policy*, **38** (3), 1229–40.

9. Exporting the good example? European energy policy and socialization in south-east Europe

Andrea Ciambra

9.1 INTRODUCTION

As a key strategic goal for the European energy policy, diversification of supply is commonly perceived as the keystone for future short- and long-term energy sustainability. While consuming countries can realistically pursue a diversification of supply – that is, relying on different kinds of sources – the diversification of suppliers has, on the contrary, proven difficult and is highly dependent on exogenous factors: monopoly energy markets, constraining physical reserves and unsettling local politics. Against this backdrop, the EU has been following the path marked by the Commission's Green Paper on security of energy supply, which set out explicitly that

> [t]he European Union's long-term strategy for energy supply security must be geared to ensuring, for the well-being of its citizens and the proper functioning of the economy, the uninterrupted physical availability of energy products on the market, at a price which is affordable for all consumers (private and industrial), while respecting environmental concerns and looking towards sustainable develop-ment. (European Commission, 2000a, p. 3)

Therefore, in parallel to the construction of a European energy policy, the EU has been urging for a comprehensive approach to the diversification issue. In this sense, the European Commission's 2006 Green Paper *A European Strategy for Sustainable, Competitive and Secure Energy* remarked on the need to diversify 'EU's energy mix with greater use of competitive indigenous and renewable energy, and ... sources and routes of supply of imported energy' (European Commission 2006, p. 18, our emphasis), a vision consoli-dated with the emergence of a consistent EU energy policy framework in 2007 (see Chapter 1 by Solorio Sandoval and Morata).

This chapter investigates whether and to what extent EU external relations have become a tool for pursuing the energy trinity abroad. In other words, by means of a sociological approach, the following sections examine the role of the EU as a 'green-energy' model exporter.

The chapter develops a theoretical and empirical analysis of the role the EU has been playing in its geographical and political proximity as a norm- and model-exporter in energy policy. It focuses specifically on the environmental dimension of the EU's policy actions, as well as on south-east Europe as an apt case study for recipient partner countries. The chapter is structured as follows: Section 9.2 reviews the theoretical definition of the EU's market-oriented external energy relations. Section 9.3 identifies the instruments set up by EU institutions to achieve its strategic objectives in the broader neighborhood. Section 9.4 specifically attempts to measure the effectiveness of the EU's intervention and the socialization of western Balkan neighboring countries with the EU's energy acquis within the institutional context of the Energy Community (EnC). Section 9.5, moreover, engages discussion on the topic by providing analytical insights and suggesting research tracks on the topic. Finally, Section 9.6 draws conclusions on the actual impact that socialization dynamics can have on fostering or hindering processes of policy adaptation, harmonization and compliance in neighboring countries. This chapter argues that the EU actually exerts an autonomous foreign energy policy-making in the neighborhood and that, besides the technicality of legal diffusion in neighboring countries, the EU aims to act as a 'green-energy' model exporter in the 'proximity' area.

9.2   EXTERNAL CAPABILITIES OF THE EU: A SOCIALIZATION APPROACH

In addressing the EU's external relations – in terms of a growing and consistent external European energy policy – at least two main theoretical challenges arise: (1) the ability of EU institutions to act outside EU boundaries, and (2) the mutual interest of the EU and its neighboring countries in sharing knowledge and resources in sectoral cooperation. The mere possibility of conceiving autonomous foreign policy capabilities for the EU's institutions has generated an impressive debate in EU studies and scholarship, drawing from established international relations paradigms in the attempt to grasp the originality of the EU's external relations (see Chapter 7 by Dobbins and Tosun; Chapter 8 by Herranz Surrallés and Natorski; Chapter 10 by Carafa; Chapter 11 by Escribano-Francés and San Martín González).

A speculative upgrade has been attempted through constructivist research, by assuming two key points: first, both the structure and agents of international relations are constructed through social interaction rather than material endowment, and both continuously influence each other; second, social interaction is neither given nor accidental, but is determined by 'rules, norms, ideas and *patterns of behavior*' (White, 2004, p. 22; emphasis added). It is these patterns that entitle the actor to 'play' a role in its interactions[1] with other units and that 'motivate' the actor to 'comply with the rules of the game' (Aggestam, 2006, p. 12). This role can be defined for any actor by its identity – that is its nature, components, aims, tools – and by the intervention of both an internal and external 'expectation' of what the actor is supposed to do. Role is, there-fore, eminently a social production. With such a socially constructed ego, the actor eventually defines its role performance. This is the analytical framework (Figure 9.1) in which this work conceives of a foreign-policy-making capabil-ity for EU institutions.

This socially constructed 'role' allows an enquiry about the EU's relation-ship with its political neighborhood. Particularly with regard to central and eastern European countries (CEECs), the EU has 'exerted a powerful social-izing influence ... explicitly cast in terms of democratic governance and respect for human rights' (Hobson and Sharman, 2005, p. 79), which proved hugely appealing to ex-Soviet bloc countries after the end of the cold war. The 'desirability' of the EU model was in fact based upon 'perceptions of success' and the expectation that the EU would actually have been able to solve the problems arising in its new neighborhood, through a masterful blend of liber-alism and social awareness (Bretherton and Vogler, 1999, p. 148). Such expec-tations contributed to the definition of a role for the EU as a model, and for the neighboring countries as 'apprentices' (ibid., p. 149).

This relationship has contributed to shaping the enlargement policies that led to the EU membership of up to 27 countries (see Chapter 7 by Dobbins and

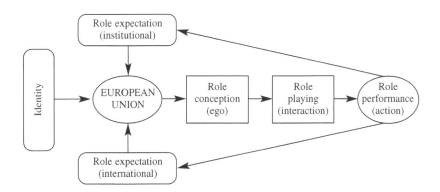

Source: Own creation.

Figure 9.1   Analytical framework for EU's role conception

Tosun) and the several facets of the EU's neighborhood policy (see Chapter 8 by Herranz Surrallés and Natorski). While the former focused on the use of external incentives to subsume candidate countries under the harmonization process with the EU's *acquis*, this chapter argues that neighborhood policies[2] are actually managed through 'different mechanisms of Europeanization' (Schimmelfennig and Sedelmeier, 2005, p. 8). The EU's role, as commonly perceived by neighboring countries, is basically that of an advocate of the 'imagined' Western international community, which is 'interstate, liberal, post-national' (Schimmelfennig, 2003, p. 77). It is this post-national, 'civic' feature of European integration that allows non-member countries to believe they can eventually become part of this community and that allows the EU to convince other parties that such an identity is 'acquirable and changeable' (Schimmelfennig, 2003, p. 80), whatever the expectation for formal membership of the EU. The adoption of rules and norms, whereby the EU spreads its governance and technical standards, is easier if such rules are legitimate (that is clearly stated and addressed, equal among members and non-members, or even co-owned), consistent with the community's identity, and 'resonant' with recipient countries' cultural and domestic factors (Schimmelfennig and Sedelmeier, 2005, p. 18–20).

9.3   EUROPEAN ENERGY POLICY OUTSIDE EU BOUNDARIES

EU institutions have supported and autonomously led two large external energy policy frameworks in the neighborhood, engaging various players within the EU's geopolitical proximity: (1) the INOGATE program, and (2) the Energy Community. The INOGATE project was first set up in 1995 under the broader umbrella of the TACIS (Technical Assistance to the CIS countries) funds, one of the first examples of the EU's consistent external relations instruments in the mid-1990s – for technical start-up and compliance with the regulations and objectives of the Energy Charter Treaty (ECT). The INOGATE program has implemented several initiatives and projects aimed at networking among the relevant stakeholders in recipient countries, devising technical assistance and substantial financial aid through the European Neighbourhood Policy Instrument (ENPI). Up to 2004, at least 26 different projects were completed, ranging from safety monitoring to actual construction of new infrastructures and buildings, thus ensuring trans-border cooperation among neighbors[3] (see also Chapter 8 by Herranz Surrallés and Natorski).

The scope of the Energy Community (EnC) is actually broader. It was the outcome of a gradual evolution prompted by the Athens Process back in 2002, when the first Athens Memorandum of Understanding (MoU) was signed by the European Commission and nine European parties.[4] The process culminated in the signing of the Treaty establishing the Energy Community (TEnC), on 25 October 2005. The treaty itself 'was consciously modeled on the European Coal and Steel Community', with the aim of allowing the parties to 'agree on one area of policy, and then to develop in common a shared outlook' (DG TREN, 2006, p. 2). Moreover, accessing the EnC was deemed as an essential and 'effective pre-accession tool' for all non-EU parties, and as a way of 'extending the benefits of the internal energy market' prior to further engagement with the EU (ibid., p. 2). Again, a narrative of conditional approximation to the EU and a discourse of socialization with EU standards and norms are elicited as part of a process under the EU institutions' control. It is therefore not imprudent to say that, since the very beginning of the Athens process, EU institutions, in concert with keen south-eastern neighbors have let new progressive dynamics come into play in the EU's energy market security. Whether this process has actually brought about an effective, market-led foreign policy tool under the control of EU institutions will be dealt with in Section 9.5, and an assessment made of the overall performance of the EnC, with suggestions for further evaluation.

The case of the EnC has been selected for its distinctive character, as its contracting parties account for all levels of engagement with the EU – candidate countries, SAP countries, simple partners. Therefore, the single case-study design here selects a 'critical case' to assess theories of rule adoption and role attribution, or for diverse levels of engagement between the EU and its partners (Yin, 2003, p. 40). Accordingly, the effectiveness of this compliance as a means for stabilizing the external energy market of the EU, while binding partners into a broader market 'community', will determine whether or not energy policies in the neighborhood can be considered as fledgling autonomous foreign policy by EU institutions, promoting the export of the 'green-energy' model.

9.4   THE ENERGY COMMUNITY IN PRACTICE

The EnC was the institutional and legal goal of the Athens Process. The TEnC entered officially into force on 1 July 2006, binding the parties – to date, the European Community, Albania, Bosnia and Herzegovina, Croatia, Kosovo, the former Yugoslavian Republic of Macedonia (FYROM), Moldova, Montenegro, Serbia, and Ukraine[5] – in an attempt 'to promote high levels of gas and electricity provisions to all citizens', while enhancing security of supply and improving environmental protection, energy efficiency and use of RES – as stated in the Treaty's preamble. To do so, the TEnC provides the EnC with a permanent institutional endowment[6] and its own mechanism of dispute settlement, modeled on the infringement procedure of the EU. Two principles are enshrined in the Community's dispute settlement system: decisions on compliance by the Ministerial Council are not judicial decisions and therefore not binding, and private bodies or individuals can raise an issue of non-compliance against national legislations in front of the Secretariat.

Moreover, membership is regarded as internally fluid: the ambition of the TEnC is to create a stable energy market and distribution grid on the whole of 'Europe's landmass', hence all neighboring countries are potentially eligible to commit to the process, or rather socialize themselves with the purpose, tools and benefits of the EnC through the status of 'observers'. Finally, all EU member states are entitled to enter the EnC as 'participants'. As of April 2011, 14 EU countries[7] have taken part in the EnC with this peculiar status: as members of the EU, all 'participants' have already clearly accepted and possibly implemented the energy *acquis communautaire*. Despite such redundancy, the specification of a 'participant' status reserved for EU countries is politically salient. The construction of the EnC, since its inception in 2006, has been governed autonomously by the European Commission and all concerned bodies within the scope of the EU's supranational agency. Member states have not been involved in the process except as concerned parties and have not even been included as signatory parties of the TEnC. This element of self-reliance by the EU's supranational agency surely demonstrates that EU entrepreneurship in external market relations is strong and opens up new opportunities for a single-voiced foreign policy capability of the EU.

A fledgling experiment in shared governance and technical cooperation, the EnC has engaged nine neighboring countries with high EU-level standards. There are at least two feasible ways to assess the efficiency of the EnC's institutional machinery in pursuing its strategic objectives of 'a stable regulatory and market framework' and a 'single regulatory space'. First, the implementation (Title II of the TEnC) of the EU's *acquis* on energy; and second, the adoption of secondary legislation (Articles 76 ff. TEnC) enacted by the EnC's Ministerial Council (MC).

In an effort to sustain accountability and transparency, the EnC provides an up-to-date list of all decisions enacted after receiving the MC's approval. Moreover, it periodically publishes official reports on the implementation status of the *acquis*. This work will take into account the current implementation process in the seven western Balkan members of the EnC. This choice is justified, first, according to a criterion of geographical, sociopolitical and historical consistency and, second, by the lack of established and reliable data on the performance within the EnC by the two newly accessed members – namely, Moldova and Ukraine. This section will build on a report (Energy Community Secretariat 2008) about the implementation of the environmental, RES and competition *acquis* (November 2008) and a report (Energy

Community Secretariat, 2009) on the electricity and gas *acquis* (April 2009), which also includes the latest developments in the contracting parties' national legislation and infrastructure. Newer reports on the electricity and gas legislation implementation (September 2010), which also include a preliminary assessment of Moldova's performance, will nonetheless be analyzed in order to track down potential changes in the implementation pattern (Energy Community Secretariat, 2010).

Reports allow both a general and a detailed, state-by-state appraisal. In an extensive overview, the Secretariat has stressed that the deadlines agreed by the parties have not been respected – except by fully complying Croatia. Moreover, the energy markets for both electricity and gas in contracting parties are structurally weakened by an overwhelming state presence, which led to anti-competitive subsidies to retail consumers and also made the unbundling of ownership (distribution and supply) even more difficult; and subsidized tariffs generally do not allow private suppliers or distributors to enter competitively into the market. Lack or absence of efficient infrastructure prevents the creation of a truly regionally integrated energy market, which is obviously regarded as a precondition for any integration with the EU network. This notwithstanding, dispute settlement procedures have only been initiated once against FYROM, for failing to comply with the EU acquis.

At the state level, the reports by the EnC Secretariat give a detailed assessment of the implementation of the electricity and natural-gas directives. Results are standardized to some extent on the overall model performance of Croatia, which has recorded an almost flawless adoption of EU rules into its national system. Table 9.1 shows the performance of the contracting parties in the implementation of the electricity *acquis* and the achievements in the natural-gas field.

It is worth noticing, however, that in the latest 2010 report on implementation, the EnC Secretariat has explicitly singled out delays and underperformance in the implementation and legislation amendment processes in Albania and Bosnia and Herzegovina. In fact, despite an optimistic assessment in the 2009 reports, neither country has shown any significant progress, and the integration process 'is still at an early stage' (Energy Community Secretariat, 2010, p. 16).

9.5 DISCUSSION: POTENTIAL TRENDS AND RESEARCH AGENDAS

Drawing on the results presented above, the analysis of the implementation of natural-gas rules certainly offers intriguing insights: three of the seven contracting parties investigated here did not even own any gas infrastructure

Table 9.1 Compliance of the EnC's contracting parties with electricity and gas acquis (1 = low to 3 = high)

	Electricity										
	Institutional organization	PSO† and consumer protection	Security of supply	Technical rules	Unbundling and access to accounts	Third-party access	Authorization and tendering	Market opening	Cross-border trande	Overall trend (improving/worsening)	EnC Secretariat's expectation
Albania	2	1	1	3	2	2	1	1	1	←	Fair
B and H	2	1	2	2	2	2	1	2	1	←	Modest
Croatia*	3	3	3	3	3	3	3	3	3	←	Good
FYROM*	2	1	2	2	1	1	n.a.	1	1	→	Low
Montenegro	2	1	2	2	2	2	1	1	2	↘	Good
Serbia	2	2	2	2	1	2	1	2	1	↑	Low
UNMIK	2	2	1	2	2	2	2	2	2	←	Fair

* Candidate countries for EU membership. † Public service obligation. n.a. = not applicable.

Natural Gas

	Institutional organization	PSO† and consumer protection	Security of supply	Technical rules	Unbundling and access to accounts	Third-party access	Authorization and tendering	Market opening	Cross-border trade	Overall trend (improving/worsening)	EnC Secretariat's expectation
Albania**	3	1	–	2	2	2	3	2	2	←	Fair
B and H	n.a.	n.a.	n.a.	n.a.	n.a.	n.a.	n.a.	n.a.	n.a.	→	Low
Croatia*	3	3	3	3	3	3	3	3	3	←	Good
FYROM*	2	2	2	2	1	1	2	–	2	↑	Modest
Montenegro**	2	3	–	2	2	2	3	3	2	←	Good
Serbia	3	2	2	2	1	2	1	3	1	←	Low
UNMIK**	2	2	1	3	3	3	2	2	–	↑	Modest

* Candidate country for EU membership. ** Country with no domestic natural gas market. † Public service obligation. n.a. = not applicable.

Source: Own creation.

on their territories as of September 2010. Nonetheless, these countries (Albania, Kosovo and Montenegro) have significantly begun to implement the provisions of the EU's gas directives in an attempt to show the most cooperative attitude toward the creation of an efficient network in line with the expectations and thresholds of the European market. This is even more surprising when the positive trends and results of the implementation process in all these three countries (where only minor changes are needed, the adoption process is in line with the directive's requirements and in an advanced stage of ratification) are compared with the deficient or unsatisfactory performances of other parties that already have a functioning gas market. Besides the prospective benefits of taking part in the regional and European gas market sometime in the future, the positive attitude of Albania, Kosovo and Montenegro needs to find some other justification beyond the material consequences of their behavior.

However, legal compliance does not tell the whole story of external Europeanization in partner countries: dispute settlement procedures for noncompliance in front of the Ministerial Council do not have any binding effect, and even any 'reputation loss' – the Athens Process now being only 7 years old – would be hardly effective. Their prompt reaction to the EU's stimuli, regardless of the structural deficit of their own resources, might demonstrate a perception of the 'need to participate' (or at least 'not to lag behind'), and also the recognition of the inner added value of an EU-led policy framework in terms of efficiency, legitimacy and development. This would be consistent with the theoretical pattern outlined above: a constant mutual attribution of roles and expectations defining the boundaries of an unbalanced relationship that the EU controls in pursuit of given (external energy) policy objectives.

Also, in the case of the gas directives, the 2010 report does not show any major changes in the overall trends of implementation and national reform. Infrastructure unbundling, third-party access, and generally competition-related norms are still undergoing a controversial implementation process: whereas progress in opening the energy market has been overtly lacking in Albania, Bosnia and Herzegovina, and FYROM, the Secretariat's report explicitly singles out Serbia's reluctance to adopt and implement Regulation 1775/2005 on the access to gas transit networks – an assessment that overturns the optimism of the 2009 report.

As for general findings and insights, the 2010 report on the implementation of the gas Directives has also drawn attention to and highlighted the singularity of the swift and straightforward implementation process of gas Directives in those countries that still lack a proper gas market. Overall, after one year, the Secretariat is still quite firm in admitting that the processes of harmonization and compliance with the electricity and gas *acquis* are both 'still not satisfactory' (Energy Community Secretariat, 2010, pp. 16–19).

Conversely, the *acquis* on environmental protection and the use of renewable energy sources (RES) is more diverse than that on electricity and natural gas. It also touches on significant political issues – such as the upgrade of the EnC parties' main industries, as well as their capability to resist disruption in energy supply. As far as environmental protection is concerned, the scope of this assessment will only cover the three main directives that the EU acknowledged as the bulk of its energy-related environmental legislation: Directives 2003/35/EC (the so-called 'Impact Assessment Directive'), 1999/32/EC (sulfur content in fuels) and 2001/80/EC (on large combustion plants). The acquis on RES includes Directive 2001/77/EC on the promotion of electricity obtained through RES, and Directive 2003/30/EC on biofuels.

The market-oriented bias underlying the EU's approach to the EnC is clear, as environmental protection is deemed as a key feature for the contracting parties to further attract foreign investments in the region. As an overall assessment, all parties have accessed the Kyoto regime[8] on climate change control and all parties have at least introduced a legal framework to fully implement Directive 2003/35/EC, even though effective secondary legislation is still lacking. Indeed, problems concerning the full transposition of norms lie more in procedural and judicial matters than in content and implementation. Again, the outstanding performance of Croatia, which has fully adopted the *acquis* on environment with what the Secretariat defines as 'a quantum leap of full transposition' (Energy Community Secretariat 2008, p. 7), is a noteworthy step forward on the road to EU membership.

The EnC's approach to RES was presented as 'strategic': all efforts towards harmonization by each contracting party should be consistent with a regional strategy to exploit huge potentials in order to fight import dependency and crises of disruption. So far, however, only Croatia and Montenegro have adopted minimum quotas; most contracting parties have instead adopted subsidized tariffs for the diffusion of renewable energy sources (RES) in the market. This has given the market a new thrust, but again procedural obstacles, unfit bureaucracies and regulatory barriers keep private investments adrift. Current developments, however, show steadily increasing market entries: in Croatia, also a top-performer country in RES, more than 250 applications for building permits have been submitted to national offices, according to the Secretariat's report.

The comprehensive objective of the EnC is the construction of an efficient regional energy infrastructure, whose distribution and production networks are connected with the EU's internal energy market. Reports from the EnC's secretariat provide the necessary information on the effectiveness of the process, on the achievements of each contracting party, as well as on the overall success of the EnC as a piece in the jigsaw puzzle of EU strategy outside its boundaries. If we were to grasp, nonetheless, the impact of the EnC upon the EU's capacity to create and lead foreign-policy actions, implementation alone would not help. There is an issue of socialization, which entails a deeper knowledge, contact and familiarity with the EU's prescriptions, objectives, and ambitions, as opposed to what ordinary rule adoption or harmonization would achieve.

The case of the gas market directives presented earlier in this section is a remarkable example. There is no purely rationalist explanation as to why Albania, Kosovo and Montenegro would accept exogenous regulation in this policy field, even though they cannot provide any basic gas market infrastructure. There are neither prospective absolute nor prospective relative gains *vis-à-vis* potential competitors in the region; there is no well-grounded domestic preference leading to compliance and, in fact, market closure and centralization are the major obstacles to harmonization. Moreover, these countries do not hold any realistic expectation of accession to the EU, but at best the opportunity to enter into closer and more ambitious partnership engagements.

Consequently, there must be some factor leading governments to accept their role in the pattern of the south-east European energy market – and that role is to promptly comply with EU norms. It has rightly been pointed out that a compliant EnC party with no gas market faces no costs at all, while enjoying maximum benefits in terms of reputation *vis-à-vis* both other parties and EU institutions. Nonetheless, governments that only implement harmonization today will probably face domestic political costs over the construction of adequate market and infrastructures that will 'suffer' from legal constraints undertaken under different circumstances at another time and under a different political framework: the 'blank check' these countries are signing now may well become a test of the democratic foresight of their own governments in the future. Finally, it could be stressed that this kind of market-driven socialization eases the construction of an overarching market culture in Europe's 'energy space', without inducing any significant change in the political culture and maturity of the neighboring countries involved. Yet, one of the assumptions of this work is exactly that EU institutions are trying to gather authority and autonomy via market-led initiatives: that is, by projecting beyond EU borders the very same competences they already exert within. Only an expansion of internal capabilities can lead to a fully-fledged external European energy policy in the long run.

9.6   CONCLUSIONS

This chapter has had two main objectives: (1) on a theoretical level, to assess the consistency of a sociological institutionalist approach to the EU's external relations; and (2) on an empirical level, to assess the performance of the EnC, an EU-led project that involves several states of its closest neighborhood at different degrees of engagement.

The empirical findings have shown that the process of implementation and compliance with the EU law on electricity, natural gas, environmental protection and RES has progressed steadily according to the yearly evaluations by the EnC's Secretariat. Overall shortcomings, such as concentration and centralization of energy markets, bundled ownership of supply and distribution infrastructures, as well as bureaucratic difficulties and bottlenecks, still negatively affect the construction of an integrated regional energy market. Conversely, by participating in international systems, such as the Kyoto framework, several contracting parties have been afforded a good legal basis on environmental care. Nevertheless, an efficient production stream dictates that the south-east European market should be entirely open, so as to attract further foreign investment seeking to benefit from a massive (and as yet unexploited) potential for RES production. The EU is actively engaged in the process: not only does it provide the regulatory structure, which the parties have an obligation to implement, but it also contributes more than 98 per cent of the EnC budget. According to the way in which the EU controls and governs the relationship, one would expect compliance and conditionality mechanisms for the EnC in the same way that these already work for the ENP, the Stabilization and Accession Process, and with the candidacy process for EU membership.

Nevertheless, the assumption of this work is that, in the case of the EnC, compliance and socialization with EU norms stem from a process of role attribution: the EU presents its neighbors with the opportunity to open, stabilize and make their energy markets competitive in a broader European framework, therefore acting as a norm-exporter and a policy-entrepreneur, while the contracting parties of the EnC perceive themselves as potential contributors to this framework – as adequate partners for richer, more-developed and freer European countries, with whom they nonetheless share basic identities and values; that is, a common idea of Europeanness. This reciprocal recognition as 'significant others' allows the EnC to work with the long-run objective of mutual benefits from an integrated regional market, despite the lack of either a clear membership expectation for the contracting parties or joint responsibility over the leadership of the Community.

The possibility to participate, to enter a new level of development and engagement is sufficient incentive for the contracting parties to accept exogenous policy-making and limitations to national authority. In line with the environmental approach of this book, energy, environmental protection and the development of RES have proved to be interesting cases for analysis. Nonetheless, the experience of the EnC is so recent that no effective or exhaustive data can yet be collected in order to prove whether a role-attribution argument is entirely consistent, or arguable. This chapter has also suggested the opportunity for methodological borrowing, by analogy, from extensive literature on compliance and socialization across the various policy fields in which the EU and its partners have cooperated to date. The hope is that empirical assessment, methodological clarity and a wider choice for case studies may further confirm the underlying assumption: EU institutions already hold socialization tools, enough regulatory weight and political autonomy to develop their own foreign policy capabilities and strengthen their position as autonomous players in the international arena – not least, as influential 'green-energy' model exporters.

NOTES

1. The word 'role' and the term 'actor' hint at a theatrical metaphor particularly common to sociological theories of interaction (see Holsti, 1970).
2. This work adopts a broader definition of the EU's policies addressed to its neighborhood, including not only the European Neighbourhood Policy but also other platforms of engagement with the EU: candidate countries (Croatia, the Former Yugoslavian Republic of Macedonia (FYROM), Turkey) as well as parties of the Stabilization and Association Process (SAP, namely Albania, Bosnia and Herzegovina, Montenegro and Serbia).
3. However, the program gathered fresh momentum in 2004, with the signing of the so-called Baku Initiative, and in 2006, when the Astana Declaration was approved: both documents aimed to include the dynamics and process triggered by the 2004 EU enlargement and the ENP. Within this new political framework, the Baku Initiative signatories undertook to 'progressively approximat[e] the legal and technical standards' of the EU, while 'promoting security of supply' through 'environmentally-viable energy projects of common interest' (INOGATE, 2004, p. 3). Despite the calls for a truly joint construction of the political dialogue, the relationship enshrined in the INOGATE framework can still be interpreted through what Emerson and Noutcheva call a 'gravity model' of Europeanization (Emerson and Noutcheva, 2004, p. 2). The EU makes both political and economic 'exceptions' that make it clearly attractive to developing, non-fully-democratic neighbors. This not only contributes to the process of social attribution of roles described above, but also deepens the divide between a center and a dependent periphery – making the political leverage utterly unbalanced toward the EU.
4. The signatories of the first MoU included Albania, Bosnia and Herzegovina, Bulgaria, Croatia (signed the document after 2002), Greece, Romania, Turkey, Serbia and Montenegro (still united at that time), and FYROM. A second MoU was then signed on 8 December 2003, by the same parties plus Kosovo (under UNSCR 1244).
5. Moldova became a fully fledged member of the EnC on 1 May 2010, while Ukraine accessed the Community on 1 February 2011. All other members are signatory and founding parties.
6. Policy decisions and comprehensive agreements are taken by the Ministerial Council (MC), which gathers representatives from all parties. Reports on the process and enforcement toward successful implementation are carried out by the Energy Community's Secretariat, which is also responsible for the Community's budget. Diplomatic negotiation takes place in the Permanent High Level Group, convening national senior officials with expertise in the field. A committee of national regulatory bodies (the Regulatory Board) and topic-based Forums – where the European Commission's representatives meet with industry experts and national interest groups – complete the institutional framework.
7. Austria, Bulgaria (a signatory party before accession in 2007), Cyprus, Czech Republic, France, Germany, Greece, Hungary, Italy, Netherlands, Romania (signatory party before accession in 2007), Slovakia, Slovenia and United Kingdom.

8. It should be noticed however that all contracting parties bar Croatia have signed the Kyoto Protocol as 'non-Annex B' parties, and are therefore not bound to the related criteria on emissions of greenhouse gases.

REFERENCES

Aggestam, L. (2006), 'Role theory and European foreign policy', in O. Elgstrom and M. Smith (eds), *The European Union's Roles in International Politics: Concepts and Analysis*, London: Routledge.
Checkel, J. (2001), 'Why comply? Social learning and European identity change', *International Organization*, **55** (3), 553–88.
Directorate General Energy and Transport – DG TREN (2006) 'Memo: an integrated market for electricity and gas across 34 European countries', DG TREN Strategy, Coordination, Information and Communication Unit, Brussels.
Ehricke, U. and D. Hackländer (2009), 'European energy policy on the basis of the new provisions in the Treaty of Lisbon', in A. Bausch and B. Schwenker (eds), *Handbook Utility Management*, Berlin–Heidelberg: Springer, pp. 741–60.
Emerson, M. and G. Noutcheva (2004), 'Europeanisation as a gravity model of democratisation', Centre for European Political Studies working document no. 214, Brussels.
Energy Community Secreteriat (2008), *Report on the Implementation of the Acquis under Title II of the Treaty Establishing the Energy Community: Environment, Competition and Renewables*, 11 PHLG/10/12/08 Annex 1, Vienna, 20 November, accessed 8 April 2011 at www.energy-community.org/pls/portal/docs/220177.PDF.
Energy Community Secreteriat (2009), *Report on the Implementation of the Acquis under the Treaty Establishing the Energy Community: Status of Electricity and Gas Market Development*, 6th MC/26/06/09 Annex 12, 09 September, Vienna, accessed 8 April 2011 at www.energy-community.org/pls/portal/docs/404179.PDF.
Energy Community Secreteriat (2010), *Annual Report on the Implementation of the Acquis under the Treaty Establishing the Energy Community*, Vienna: Energy Community Secretariat, accessed 8 April 2011 at www.energy-community.org/pls/portal/docs/722178.PDF.
European Commission (2000), Towards a European Strategy for the Security of Energy Supply, COM(2000) 769 final, 29 November 2000, Brussels.
Finon, D. and C. Locatelli (2008), 'Russian and European gas interdependence: could contractual trade channel geopolitics?', *Energy Policy*, **36** (1), 423–42.
Hobson, J.M., and J.C. Sharman (2005), 'The enduring place of hierarchy in world politics: tracing the social logics of hierarchy and political change', *European Journal of International Relations*, **11** (1), 63–98.
Holsti, K.J. (1970), 'Role conceptions and the politics of identity in foreign policy', *International Studies Quarterly*, **14** (3), 233–309.
INOGATE (2004), *Conclusions of the Ministerial Conference on Energy Cooperation between the EU, the Caspian Littoral States and Their Neighbouring Countries*, accessed 8 April 2011 at www1.inogate.org/inogate_programme/inogate_resource_center/ministerial-agreements/Baku_Conclusions_Annexes.pdf.
Schimmelfennig, F. (2003), *The EU, NATO and the Integration of Europe: Rules and Rhetoric*, Cambridge: Cambridge University Press.
Schimmelfennig, F. and U. Sedelmeier (2005), 'Introduction: conceptualizing the

Europeanization of Central and Eastern Europe', in F. Schimmelfennig and U. Sedelmeier (eds), *The Europeanization of Central and Eastern Europe*, Ithaca, NY–London: Cornell University Press, pp. 1–28.

Schimmelfennig, F. and U. Sedelmeier (2008), 'After conditionality: post-accession compliance with EU law in East Central Europe', *Journal of European Public Policy*, **15** (6), 806–25.

White, B. (2004), 'Foreign policy analysis and the new Europe', in W. Carlsnaes, H. Sjursen and B. White (eds), *Contemporary European Foreign Policy*, London–Thousand Oaks, CA: Sage, pp. 11–31

Yin, R.K. (2003), *Case Study Research: Designs and Methods*, 3rd edn, London–Thousand Oaks, CA–New Delhi: Sage.

10. Domestically driven, differentiated EU rule adoption: the case of energy sector reform in Turkey

Luigi Carafa[1]

10.1 INTRODUCTION

The question of how EU ideas, rules and institutions travel abroad has engendered various academic debates based on analytical concepts such as 'normative power Europe', external governance, idea diffusion and external Europeanization.[2] Within these debates, increasing attention is being devoted to energy in more recent years (Lavenex and Stulberg, 2007; Dimitrova and Dragneva, 2009; Escribano, 2010; Carafa, 2011; also Chapter 7 by Dobbins and Tosun; Chapter 8 by Herranz Surrallés and Natorski; Chapter 9 by Ciambra; Chapter 11 by Escribano-Francés and San Martín Gonzáles).

Energy offers a remarkable internal variation in rule systems and therefore constitutes a fertile field for researching the expansion of EU governance beyond EU borders (that is the 'green-energy' model exporter). In the early 1990s energy re-emerged as a global problem requiring supranational coordination but the landscape was rather complex at that time: there was no legal basis for energy in the Treaties and EU member states were opposed to any major developments in this field. In response to this the Commission forged a specific *modus operandi* to lock energy issues into three overlapping policy areas falling under its legislative competence: the single market, the environment, and external relations (Matláry, 1997; Solorio Sandoval, forthcoming; see also Chapter 1 by Solorio Sandoval and Morata). While a fragmented body of energy legislation was being created over one and a half decades, the Commission projected internal energy activities onto its relations with candidate and non-candidate countries in the Mediterranean region, the western Balkans and the eastern surroundings (including Russia). Only recently the Lisbon Treaty established the entry of energy among the shared competences between the Union and its member states (Zapater, 2009; Solorio Sandoval, 2011; also Chapter 1 by Solorio Sandoval and

Morata). Ultimately the Commission's competences are still limited, intra-EU energy integration is progressing slowly and the EU does not speak with one voice in its external energy relations. Nevertheless a European Community (EC) energy regulatory framework exists already and provides the templates for the Commission's external energy initiatives.

Conventional explanations in the 'top-out' literature[3] usually link effective EU rule transfer to candidate countries with a credible membership conditionality (Schimmelfennig and Sedelmeier, 2004). Consequently EU capacity to shape external regulatory environments is expected to be weaker in acceding countries whose conditional membership perspective loses credibility over time. In this context, the case of energy sector reform in Turkey is puzzling because the credibility of conditionality per se has an insufficient explanatory power. On one hand, Turkey has had candidacy status since 1999 and started accession negotiations in 2005. In 2006, the negotiations were partially suspended because of a dispute between Turkey and Cyprus. Coupled with this, the opposition of key member states such as France and Germany to the Turkish accession eventually diminished the credibility of conditionality. On the other hand, however, Turkey has considerably reformed its energy sector in line with EU rules since 2001. This happened anyway, with or without a credible conditional membership perspective.

This chapter investigates the trajectory of EU rule-based energy sector reform in Turkey between 1999 and 2010. It seeks to isolate and measure the individual contribution of external and domestic structures to the explanation of EU energy rule adoption in Turkey. By contrasting an EU institutionalist account with a domestic structures explanation, this chapter substantiates the thesis of EU–Turkey energy regulatory harmonization as a mainly domestically driven, subsectorally differentiated process. As it will be shown, domestic structures have overall a stronger causal relevance than EU variables in explaining rule adoption throughout the sector reform trajectory. They ultimately shape the timing and extent of subsector reform. Interestingly, this contribution has also found that the quality of EU rules does matter. In fact, rule adoption patterns in Turkey generally reflect internal differentiated dynamics regarding the different components of the European energy policy.

The enquiry proceeds in four steps. Section 10.2 bridges over the concepts of external governance and external diffusion. Section 10.3 devises a framework for analyzing the patterns of EU rule-based energy sector reform in Turkey. Section 10.4 is devoted to discuss the empirical analysis. Finally, Section 10.5 summarizes the findings and conclusions.

10.2   BRIDGING OVER EXTERNAL GOVERNANCE AND DIFFUSION

The notion of external governance points to institutional forms of interaction with target countries, by means of which the EU seeks to expand its rules beyond EU borders (Lavenex and Schimmelfennig, 2009). Scholars of external governance refuse to project the unitary state actor model onto the EU and move away from traditional foreign policy analysis by examining processes of norm diffusion and policy transfer (ibid., p. 794). The concept of external governance is deeply rooted in debates on international relations and comparative politics, based on the assumption that high interdependence between political units generates demand for governance. Institutionalized modes of interaction are the structures through which political units seek to coordinate this interdependence (Lavenex et al., 2009, p. 814). Three ideal types are theorized in the literature: hierarchy, network, and market modes of external governance (Lavenex et al., 2007; Lavenex, 2008; Lavenex and Schimmelfennig, 2009). They are characterized by different levels of legalization and institutionalization, ranging from more legalized and asymmetrical interactions with little room for 'the ruled' to negotiate (Lavenex et al., 2009, p. 815) to more horizontal and decentralized interactions between political units (see Lavenex and Schimmelfennig, 2009).

   Diffusion can be defined as a process through which policy ideas spread across time and space (cf. Strang and Meyer, 1993). When it comes to the EU, diffusion studies address both the internal and external diffusion processes. Although internal diffusion has been extensively researched (see Chapter 4 by Busch and Jörgens), this is less the case for external diffusion processes through which the EU seeks to export its ideas to third countries. Linking to external diffusion adds a new dimension to the present enquiry: ideas, not just rules. On one hand ideas are conceived here as causal beliefs, that is shared claims regarding cause–effect relationships and states of the world (Börzel and Risse, 2009, p. 6). On the other hand ideas are seen as principled beliefs or norms encapsulating shared expectations on the appropriate way to behave in a given context (Goldstein and Keohane, 1993; Jepperson et al., 1996). Diffusion is mediated by a wide range of channels of influence between countries, varying from more coercive mechanisms (such as imposition of policies or binding international norms) to voluntary adoption of foreign policy models (see Knill, 2005; see also Chapter 4 by Busch and Jörgens).

   Even though they are not equivalent concepts, external diffusion and external governance can be consistently mixed up. In both cases the analytical focus is on process. External governance research analyzes the factors that account for empirically observed processes of EU norm diffusion and transfer to target countries. Similarly, external diffusion studies focus on the process of spreading EU policy models across countries or within a political system. When it comes to the empirical focus, external governance is concerned with systems of rules (including norms, as well as procedures of coordination). External diffusion is more concerned with ideas (causal beliefs and norms). Interestingly rules entail causal ideas and norms to different extents. In other words, rules may encapsulate ideas on what is the cause–effect of a policy problem and how to appropriately deal with the problem per se at the same time.

Both external governance and external diffusion are related to the study of policy change, but they slightly differ in their dependent variable. On one hand external governance investigates the forms in which the EU seeks to expand its rules beyond its borders. In this respect Lavenex et al. (2009) have found that external modes of sectoral governance follow internal modes of sectoral governance. This means that the forms of external governance reflect sector-specific rather than overarching policy logic. On the other hand external governance studies seek to systematize the theoretical discussion on the effects of external governance at three levels: rule selection, rule adoption and rule application (Schimmelfennig and Sedelmeier, 2004; Lavenex and Schimmelfennig, 2009; Barbé et. al., 2009). However, authors have mainly elaborated on individual or combined explanations anchored in specific EU, power and domestic variables. Thus there is a need to test systematically the contribution of the different variables in more comparative designs (Lavenex and Schimmelfennig, 2009, p. 809). By contrast the focus of external diffusion is on the explanation of adoption patterns characterizing the spread of innovations within or across countries (Knill, 2005, p. 767). The research design here is devoted to finding robust general patterns over time. In this respect authors have largely investigated the different mechanisms through which ideas spread across countries (Powell and DiMaggio, 1991; Strang and Soule, 1998; Simmons et al., 2006; Börzel and Risse, 2009) and have found that foreign ideas must be made socially meaningful in order to make domestic adoption practicable. From this perspective, cultural and institutional similarities are conceived as significant factors for facilitating diffusion (Strang and Meyer, 1993).

To bridge over these two analytical concepts, this enquiry confines its focus to testing the individual contribution of EU and domestic structures to the explanation of EU energy rule adoption in the critical case of Turkey. It therefore excludes rule selection and rule application.

10.3 EU EXPLANATION VERSUS DOMESTIC-STRUCTURE EXPLANATION

In order to test the individual contribution of external and domestic structures to EU energy rule adoption in Turkey, this chapter advocates an interdisciplinary approach that links external governance and diffusion research with scholarship on new institutionalism. Drawing on rational-choice and sociological institutionalist approaches (Bulmer, 1994; Scharpf, 1997; March and Olsen, 1998, 2004; Aspinwall and Schneider, 2000; Peters, 2005), this chapter contrasts an EU explanation with a domestic structure explanation. Although they may be partly complementary explanations, these accounts are employed here only as competing explanations. In fact this enquiry does not intend to find the best combinations of external factors and domestic considerations: rather, it traces EU and domestic variables within the process of energy sector reform in Turkey and measures their individual value for EU rule adoption.

10.3.1 EU Explanation

Based on two complementary perspectives, the EU explanation asserts that EU structures substantively shape the patterns of EU-rule-based energy sector reform in Turkey. From a rational-choice institutionalist perspective, the mode of sector reform in a target country follows the templates of formal EU institutions (that is norms, sectoral rules and overarching procedures). In the present case, pre-accession/accession procedures and existing sectoral rules take center stage. The preferences of the taker are exogenously formed. Established patterns of cooperation constitute equilibrium contracts among self-seeking actors. To influence sector reform processes in a target country, the Union uses a key mechanism: the manipulation of utility calculations. This refers to the ability of inducing a target country into adopting EU rules via negative and positive incentives. As Turkey is an accession country, the key instrument at disposal is *acquis* conditionality, that is the adoption of the sectoral rules of the *acquis communautaire* as a condition for membership (Schimmelfennig and Sedelmeier, 2004, p. 677). In the case of Turkey, this instrument has been in place even since the pre-accession phase. Then it is employed in a tighter, more systematic manner during the accession phase. The EU also makes use of other incentives at the level of sectors such as financial assistance, loans and support for business investment.

The crucial point here is that the EU influences domestic reform in a target country by altering the state actors' behavior. From a rational-choice institutionalist point of view, successful EU rule adoption therefore varies with the quality of incentives. In the present case, EU rule adoption depends on a key condition: the credibility of membership conditionality (ibid., p. 673). The more a candidate country loses the big incentive of a credible conditional prospect of membership, the less it will adopt EU rules. The value for this variable is strong, if the speed of conditional rewards towards Turkey is high (that is the launching of formal accession negotiations, the opening of the energy accession chapter and the final reward of membership) and energy accession negotiations are depoliticized – and weak, if the speed of conditional rewards is slow and negotiations are heavily politicized. Following this line of argument, EU energy rule adoption in Turkey would have dropped substantially after 2005.

From a sociological institutionalist perspective, the mode of sector reform in a target country is shaped by formal and informal EU institutions. These include overarching procedures and sectoral rules on the one hand, as well as cognitive scripts, symbol systems and normative ideas on the other. The preferences of the taker reshape within cooperation. Ideas and rules provide the 'frames of meaning' that guide the action of target state actors (by the logic of appropriateness). Rule adoption takes place through two interrelated mechanisms: persuasion, which pertains to the practices through which target state actors internalize EU causal beliefs (that is ideas on what is the cause–effect of a policy problem); and socialization, which refers to the practices through which target state actors learn to internalize EU principled beliefs (that is ideas on how to appropriately deal with a specific policy problem). In the present case, the EU deploys these mechanisms via regulatory cooperation under pre-accession and accession programs such as twinning, SIGMA (Support for Improvement in Governance and Management) and TAIEX (Technical Assistance and Information Exchange).

The key here is that the EU influences both the preferences and behavior of state actors in the target country under consideration. From a sociological institutionalist point of view, successful EU rule adoption depends largely on the quality of EU rules (ibid., p. 676). The higher the codification of causal and/or normative ideas in sectoral rules and the higher the legitimacy of these rules within the EU, the more likely rule adoption will be in a target country. The value for this variable is strong if causal beliefs and energy principles are precisely legalized in the sectoral *acquis*, and most EU member states adapt to the these rules; it is weak if causal beliefs and energy principles are not or only loosely legalized in the sectoral *acquis* or at least a group of member states (or a few 'big' ones) oppose rule adaptation.

10.3.2   Domestic Structure Explanation

Based on two complementary perspectives, the domestic structure explanation contends that domestic variables shape the patterns of EU-rule-based energy sector reform in Turkey. From a rational-choice institutionalist perspective the mode of sector reform looks after the domestic institutions and legislation (that is more exactly the formal structures: norms, Decision rules, and procedures). Preference formation is endogenous but takes place outside formal institutions. The behavior of domestic actors draws on a pure logic of consequentiality. Rule adoption attains to a particular mechanism: instrumental problem-solving. This refers to the ability to solve domestic problems and maximizing advantages. Domestic actors thus adopt specific rules that match the sectoral preferences of domestic actors. But it is not all about efficiency. At the same time rule adoption is beneficial for other purposes. Rules constitute opportunity structures for domestic actors to maximize benefits from cooperation with external actors.

The crucial point here is that domestic agents pick up and adopt EU/foreign rules instrumentally. From a rational-choice institutionalist point of view, effective EU rule adoption depends on the perceived usefulness of rules for domestic scopes (Casier, 2011, p. 46). The underlying assumption here is a substantial dissatisfaction of domestic actors with the status quo or the compelling urgency to solve particular domestic problems (Rose, 1991, pp. 10–12). The better that EU rules respond to sector-specific problems and maximize macrolevel advantages, the more likely will be their adoption at a domestic level. The value for this variable is strong if EU energy rules match sectoral priorities and are perceived as legitimacy-seeking opportunity structures to unblocking accession chapter negotiations; it is weak if EU energy rules do not match sectoral priorities and do not provide such opportunity structures.

From a sociological institutionalist perspective the mode of sector reform is shaped by both formal and informal institutions at domestic level. These include domestic norms, rules and procedures, as well as ideas, values, discourse symbol systems and cognitive scripts. Preference formation takes place within domestic institutions. The behavior of domestic actors follows the logic of appropriateness. Cooperation with external actors is appropriate in so far as it contributes to the exchange of information and best practice between the parties. But preferences are not reshaped by cooperation. The mechanism of rule adoption is mimicry, which refers to the adoption by domestic actors of specific EU policy ideas, models and rules that are seen as correct solutions to a problem at hand.

The key here is that domestic structures are conceived as normative-cognitive vessels that guide domestic actors towards rule adoption. From a sociological institutionalist point of view, successful EU rule adoption hinges on the domestic resonance of EU rules (Schimmelfennig and Sedelmeier, 2004, p. 676). The more the cultural and institutional structures of the EU resemble domestic structures, the more likely it is that EU rules will be adopted (Strang

Table 10.1 An analytical framework for explaining EU energy rule adoption in Turkey

	EU explanation		Domestic structure explanation	
	Rational choice institutionalism	Sociological institutionalism	Rational choice institutionalism	Sociological institutionalism
Mode of energy sector reform in the target country	Follows EU formal institutions: sectoral rules and overarching accession procedures.	Is shaped by EU formal and informal institutions: (1) sectoral rules and overarching accession procedures; (2) ideas, discourse symbol systems, cognitive scripts.	Follows the templates of domestic institutions, more exactly the formal structures: norms, decision rules, procedures.	Follows the templates of domestic institutions, more exactly the formal and informal structures: (1) norms, rules and procedures; (2) ideas, values, discourse symbol systems, cognitive scripts.
Preferences of the taker	Exogenous formation.	Endogenous formation (within cooperation structures).	Domestic formation but outside formal institutions.	Domestic formation within institutions.
Behavior of the taker	Logic of consequentiality moderated by EU formal institutions.	Logic of appropriateness.	Logic of consequentiality.	Logic of appropriateness.
Mechanism of rule adoption	Manipulation of utility calculations. Key instrument of external influence. *Acquis* conditionality.	Persuasion (cognitive ideas are internalised by the taker). Socialisation (normative ideas are internalised by the taker). Key instrument of external influence: Regulatory cooperation.	Instrumental problem-solving (foreign rules are seen as opportunity structures).	Mimicry (foreign rules are seen as appropriate models).

	EU explanation		Domestic structure explanation	
	Rational choice institutionalism	Sociological institutionalism	Rational choice institutionalism	Sociological institutionalism
Rule adoption	EU formal institutions heavily influence rule adoption.	EU sectoral rules are normative-cognitive vessels that guide the rule taker towards rule adoption.	Rational purposive agents adopt EU/foreign rules instrumentally.	Domestic institutions are normative-cognitive vessels that guide rule actors towards rule adoption.
Conditions	Credibility of EU membership conditionality (Speed of rewards; politicisation of accession negotiations.)	Quality of EU rules (Codification of ideas into rules; internal legitimacy of rules.)	Usefulness of rules for domestic scopes (Perceived rule efficiency; perception of rules as legitimacy-seeking opportunity structures.)	Domestic resonance of rules (Similarity of traditional or pre-existing domestic rules and administrative culture.)

Source: Own elaboration

and Meyer, 1993; Lenschow et al., 2005). The value for this variable is strong if EU energy rules tie in with traditional or pre-existing domestic rules and administrative practices; and weak if EU energy rules conflict with domestic rules or administrative practices. Table 10.1 summarizes these considerations and sets out the guidelines for the empirical analysis.

10.4 DISCUSSION

Located in a crucial geopolitical position between Europe and Asia, Turkey is among the top ten big emerging markets (GlobalEDGE, 2011), as well as the fastest-growing energy markets and CO_2 emitters in the world (see IEA, 2010). It is a secular constitutional republic ruled by a three-party coalition government under Bulent Ecevit from 1999 to 2002 and by the conservative Justice and Development Party (AKP) governments under Recep Tayyip Erdoğan since 2003. Turkey has had EU candidacy status since the Helsinki European Council of December 1999 and has been involved in accession negotiations since 2005. However accession progress has slowed down owing to the increasing politicization of negotiations since 2006. Turkey has also participated in the Barcelona process since 1995 and the Union for the Mediterranean since 2008.

This section discusses the trajectory of EU rule-based energy sector reform in Turkey between 1999 and 2010. It provides the results of the empirical analysis concerning the adoption as well as non-adoption of EU energy rules on competitiveness, security and sustainability. The analysis is based on semi-structured elite interviews conducted in 2009 and 2010 in Brussels and Ankara, as well as on official documents and reports.

10.4.1 Energy Competitiveness

The EU asserts that a more competitive use of energy can be achieved by opening up internal markets for gas and electricity and ensuring the efficient functioning of markets, as well as competitive prices (European Commission, 2006a, p. 17; see also Chapter 1 by Solorio Sandoval and Morata). This principle is strongly coded in EC internal energy market rules and loosely incorporated in relevant international rules.[4] However the overall value for quality of internal energy market rules was strong in 1999–2001 and has decreased to weak since 2002. Whereas most member states implemented the first Directive package[5] by September 2000, the making of the second and third Directive packages[6] has been characterized by increasing opposition from key member states, such as France and Germany, to the liberalization model pushed by the Commission (See Eberlein, 2008).

As regards domestic adaptation, Turkey has made important progress in the field of energy competitiveness, mainly between 1999 and 2001, that is the first years of pre-accession alignment with the *acquis*. A key addendum to the constitution of Turkey was adopted in 1999, paving the way to gradual privatization and liberalization of all sectors. In this context, Directives 96/92/EC and 98/30/EC resonated well at a domestic level and tied in with a strong internal drive (Interviews Turkey 2009, 2, 7, 23). The Laws on the Electricity Market (Parliament of Turkey 2001a, EML) and Natural Gas Market (Parliament of Turkey 2001b, NGML) of 2001 set the basis for market restructuring, liberalization and harmonization with the first directive package. These reforms were complemented by the creation of the Energy Market Regulatory Authority (EMRA) and subsequent implementing legislation (European Commission, 2002). However a close analysis of subsector reform reveals a set of interesting findings. First, the strong need to cope with electricity-specific problems suggests that market restructuring was indeed a sectoral priority for Turkey. In fact until 2001 Turkey was not self-sufficient in satisfying its electricity demand with its domestic production (Interview Turkey 2009, 7). Thus the shortage was met by imported electricity, mainly from Bulgaria and Russia (ibid.). With respect to electricity subsector reform, Turkey demonstrated that it was even more prone than other member states to align with EU specific provisions on unbundling, that is separating the energy transmission networks from the production and supply side (Interview Turkey 2009, 19). In 2001 the national electricity champion TEDAS unbundled into three companies: EUAS (generation), TEIAS (transmission and market operator) and TETAS (wholesale). TEDAS and its seven regional distribution companies were rearranged and Turkey's distribution network was divided into 21 regions (ibid.). Second, the fact that Turkey fairly adopted the electricity unbundling is a telling message, considering that the Commission's unbundling credo met strong opposition from some member state governments and national champions, who strongly pushed for the second and third Directives on the liberalization of the electricity and gas markets approved in 2003 and 2009. Third, the case of NGML suggests a different story: unlike the EML, the NGML called for the unbundling of the national gas champion BOTAS by 2009. In the NGML unbundling of distribution activities was not required, although it was mandatory for the EC directive. Despite largely reforming the gas sector, the Law was enacted without any significant distributional domestic conflict (Interview Turkey 2009, 13). Whereas the phase of policy formulation-adoption was 'captured' (escaping from the wider constellation of actors), policy implementation later on encountered veto players notably limiting the application and effectiveness of the adopted reforms (ibid.). As a result of this, the discrepancy between the NGML and developments in the market now requires substantial revision of the Law (ibid.).

The credibility of membership conditionality was strong between 1999 and 2005 (pre-accession period) and largely weakened since 2006. At the sectoral level it must be highlighted that the adoption of the two key Laws (EML and NGML) and the creation of an energy regulatory board was a strict condition for the International Monetary Fund's (IMF) support for Turkey (European Commission, 2001, p. 70). Although alignment with the second directive package has always been explicitly required by the EU (see Council of the European Union, 2003, 2006, 2009), EU rule transfer did not occur either with or without a credible conditional membership offer to Ankara. This EU request did not meet the domestic sectoral priorities between 2003 and 2005 (Interview Turkey 2009, 19).[7] It resonated badly domestically and hardly questioned the national adaptation capacity only a few years after the adoption of EML and NGML (ibid.). Coupled with this the decreasing internal legitimacy of the second directive package's rules well explains their non-adoption by Turkey even after 2005, that is when the credibility of conditionality has decreased.

10.3.2   Energy Security

The EU contends that energy supply can be secured through an integrated approach that mainly consists of reducing demand, diversifying the energy mix as well as sources and routes of energy imports, stimulating infrastructure and technology investments, and addressing energy emergencies at EU level (European Commission, 2006a, p. 17; see also Chapter 9 by Ciambra). The EC principle of energy security is weakly coded in the *acquis*, being mainly incorporated in rules concerning oil stocks, the safeguard of natural-gas supply security, and the preservation of electricity supply security and infrastructure investment (see Chapter 8 by Herranz-Surrallés and Natorski). Causal and normative energy security ideas are loosely encapsulated in subsequent Decisions 96/391/EC, 1229/2003/EC and 1364/2006/EC, laying down guidelines for Trans-European Energy Networks (TEN-E) activities. Key decisions on the energy mix and imported energy sources still remain a matter of national politics, thus undermining the basis of the energy security principle. As a result the value for quality of rules is strikingly weak.

With respect to domestic adaptation, important steps were already taken in 1999 to comply with IEA commitments on emergency preparedness (European Commission, 2000, p. 52). The Petroleum Law of 2003 (Parliament of Turkey, 2003) advanced legal alignment with Directives 68/414/EEC and 98/93/EC. This Law established a management system with the objective of maintaining oil stocks for at least 90 days amounting to the net import share of the daily average consumption of the previous year (Council of Ministers of Turkey, 2003, p. 525). Turkey strategically selected and placed these 'easy rules' under the 2003 National Programme (NP) for the adoption of the *acquis* (Interview Turkey 2009, 7).[8] Ultimately, the adoption of EU rules on oil stocks was arising more from international commitments with the IEA (of which Turkey is a permanent member) than from the pre-accession process per se (ibid.).

To overcome the lack of an EU strong competence in energy security matters, the European Commission centered cooperation on ambitious infra-structure-building projects[9] with the aim of diversifying energy routes, sources and suppliers (Interviews EU, 2010, 27, 31). In this respect Turkey clearly took action in order to cope with its high-energy import dependency and strengthen its position as a key energy hub for Europe (Interviews Turkey 2009, 7, 26). EU–Turkey energy security cooperation builds on a set of positive experiences: (1) the construction of the Turkey–Greece gas interconnector, begun in 2002 and completed in 2008; (2) the technical preparations for building the Turkey–Greece–Italy Interconnector natural-gas pipeline; and (3) the construction of the Babaeski–Filippi line, which was completed in June 2008 (European Commission, 2009). To fully integrate into the internal electricity market, Turkey needs not only regulatory harmonization, but also the synchronous physical connection of the national power system with the Union for the Coordination of Transmission of Electricity (UCTE). To that end Turkey is working on a number of projects that contribute towards the completion of priority axes number 4 (Greece–Balkan Countries UCTE system) and number 9 (Mediterranean Electricity Ring) under the TEN-E umbrella (ibid., p. 68).

Another clear example of this physical approach of cooperation followed by the Commission is Nabucco, that is a natural-gas pipeline project stretching from the Caspian and central Asian region to the EU via Turkey. Unfortunately preparations for the Nabucco project coincided with the growing politicization of accession negotiations and a drastic slowdown of conditional rewards. Turkey engaged in accession talks with the EU in October 2005 thanks to a compromise. Ankara unilaterally recognizes the Turkish Republic of Northern Cyprus and traditionally refuses to give international recognition to Cyprus, a member state since 2004. As the price for initiating the accession process, the negotiating framework included a commitment for Turkey to extend its customs union to Cyprus and give ships and airplanes coming from Cyprus free access to its national harbors and airports by the end of 2006 (Euractiv, 2005). Following Ankara's non-compliance, the EU partially suspended the accession negotiations. Coupled with this, increasing opposition of key member states such as France and Germany to the Turkish accession further diminished the credibility of membership conditionality. That politics matters is even more striking at the sectoral level. Although Turkey adopted the key bulk of EU energy rules before 2006 (see also subsection 10.3.3), the energy accession chapter opening is being blocked by a specific veto by Cyprus. Since 2007 Cyprus has been preparing off-shore oil explorations which are being obstructed by Ankara's claim that research ships invade its continental shelf. In response to this, Cyprus is vetoing the advancement of accession negotiations in the energy field. Nabucco was not exempt from politicization, leading Erdoğan to play the pipeline card more than once in Brussels to unblock the energy chapter (Euractiv, 2009).

To circumvent the politicization of negotiations on the energy accession chapter opening and the lack of a strong EU competence in the energy security field, the European Commission moved to more horizontal, process-oriented modes of interaction with Turkey in late 2008 (Interviews EU 2010, 33, 34). This in turn had some positive effects. After months of difficult negotiations, an intergovernmental agreement on Nabucco between Austria, Bulgaria, Hungary, Romania and Turkey was signed in Ankara in July 2009. More importantly, horizontal coordination on Nabucco contributed positively to building a 'sense of trust' among high-level officials (Interview Turkey, 2009, 7). As a result of this, in September 2009 the Commission started negotiations with Turkey on accession to the Energy Community Treaty (ibid.), which would be of particular importance in further advancing regulatory alignment with EU energy rules (European Commission, 2009, p. 59).

10.3.3   Energy sustainability

The principle of energy sustainability is deeply rooted in the shift towards a low-carbon economy. The EU sees that a sustainable use of energy can be achieved by developing renewable energy sources (RES) and other low-carbon energy sources, by boosting energy efficiency and by combating global climate change (European Commission, 2006a, p. 17). This principle is strongly coded in EU rules (see Chapter 3 by Knudsen; Chapter 6 by Solorio Sandoval and Zapater). The central bulk of this *acquis* is composed of norms on the promotion of electricity from RES (RES-E), energy end-use efficiency and energy services, geological storage of carbon dioxide (see Chapter 5 by Fischer for further information on CCS) and energy performance of buildings.[10] For their part, most member states are keen on developing their RES and energy efficiency subsectors.[11] Eventually the *acquis* on energy sustainability is an evolving output within largely legitimate EU sector-specific policy-making. Consequently the overall value for quality of rules is strong.

With or without a credible conditional membership offer to Turkey, regulatory harmonization in the subfield of energy sustainability has always been a priority for the EU (Council of the European Union, 2003, 2006, 2009). Interestingly a close analysis of Turkey's reform trajectory suggests that domestic structures ultimately shaped the patterns of EU rule adoption. EU rule transfer did not happen between 2001 and 2004, that is a period of credible conditionality and high quality of rules. Liberalization of the gas and electricity markets was topping the priority list of sectoral reforms to be undertaken by the Ecevit government (Interviews Turkey 2009, 3, 19). Once these key reforms were accomplished, the usefulness of EU rules on energy sustainability became increasingly strong after 2004.

The following government under Erdoğan had an urgent need to address the problem of a considerable electricity consumption growth, averaging 8.8 percent a year since 2001 (IEA, 2009, p. 110). EU rules tied well with the domestic agenda of sectoral reform. In response to these concerns *The Law on the Use of Renewable Energy Sources in Electricity Generation* (Parliament of Turkey, 2005) of 2005 set out a general framework for promoting competitive prices for RES-E, notably aligning legislation with Directive 2001/77/EC (European Commission, 2006b). To scale-up clean electricity generation it established specific measures such as (1) a feed-in tariff level of the wholesale market price plus a 20 percent premium; (2) initial licensing fees for RES-E generators reduced by 99 percent compared with the license fees of non RES-E generators; and (3) 10-year reduced land-use fees for new plants commissioned before 2012. Contrary to the above rules this law did not set a target for RES-E (European Commission, 2007, p. 50). Only in 2009 did the revised strategy paper for the electricity sector establish a share of 25 percent of electricity to be produced from RES by the end of 2020 (Interview Turkey, 2009, 3). By the end of the same year Turkey was already producing 19.6 percent of its electricity from RES (European Commission 2010, p. 65).

The considerable reform of the energy efficiency subsector is indeed a telling case. In fact EU relevant rules were adopted after that the time of 'conditionality bonanza' turned out badly in 2006 (see subsection 10.3.2 on the politicization of negotiations). Yet again the usefulness of EU rules for domestic scopes constituted a key facilitating factor of regulatory harmonization. On one hand the government had to manage a (projected) doubling of the total final energy consumption from 2007 to 2020 (IEA, 2010, p. 35). One the other hand, EU rules on energy efficiency were perceived by the government as less costly than realignment of legislation with the second directive package on energy market liberalization and instrumentally selected to increase the external legitimacy of Turkey as an acceding country in good standing with regard to the energy field (Interviews Turkey, 2009, 3, 19). Notably aligning legislation with Directive 2006/32/EC, the framework Law on Energy Efficiency (Parliament of Turkey, 2007, EEL) of 2007 set out the general guidelines and instruments for reducing energy intensity in the largest energy-using sectors (manufacturing industry, transport, services, buildings and the electricity subsector). Unlike the European Directive, this law did not include either targets or provisions on the promotion of high-efficiency cogeneration

Table 10.2 Summary of the empirical analysis

	Competitiveness			Security			Sustainability		
	1999–2001	NAP* 2002–05	2006–10	1999–2003	NAP* 2004–05	2006–10	1999–2003	NAP* 2004–05	2006–10
Credibility of EU membership conditionality	+	+	–	+	+	–	+	+	–
Quality of EU rules	+	–	–	–	–	–	+	+	+
Usefulness of rules for domestic scopes scopes	+	–	–	+	n.a.	n.a.	–	+	+
Domestic resonance of rules	+	–	–	+	n.a.	n.a.	+	+	+

Note: NAP = non-adoption period; n.a. = not applicable.

Source: Own elaboration.

(European Commission, 2007, p. 50). More importantly, EU rule alignment continued with the adoption of implementing laws at the level of energy-using sectors. Between 2008 and 2009 secondary legislation on energy efficiency in buildings, appliances and industry was adopted in line with Directives 94/2/EC, 2002/91/EC and 2005/32/EC. Significantly, Turkey also adopted some pieces of legislation from the Japanese and Dutch energy efficiency regulations as follows: (1) the Energy Efficiency Coordination Board; (2) as regards energy efficiency measures for the industry sector, industries must compulsorily set up an energy management system and nominate an energy manager trained at the Energy Efficiency Training Centre; (3) following the Dutch model, voluntary agreements with industrial factories have been established (Interviews Turkey, 2009, 21–23). This shows that Turkey not only strategically chose from the EU menu but also perceived other particular foreign norms as more appropriate for addressing particular sector-specific issues. Table 10.2 summarizes the results of the empirical analysis.

10.5   CONCLUSIONS

This chapter has investigated the case of EU energy rule transfer to a *sui generis* candidate country, that is Turkey. Engaged in pre-accession programs from 1999, Ankara started accession negotiations in 2005. However the negotiations were partially suspended in 2006 because of a dispute between Turkey and Cyprus. In addition to these European debates saw an increase in opposition by key member states such as France and Germany to the Turkish accession. Contrary to the conventional explanations in the 'top-out' literature, linking effective rule transfer to candidate states with the credibility of conditionality, Turkey has considerably reformed its energy sector in line with EU rules since 2001. Strikingly, this has occurred anyway with or without a credible conditional membership perspective.

This chapter has explored the case of energy sector reform in Turkey with the aim of testing the individual contribution of external and domestic structures to the explanation of EU energy rule adoption in Turkey. In other words, this enquiry did not intend to find the best combinations of EU factors and domestic considerations capable of explaining rule transfer. Instead it sought to isolate and control 'two sides of the same coin' with a comparative research design. It thus contrasted an EU institutionalist account, emphasizing the relevance of credibility of conditionality and quality of rules, with a domestic structure explanation, giving high ranking to the strategic usefulness and resonance of EU rules in Turkey.

Two outcome patterns can be easily detected: first, this research has shown that EU–Turkey regulatory alignment was mainly domestically driven. EU energy rule adoption varied with the usefulness of EU rules for addressing country-specific energy problems (such as the elevated energy inefficiency of the industrial and building sectors) and maximizing sector utilities (such as developing the RES subsector). With and especially without a credible conditionality, Turkey selectively but regularly adopted EU energy rules with the aim of strengthening its external legitimacy as a candidate country in good standing and consolidating its geopolitical ambition to become an energy hub for Europe. Yet it is not all about utility calculations: rather, there is evidence that mimicry took place when technocrats considered a foreign model to be appropriate for addressing a sector-specific problem at hand. Despite the blockage of the energy chapter opening and the fading credibility of membership conditionality, the end result has been a progressive alignment with EU energy rules.

Second, this chapter has shown that the quality of rules does matter. Rule adoption patterns reflect the internal dynamics of EU sectoral governance formation. Domestic alignment is differentiated across the three constituent axes of the European energy policy. The high quality of EU rules on energy sustainability increased the likelihood of rule transfer with the pace of domestic structures. By contrast, the low codification of energy security ideas into the sectoral *acquis*, and the declining legitimacy of the energy competitiveness rule-making process, contributed to decreasing the likelihood of rule adoption.

NOTES

1. The author would like to thank Fulvio Attinà, Gonzalo Escribano, Anna Herranz, Stefania Panebianco, and Francesc Serra for their valuable comments on previous versions of this chapter.
2. For reviews, see Manners (2002); Lavenex and Ucarer (2004); Schimmelfennig and Sedelmeier (2004, 2005; Diez, 2005); Escribano (2006); Schimmelfennig (2007); Lavenex (2004, 2008); Lavenex and Schimmelfennig (2009); Barbé et al. (2009); Börzel and Risse (2009); Börzel (2010).
3. For reviews, see Magen (2007).
4. GATT/WTO rules contain relevant rules for general application, but do not deal specifically with energy matters (see World Energy Council, 2009).
5. Directives 96/92/EC and 98/30/EC.
6. Directives 2003/54/EC and 2003/55/EC (second directive package); Directives 2009/72/EC and 2009/73/EC (third directive package).
7. In this period, developing the RES subsector was a top priority at domestic level (see subsection 10.3.3).
8. Although not mandatory, pre-accession and acceding countries are expected to adopt an NP for each Accession Partnership Document (APD) adopted by the Council of the EU.
9. More precisely on the following projects: Turkey–Iran gas pipeline, Blue Stream, Caspian–Mediterranean, Baku–Tbilisi–Erzurum.
10. More exactly, Directives 2001/77/EC, 2009/28/EC, 94/2/EC, 2002/91/EC and 2005/32/EC (RES); Directive 93/76/EEC and Directive 2006/32/EC (energy efficiency) and Directives 2002/91/EC and 2010/31/EU (energy performance in buildings); Directives 2000/60/EC,

2001/80/EC, 2004/35/EC, 2006/12/EC, 2008/1/EC, 2009/31/EC (geological storage of carbon dioxide).

11. Unlike in the case of energy competitiveness, key member states such as Germany have been facilitating rather than constraining the formation of EU rules on energy sustainability.

REFERENCES

Aspinwall, M.D. and G. Schneider (2000), 'Same menu, separate tables: the Institutionalist turn in political science and the study of European integration', *European Journal of Political Research*, **38** (1), 1–36.

Barbé, E., O. Costa, A. Herranz-Surrallés, M. Natorski (2009), 'Which rules shape EU external governance? Patterns of rule selection in foreign and security policies', *Journal of European Public Policy*, **16** (6): 834–52.

Börzel, T. (2010), 'The transformative power of Europe reloaded: the limits of external Europeanization', *KFG working paper* no.11, accessed 6 March at www.polsoz. fu-berlin.de/en/v/transformeurope/publications/working_paper/WP_11_February_ Boerzel1.pdf.

Börzel, T. and T. Risse (2009), 'The transformative power of Europe: the European Union and the diffusion of ideas', *KFG* working paper no. 1, accessed 21 November at http://www.polsoz.fu-berlin.de/en/v/transformeurope/publications/working_ paper/ wp_01_boerzel_risse.pdf.

Bulmer, S.J. (1994), 'The governance of the European Union: a new Institutionalist approach', *Journal of Public Policy*, **13** (4): 351–80.

Carafa, L. (2011) 'The Mediterranean Solar Plan through the prism of external governance', *EuroMeSCo-IEMed Papers*, **5**, last accessed 1 August at www.iemed.org/ documents/paperseuromesco5.pdf.

Casier, T. (2011), 'To adopt or not to adopt: explaining selective rule transfer under the European neighbourhood policy', *Journal of European Integration*, **33** (1): 37–53.

Council of the European Union (2003), *Regulations on the Principles, Priorities and Conditions Contained in the Accession Partnership with Turkey*, 2003/398/EC, 19 May, Brussels.

Council of the European Union (2006), Regulations on the Principles, Priorities and Conditions Contained in the Accession Partnership with Turkey, 2006/35/EC, 23 January, Brussels.

Council of the European Union (2009), *Regulations on the Principles, Priorities and Conditions Contained in the Accession Partnership with Turkey*, 2008/157/EC, 18 February, Brussels.

Council of Ministers of Turkey (2003), *Decision on the National Programme for the Adoption of the Acquis*, 2003/5930, 23 June, Ankara.

Diez, T. (2005), 'Constructing the self and changing others: reconsidering "normative power Europe" ', *Millennium*, **33** (3), 613–36.

Dimitrova, A., R. Dragneva (2009), 'Constraining external governance: interdependence with Russia and the CIS as limits to the EU's rule transfer in the Ukraine', *Journal of European Public Policy*, **16** (6), 853–72.

Eberlein, B. (2008), 'The making of the European energy market: the interplay of governance and government', *Journal of Public Policy*, **28** (1): 73–92.

Escribano, G. (2006), 'Europeanisation without Europe? The Mediterranean and the Neighbourhood policy', European University Institute working paper RSCA no. 19, Fiesole, Italy.

Escribano, G. (2010), 'Convergence towards differentiation: the case of Mediterranean energy corridors', *Mediterranean Politics*, **15** (2): 211–29.

EurActiv (2005), 'Turkey talks deadlock broken', 20 September, accessed 2 May 2011 at www.euractiv.com/en/enlargement/turkey-talks-deadlock-broken/article-144575.

EurActiv (2009), 'Turkey plays energy card in stalled EU accession talks', 20 January, accessed on 2 May 2011 at www.euractiv.com/en/enlargement/turkey-plays-energy-card-stalled-eu-accession-talks/article-178623.

European Commission (2000), *Regular Report on Turkey's Progress Towards Accession*, 8 November, Brussels,

European Commission (2001), *Regular Report on Turkey's Progress Towards Accession*, SEC (2001) 1756, 13 November 2001, Brussels.

European Commission (2002), *Regular Report on Turkey's Progress Towards Accession*, COM (2002) 700 final, 9 October, Brussels.

European Commission (2006a), *Green Paper: A European Strategy for Sustainable, Competitive and Secure Energy*, COM (2006) 105, 8 March, Brussels.

European Commission (2006b), *Turkey 2006 Progress Report*, COM(2006) 649 final, 8 November, Brussels.

European Commission (2007), *Turkey 2007 Progress Report*, COM(2007) 663 final, 6 November, Brussels.

European Commission (2009), *Turkey 2009 Progress Report*, COM(2009) 533, 14 October, Brussels.

European Commission (2010), *Turkey 2010 Progress Report*, COM(2010) 660, 9 November, Brussels.

GlobalEDGE (2011), *Market Potential Index for Emerging Markets: 2010*, MPI Archive, Michigan State University, East Lansing, accessed on March 2011 at http://globaledge.msu.edu/resourcedesk/mpi/.

Goldstein, J. and R. O. Keohane (1993), 'Ideas and foreign policy: an analytical framework', in J. Goldstein and R.O. Keohane (eds), *Ideas and Foreign Policy. Beliefs, Institutions and Political Change*, Ithaca, NY: Cornell University Press, pp. 3–30.

International Energy Agency (IEA) (2010) *Energy Policies of IEA Countries: Turkey 2009 Review*, Paris: IEA.

Interviews (2009), Turkey 1–26.

Interviews (2010), EU 27–34.

Jepperson, R., A. Wendt and P. Katzenstein (1996), 'Norms, identity, and culture in national security', in P. Katzenstein (ed.), *The Culture of National Security: Norms and Identity in World Politics*, New York: Columbia University Press, pp. 33–75.

Knill, C. (2005), 'Introduction: cross-national policy convergence: concepts, approaches and explanatory factors', *Journal of European Public Policy*, **12** (5), 764–74.

Lavenex, S. (2004), 'EU external governance in "wider Europe"', *Journal of European Public Policy*, **11** (4), 680–701.

Lavenex, S. (2008), 'A governance perspective on the European neighborhood policy: integration beyond conditionality?', *Journal of European Public Policy*, **15** (6), 938–55.

Lavenex, S. and Schimmelfennig, F. (2009), 'EU rules beyond EU borders: theorizing external governance in European politics', *Journal of European Public Policy*, **16** (6), 791–812.

Lavenex, S. and Stulberg, A. (2009), 'Connecting the neighborhood: energy and environment', in K. Weber, M.E. Smith and M. Baun (eds), *Governing Europe's New Neighborhood: Partners or Periphery?*, Manchester: Manchester University Press, 134–55.

Lavenex, S. and E. Uçarer (2004), 'The external dimension of Europeanization: the case of immigration policies', *Cooperation and Conflict*, **39** (4), 417–43.

Lavenex, S., D. Lehmkuhl and N. Wichmann (2007) 'Die Nachbarschaftspolitiken der Europäischen Union: zwischen Hegemonie und erweiteter Governance', in I. Tömmel (ed.), *Die Europäische Union: Governance und Policy-Making, PVS-Sonderheft*, **40**, Wiesbaden, Germany: VS-Verlag, pp. 367–88.

Lavenex, S., D. Lehmkuhl and N. Wichmann (2009), 'Modes of External Governance: A Cross-National and Cross-Sectoral Comparison', *Journal of European Public Policy*, **16** (6), 813–33.

Lenschow, A., D. Liefferink and S. Veenman (2005), 'When the birds sing: a framework for analysing domestic factors behind policy convergence', *Journal of European Public Policy*, **12** (5), 797–816.

Magen, A. (2007), 'Transformative engagement through law: the Acquis Communautaire as an instrument of EU external influence', *European Journal of Law Reform*, **9** (3), 361–92.

Manners, I. (2002), 'Normative power Europe: a contradiction in terms?', *Journal of Common Market Studies*, **40** (2), 193–379.

March, J., G. and J.P Olson (1998), 'The institutional dynamics of international political orders', *International Organization*, **52** (4), 943–70.

March, J.G. and J.P. Olson (2004), 'The logic of appropriateness', *Arena working papers*, **04** (09), Oslo, accessed 5 October 2009 at http://www.arena.uio.no/publications/working-papers2004/papers/wp04_9.pdf.

Matláry, J. (1997), *Energy Policy in the European Union*, New York: St Martin's Press.

Parliament of Turkey (2001a), *Law on Electricity Market*, Law no. 4628, 3 March.

Parliament of Turkey (2001b), *Law on Natural Gas Market*, Law no. 4646, 7 May.

Parliament of Turkey (2003), *Petroleum Law*, Law no. 5015, 20 December.

Parliament of Turkey (2005), *Law on the Use of Renewable Energy Sources in Electricity Generation*, Law no. 5346, 18 May.

Parliament of Turkey (2007), *Energy Efficiency Law*, Law no. 5627, 2 May.

Parliament of Turkey (2009), *Kabul Law*, Law no. 5836, 17 February.

Peters, B.G. (2005), *Institutional Theory in Political Science: The 'New' Institutionalism*, 2nd edn, London: Continuum.

Powell, W. and P. DiMaggio (eds) (1991), *The New Institutionalism in Organizational Analysis*, Chicago–London: University of Chicago Press.

Rose, R. (1991), 'What is lesson-drawing?', *Journal of Public Policy*, **11** (1), 3–30.

Scharpf, F., W. (1997), *Games Real Actors Play: Actor-Centered Institutionalism in Policy Research, Theoretical Lenses on Public Policy Series*, Boulder, CO: Westview Press.

Schimmelfennig, F. (2007), 'Europeanization beyond Europe', *Living Reviews in European Governance*, **2** (1), accessed 6 March 2009 at www.livingreviews.org/lreg-2007–1.

Schimmelfennig, F. and U. Sedelmeier (2004) 'Governance by conditionality: EU rule transfer to the candidate countries of Central and Eastern Europe', *Journal of European Public Policy*, **11** (4), 661–79.

Schimmelfennig, F. and U. Sedelmeier (2005), *The Europeanization of Central and Eastern Europe*, Ithaca, NY: Cornell University Press.

Solorio Sandoval, I. (2011), 'Bridging the gap between environmental policy integration and the EU's energy policy: mapping out the "green Europeanisation" of energy governance', *Journal of Contemporary European Research*, **7** (3).

Simmons, B.A., F. Dobbin and G. Garrett (2006) 'Introduction: the international diffusion of liberalism', *International Organization*, **60** (4), 781–810.

Strang, D. and J. Meyer (1993), 'Institutional conditions for diffusion', *Theory and Society*, **22** (4): 487–511.

Strang, D. and S.A. Soule (1998), 'Diffusion in organizations and social movements: from hybrid corn to poison pills', *Annual Review of Sociology*, **24**, 265–90.

World Energy Council (WEC) (2009), *Trade and Investment Rules for Energy*, WEC Task Force Report, London.

Zapater, E. (2009) 'La seguridad energética de la Unión Europea en el contexto de la nueva política energética y el tratado de Lisboa', in F. Morata (ed.), *La Energía del Siglo XXI: Perspectivas europeas y tendencias globales*, Barcelona: Institut Universitari d'Estudis Europeus, pp. 49–79.

11. Morocco, the European energy policy and the Mediterranean Solar Plan

Gonzalo Escribano-Francés and Enrique San Martín González[1]

11.1 INTRODUCTION

The development of renewable energy sources (RES) is one of the pillars of the emerging European policy, which has become a world leader in the promotion of clean energies, making the fight against climate change one of its signs of identity in the international arena (see Chapter 1 by Solorio Sandoval and Morata; Chapter 2 by Adelle et al.). Within the framework of the Union for the Mediterranean (UfM) there has been launched a proposal for a Mediterranean Solar Plan for the deployment of RES in the southern shore of the Mediterranean, with EU support. This initiative could also be envisaged as a way of counterbalancing the 'eastward turn' that has occurred in the EU energy supply since the fall of the Berlin Wall (Escribano et al., 2006; San Martín, 2010; see also Chapter 8 by Herranz Surrallés and Natorski).

Morocco has expressed its interest in participating in the Mediterranean Solar Plan as it is an energy-dependent country that imports 85 percent of its energy needs. In order to reduce its vulnerability while improving its environmental status, the country is committed to producing 42 percent of its electricity through RES by 2020 and to becoming a net exporter of electricity to the EU via the Straits of Gibraltar. A major goal, implicitly included within this commitment, would also be the creation of employment associated with the renewable energy companies created or established in Morocco, a country with almost a third of its young population unemployed.

Although most of the Maghreb countries have committed to developing RES (Brand and Zingerle, 2011), Morocco is probably the best-positioned country in the southern Mediterranean region to implement the Mediterranean Solar Plan, taking into account its internal drivers, combined with its vast solar and wind potential and its geographic location. Besides, it already has a relatively significant solar and wind energy installed capacity, and given its proximity to Spain (14 km) it has the only relevant and functional electricity interconnection with the EU in the whole region. This link could be used as the first step towards the Mediterranean Solar Plan (Marín and Escribano, 2010a).

At the start it is expected that the Solar Plan will help Morocco supply its domestic electricity markets; later on, it will allow the electricity surplus to be exported to the EU, benefiting from the new 'green-energy' trade scheme provided for by new Directive 2009/28, art. 9. However, there was some discussion as to whether employment related to RES technologies would turn out to be created in the longer term on the north or south side of the Mediterranean Sea (Colombo and Lesser, 2010). Regarding this point it should be borne in mind that many aspects of solar technology manufacturing are not particularly labor-intensive and are already subject to strong international competition.

The purpose of this chapter is, first, to reflect on whether the Mediterranean Solar Plan can make a difference to the deployment of RES in Morocco (that is facilitate the EU role as 'green-energy' model exporter). And second, it is to consider to what extent and under what conditions the Mediterranean Solar Plan could potentially become a driver for Moroccan development or could instead be better considered as an EU-centric project for achieving its own environmental objectives, together with the promotion of European industries and engineering firms.

This chapter is structured as follows. Section 11.2 analyzes Morocco as a suitable partner for the external European energy policy. Section 11.3 zooms in on the case of RES in Morocco. Section 11.4 goes in depth into the Mediterranean Solar Plan and Morocco. Section 11.5 explores further perspectives for RES development in Morocco in the context of the Euro-Mediterranean partnership. Finally, Section 11.6 concludes with some elements of the analysis of the EU's role as a 'green-energy' exporter and the case of Morocco.

11.2   MOROCCO: A SUITABLE PARTNER FOR EUROPE?

Since 2000 Morocco has experienced a significant leap forward in its gross domestic product (GDP) growth rates and most forecasts point to growth rates stabilizing at around 3 to 5 percent. The government's objective is to attain a sustained growth rate of around 6 percent. This acceleration of economic growth together with significant demographic dynamism implies an increasing energy demand. Energy demand has been rising by around 5 percent per annum in the last decade, in line with economic growth figures. The projections for future increases are even higher, especially in electricity, owing to the current low per capita consumption levels and the limited penetration of electrical appliances in most Moroccan households (OME, 2008).

In 2007 total primary energy consumption per capita in Morocco was around a tenth of German or Spanish rates. The gradual improvement in living conditions, economic modernization, urbanization and the progressive adoption of Western lifestyles by some population segments will certainly imply an increase in per capita energy consumption levels. In addition to this, the Moroccan growth model is quite energy-intensive: in absolute terms, Morocco needs almost double the energy of Germany to produce one US dollar of GDP. This is a typical feature of developing countries, reflecting low productivity levels and GDP figures. But given that energy intensity figures do not include traditional biomass the real energy intensity is in fact much higher and as a consequence energy use is economically very inefficient.

But in the Moroccan case this also reflects its economic specialization in productive sectors with relatively high levels of energy consumption, such as the chemical industry associated with its phosphate resources, and construction or tourism within the services sector. This growth pattern is expected to intensify, according to the Moroccan economic growth strategy, based on the deployment of infrastructures to raise total factor productivity levels. Most of these infrastructures both require and entail increasing energy needs: for example, highways, ports and airports, urbanization, social housing, health system improvements, desalination and rural electrification. The emphasis on strategic sectors such as tourism, agriculture and industry further accentuates the long-term energy needs of the Moroccan economy.

Electricity demand has been growing at 8 percent during the last decade, while per capita electricity consumption remains extremely low (480 kW per capita per year). Furthermore there are strong disparities in household electricity consumption levels across different consumer categories, with rural areas and impoverished suburbs falling close to energy poverty levels when there is any (formal and safe) access to the grid at all. Despite being cross-subsidized by urban and industrial consumers, rural consumers account for a small fraction of electricity consumption. As in most developing countries the electricity load increases at sunset, making it more complex to manage an electricity system relying heavily on solar energy. Electricity generation relies mainly on coal and fuel power plants, with natural gas being marginal owing to the lack of local transport and distribution infrastructures. There is a single natural-gas combined-cycle power plant, which is run using the fee Morocco receives from Algeria for the latter's gas exports to Spain via the Maghreb–Europe gas pipeline.

Energy poverty is concentrated in rural areas, since their distance from the main electricity lines makes it uneconomical to supply them with conventional electricity. Energy poverty is one of the most pressing challenges facing the development community and Morocco is no exception. Energy poverty is closely related to human development in so far as the lack of energy services is correlated with key elements of poverty, such as low education levels and the limited opportunities for subsistence activity (Barnes and Floor, 1996; Sagar, 2005). Energy poverty also causes deforestation (30,000 ha per year), one of the major threats to Moroccan sustainable development. Traditional biomass consumption for heating and cooking in the rural areas represents more than a quarter of commercial consumption, highlighting the lack of access to energy services. Moroccan authorities have responded to this situation by means of a rural electrification program that increased the rural electrification rate from 18 percent in 1995 to 90 percent in 2008, according to the Moroccan electricity utility Office National de l'Electricité (ONE). However even in urban areas energy costs restrict access to energy services by poor households.

There are other economic implications of the Moroccan energy scenario linked to economic development. Lack of access to energy by rural entrepreneurs and the urban informal sector, together with high energy costs, also erodes business competitiveness. Compensation schemes subsidizing petroleum consumption represent a significant budget cost for Morocco. Given that the country imports over 96 percent of its energy needs, the energy bill alone (around €3.5 billion in 2008, representing 20 percent of imports) explains much of the Moroccan structural trade deficit. The energy mix is based upon fossil fuels, with coal representing 30 percent of total primary energy supply (TPES) in 2008, petroleum products 62 percent, natural gas 3 percent, wind energy 0.4 percent, hydropower 3 percent and electricity imports from Spain 1.7 percent. In addition there are geopolitical aspects, mainly Morocco's reluctance to depend excessively upon Algerian hydrocarbon exports. This forces Morocco to diversify away from Algeria and towards more distant producers, further raising the cost of energy imports. It also forces Morocco to shift towards liquefied natural gas (LNG), and incur the associated extra costs of gasification terminals, if it wants to develop a natural-gas domestic market to modernize its energy mix.

These challenges make energy a significant restrictive factor to sustainable economic growth and human development in Morocco. The long-term Moroccan strategy for confronting these challenges is articulated into a set of energy policy goals and their correlated policy instruments. They are broadly inspired by the EU's own energy trinity: energy security, sustainable development and economic competitiveness, although, as is to be expected, the sustainable development objective incorporates the alleviation of energy poverty as a fundamental contribution to human development (see Chapter 1 by Solorio Sandoval and Morata).

Energy security is to be achieved by two means. First, through the diversification of energy sources and their geographical origins: this involves introducing natural gas and reinforcing gas interconnections with Algeria, as well as reinforcing electricity interconnections with both Algeria and Spain. In addition, exploration efforts to search for hydrocarbons will be maintained, and the country has expressed its interest in advancing in the field of nuclear energy in the long run. Finally and more importantly for the purpose of this research, RES will be promoted in order to increase local energy supplies, reduce energy dependency and diversify away from imported fossil fuels. Second, these intermediate objectives also imply some more technical measures, such as upgrading refining facilities, increasing storage and port capacities to receive petroleum products, and reinforcing the electricity grid.

The environmental sustainability of energy use is approached through a twofold strategy: by limiting its carbon content and reducing traditional biomass consumption to sustainable levels. RES can make a significant contribution in both areas. The reduction of traditional biomass consumption and its substitution by modern energy services is closely related to the eradication of energy poverty in rural areas. Thus the successful Programme d'Électrification Rurale Global (PERG) will be extended to the 10 percent of the rural population still without access to electricity. Other important elements of the strategy to secure access to energy have been the development of liquefied petroleum gases (LPG) distribution and the promotion of decentralized energy services through microenterprises (*Maisons Energies*).

As regards competitiveness, the government intends to continue the gradual liberalization of the energy markets. The government has also expressed its desire to further restructure different energy sectors with measures such as tax standardization across sectors or the partial indexing of prices to the international market. The authorities also want to improve the management of energy consumption by implementing demand-side management measures, including the restructuring of tariffs.

11.3. RES IN MOROCCO AND THE MEDITERRANEAN SOLAR PLAN

To focus on RES, these account for 4 percent of the Moroccan energy balance (excluding traditional biomass) and 10 percent of electricity generation. While the figures are low, they are still significant. This RES derives mainly from hydropower, but also from wind energy of late. Nowadays, Morocco has 124 MW of wind energy installed and another 240 MW is being implemented. Despite their small contribution to the energy mix, RES constitute a diverse set of projects, including windfarms, photovoltaic farms, solar thermal plants, hydropower, waste reused for energy, desalination and solar water heaters. This diversity allows for the interaction of RES with strategies for enhancing human development, like rural electrification or sanitation. For instance, rural electrification is expected to be achieved with a 7 percent contribution from individual photovoltaic (PV) systems.

Morocco's RES are among the highest in the world (DLR 2005, OME 2007, REACCESS-DLR 2009), including solar thermal (Concentrated Solar Power-CSP), wind and PV resources. Although expectations are correlatively high, there are still some obstacles to its realization. The Programme National de Développement des Energies Renouvelables et de l'Efficacité Énergétique aims to raise the share of RES to 42 percent of the installed capacity of power generation by 2020. This would mean a veritable contribution to energy supply sustainability and access to electricity, including the provision of sustainable and decentralized energy services to 300,000 rural households.

The legal and regulatory framework for RES is being developed and includes the following elements: (1) a law on RES and energy efficiency; (2) a decree allowing independent power producers (IPPs) to access the electricity grid and an increase of the production threshold from 10 MW to 50 MW; (3) a new fund to support RES deployment and energy efficiency; and (4) transformation of the existing Centre de Développement des Energies Renouvelables (CDER) into a new operational agency devoted to implementing Moroccan RES and energy efficiency policies.

The UfM's Solar Plan is becoming a strategic element of this picture. Within the Solar Plan, the Moroccan electricity utility (ONE) has launched a pilot project for building a 5 MW photovoltaic solar farm that could be increased to 20 MW. This project is included in the first phase of the Mediterranean Solar Plan and would generate green electricity for both the Moroccan and the European market, exported to Spain through the existing interconnection and benefiting from the provisions of art. 9 in Directive 2009/28. This will be the first significant export of green electricity flowing from a Mediterranean neighbor to the EU. Within the Mediterranean Solar Plan, ONE is also developing a public–private partnership for the construction of a solar-powered desalination plant.

The Moroccan authorities also recently announced a 2000 MW and €6000 million megaproject for solar generation with a 2020 time frame. The project will be implemented in five different locations in the south and northeast of the country. In one of them, Ain Beni Mathar (north-eastern Morocco), the Spanish company Abengoa is already building a 470 MW hybrid gas combined-cycle and solar thermal plant, 20 MW of which is provided by a 183,000 m^2 solar field (equivalent in area to 25 football pitches). It is a turnkey project for ONE, the national electricity utility (Greenpeace et al., 2009). New wind parks are attracting large investments and the authorities plan to obtain 13 percent of electricity generation from wind energy in 2012, reaching an installed capacity close to 1300 MW. Morocco expects the Mediterranean Solar Plan to support this policy of promoting RES in order to boost green electricity generation for both internal consumption and exports, transforming RES into a new driver for the country's economic development. Will the Mediterranean Solar Plan fulfil these expectations?

11.4   THE MEDITERRANEAN SOLAR PLAN: ISSUES FOR MOROCCAN DEVELOPMENT[2]

As regards the context, most energy scenarios foresee a rapid expansion of RES worldwide. A significant share of these potential capacities is concentrated in the EU's Mediterranean neighborhood, thus explaining the EU's interest in securing access to these potential sources of green electricity. As mentioned in the previous section, Morocco is one of the best-positioned countries to export green electricity to Europe. Of course, there are other energy vectors of great immediate relevance in the Euro-Mediterranean energy scenario, such as those related to oil and gas (and eventually nuclear energy). However, many of the arguments for RES can be extended to the energy system as a whole. In fact, it seems that any action at the level of RES must be coordinated with energy integration within the EU itself, and especially with the role given to natural gas in an energy mix featuring a greater contribution of RES.

As put forward in Section 11.1, the promotion of RES has become one of the principal elements of European energy policy. Between 2001 and 2006, their contribution in the EU increased from 13 percent to 16 percent, but the new Directive 2009/28 seeks to double this percentage beyond 30 percent to achieve the general objective of a 20 percent contribution of RES by 2020. The Commission itself has recognized that it could be difficult for some countries to achieve the established objectives. However, under certain circumstances, the new directive allows a Member State to sell its surplus RES to another Member State that has not fulfilled its objectives. Directive 2009/8 also allows for 'physical' green-energy imports into the EU (real electricity imports generated from RES, not just investments). This possibility can generate additional incentives for shifting towards green electricity in the best-positioned Mediterranean Partner Countries (MPCs), in both geographical and industrial terms, as well as new investment opportunities for EU companies.

These regional dynamics also fit into a wider context: the Gulf Cooperation Council (GCC) countries have a growing interest in RES technologies and could be both financial and producer partners of the Mediterranean Solar Plan. In the global arena, Barack Obama's new presidential promotion of RES is also helping to consolidate their increasing contribution to the global energy mix and this process is being accompanied by other developed and developing countries. Therefore positioning the Euro-Mediterranean region within such a promising emerging global market is another significant strategic goal.

As for the Mediterranean Solar Plan, it is one of the six priority projects of the UfM, the new name given to the Barcelona Process, which was set up in 1995 to channel Euro-Mediterranean relations (Escribano and Lorca, 2008). The UfM was formally established on 13 July 2008 in the Paris summit, under the French Presidency of the EU. The summit adopted the Paris Declaration establishing an institutional structure and proposing a series of specific priority projects: de-pollution of the Mediterranean, maritime highways, civil protection, a solar plan, higher education and the development of small and medium enterprises. One of the projects listed in the annex of the Paris Declaration is the so-called 'Alternative Energies: Mediterranean Solar Plan'. Despite the precision about the Solar Plan, the sense of the Declaration calls for the mobilization of all alternative energies to export green electricity produced in the MPCs to the EU.

Tasked with developing the projects, the UfM Secretariat plays a central role in the institutional network. The delay in its operational constitution has prevented it from invigorating the process so far, but some ideas have been put forward to allow progress in the field of RES and the interconnection between the two shores of the Mediterranean.

In recent years there has been a plethora of analyses of the potential of RES (basically solar and wind) in the southern Mediterranean (DLR, 2005; European Commission, 2007; OME, 2007, 2008; Plan Bleu, 2007, 2008a, 2008b; TREC, 2007; REACCESS-DLR, 2009; REACCESS-UNED, 2009). Most of the studies coincide on the type of projects to undertake, have been tested with the public and private stakeholders and constitute the starting point for the UfM's renewable projects, even if they do not directly inspire them. The proposed projects are (1) the installation of renewable electricity generation capacities in the MPCs, (2) the construction of MPC-EU high-capacity high voltage direct current (HVDC) lines, (3) the improvement of MPC electricity grids and intraregional interconnections, (4) natural-gas capacities in MPCs to supplement RES, (5) desalination through renewable energies and finally, (6) training projects, technical cooperation and technology cooperation for development.

The installation of renewable electricity generation capacities in the MPCs mainly concerns wind, solar thermal and photovoltaic energy. The Mediterranean Solar Plan poses the initial dilemma as to which technological option should be prioritized. In the southern Mediterranean, solar thermal technology has only been developed on a small scale and therefore a short-term option would be to support new projects that demonstrate this technology, and to promote this in the medium and long term. The Moroccan hybrid solar thermal plant in Ain Beni Mathar provides the country with an advantage for exploring new and more ambitious solar thermal projects.

Wind generation seems closer to the profitability threshold, so that a wind energy plan could be the subject of a short-term undertaking, for which there is major potential on Moroccan shores. Photovoltaic energy has major potential in the rural environment, as Morocco's experience with the rural electrification program demonstrates, but it also has a significant potential for powering large and medium-sized decentralized installations, like Moroccan tourist resorts. The alternatives of generation technologies and transmission lines to the EU should be considered for all of these, as the impact for the EU and MPCs will depend to a great extent on generating capacities, as well as on the location and layout of the transmission lines.

The last point led us to the construction of high-capacity HVDC lines for transmitting the green electricity generated in the MPCs to the EU. Without the development of interconnection infrastructures between the MPCs, Mediterranean Europe and the rest of the European continent, it will not be possible to transmit electricity from the MPCs to the EU. Perhaps the greatest obstacles for undertaking these lines are the lengthy approval procedures and the lack of clarity about the role of local utilities as a support for infrastructure development in Mediterranean countries. Morocco has had the only functional interconnection to the EU through the Strait of Gibraltar since 1997, which was doubled later on. There were also plans to link Algeria to Spain following the Medgaz pipeline from Oran to Almeria, but the project has not been yet undertaken. The Mediterranean electricity ring that the EU proposes includes the Turkey–Greece, Algeria–Italy and Tunisia–Italy interconnection projects. However, the Moroccan–Spanish interconnection is the only operational one, used for balancing the Moroccan electricity system, mainly by exporting Spanish electricity to Morocco.

This issue is also closely linked to the improvement of MPC electricity grids and intraregional (MPC–MPC) interconnections. Electricity systems in MPCs are much weaker than those of Europe, and connecting their grids with the EU and among themselves will enhance their systems, but requires the modernization of local grids. A significant increase in the contribution of RES is another challenge that requires the improvement of MPC electricity systems, given that RES are very grid-intensive and require greater flexibility of the system in order to manage it appropriately. Morocco is already interconnected to Algeria (two connections, and a third underway), but the exchanges are very small and grid synchronization remains inoperative.

Moreover the deployment of RES will require establishing the necessary natural-gas infrastructures in the MPCs in order to supplement them and act as backup capacity, especially in combined-cycle power stations that can supply demand peaks. This is of special importance for Morocco, which does not have any developed gas infrastructures, apart from the segment of the Maghreb–Europe pipeline transiting from Algeria to Spain, which has allowed

Morocco to run the Beni Mathar hybrid plant with the gas transit fee paid by Algeria. Moreover, Morocco is reluctant to increase its dependency on Algeria, with which it has very problematic relations, to the point that the Moroccan–Algerian border has been closed for almost two decades. Another proposed set of projects concerns desalination facilities powered by RES, given the high energy intensity of desalination plants and the water shortages most MPCs suffer. The forecasts for hydro resources in the southern Mediterranean and the Persian Gulf point to growing water shortages from the middle of the next decade.

Last but not least, the deployment of RES in MPCs requires the upgrading of their regulatory institutions, grid management and capacities to absorb renewable technologies, including the generation of local skills concerning innovation and adaptation to local needs and circumstances. This is why the Mediterranean Solar Plan requires technical cooperation and training programs on the use and development of RES-related technologies and the management and regulation of the electricity sector and RES itself. The programs could incorporate, along with the local authorities, new actors such as education and research institutions, companies and eventually other civil society agents, in addition to regulators and network operators. These are some of the preferences that MPCs have expressed to their European partners in the framework of mutual interest and as an exercise in Euro-Mediterranean solidarity.

11.5   DISCUSSION: PERSPECTIVES FOR EXPORTING THE EU'S 'GREEN-ENERGY' MODEL TO MOROCCO

Morocco is aware that the deployment of RES requires upgraded technical and management capabilities as part of the efforts for modernizing the electricity grid, introducing natural gas and increasing green electricity generation. Furthermore Morocco expects RES to become a new source of job creation in the short run, mainly for building and maintaining the new renewable energy facilities. In the medium term, and in addition to the jobs created in maintenance and operation, the deployment of RES could mean the delocalization of the less technologically intense parts of the industrial processes (such as assembling windmills or solar panels). Both activities are labor-intensive, but require targeted training of local human capital in order to absorb the new technologies and provide the qualified human resources that are needed to operate and maintain the facilities. In the long term, preparedness to absorb technology transfers could expand local innovation capabilities. Morocco has adopted a cluster-oriented industrial policy in which training of human resources is a key feature. The Mediterranean Solar Plan could support that strategy in the field of RES.

More precisely, training and technical–technological cooperation could eventually include three different programs: first of all, training programs for professionals and technicians in the fields of both engineering and economics, to provide local human resources for the dissemination of the new energies and consumer satisfaction; second, R&D&I training on RES in leading research bodies in the respective MPCs, to foster the transfer of technology; and finally, the training of regulatory bodies, network operators and the energy authorities of MPCs, extending twinning to the field of management and regulation of RES and the electricity sector. The EU has important assets in this area. It would be important to construct a strategic relationship through broad training programs that comprise regulators, businesses, associations, universities, professional training centers and research institutions. There are European funds for financing this kind of programme and the programs already existing in the EU (Erasmus, Marie Curie, Leonardo etc.) could emphasize the aspect of RES in their extension to the MPCs (ESTELA, 2009).

Concerning Morocco, the country has experience of cooperating with EU countries on energy issues. For instance the Spanish electricity grid operator Red Eléctrica Española, which cooperates extensively with ONE, managed the technical synchronization of the Moroccan grid with the Southern European network and is currently cooperating on the synchronization of the Maghrebian grid. There are many cooperation opportunities in regulatory, industrial and services management and technological transfers between Morocco and the EU. Enhancing human capabilities and skills in the domain of RES is a precondition for Morocco to reap the benefits of the Mediterranean Solar Plan. For instance, forecasts from the solar thermal plant industry itself concerning job creation stress that every 100 MW of solar thermal plant installed will provide an equivalent 400 men/year manufacturing jobs: 600 in contracting and installation, and just 60 in operation and maintenance (ESTELA, 2009, p. 7). Therefore training programs are required for Moroccan workers if they are to participate in the parts of the industrial and construction processes where most jobs are created and where the added value is concentrated. If local workers are restricted to maintenance, this would add very little in terms of job creation, human resource training and enhancement of local innovation capabilities.

Another key issue of the Mediterranean Solar Plan concerns the institutional aspects related to regulation. RES still require support schemes in the medium term, which are supposed to be transitory until the profitability threshold is met. They also require a stable institutional context to minimize regulatory risks and to allow the heavy investments resulting from their high capital intensity, therefore generating the appropriate conditions for establishing a sustainable framework for their long-term development. RES facilities imply high sunken costs. Thus the legal security of investment (especially in a region with a high country risk) and the stability of incentives are necessary prerequisites before starting to think about different payment schemes and funding possibilities (Escribano, 2010). Another relevant aspect concerns technical standards, as the interoperability of the electricity systems requires their standardization. Although the harmonization of the technical requisites is gradually being undertaken, the need to increase technical cooperation in order to advance in this process should again be pointed out.

MPC electricity markets have historically been state monopolies. Morocco has also progressed in the liberalization of its energy market. However, relevant legislation and institutions are not yet operationally in place and the energy sector remains plagued with state interventions, from subsidies to public companies, and restrictions on competition. The Mediterranean Solar Plan calls for convergence in energy regulations and standards across Euro-Mediterranean countries, but lacks a clear strategy to achieve it. In the Moroccan case, there is a wide consensus about the need for further and deeper reforms, and the EU should conceive a way of supplying sufficient incentives to Moroccan authorities to embark on the pending reforms. Together with technical cooperation, technology transfers and training, a reform package to modernize the Moroccan energy system could be agreed and partially funded by the European Commission or the European Investment Bank (EIB).

One of the key features of the regulatory framework is the incentives it provides and under which mechanism. The most widely extended regulatory mechanism for alternative energies in the EU are feed-in tariffs (FIT), which offer a bonus to green electricity over the electricity market price. However, there are other alternatives, such as tax incentives. For instance, the United States applies a tax deduction scheme to production, known as Production Tax Credit (PTC), which is criticized for the unpredictability of its renewal and the absence of significant incentives when profits drop, owing to an economic downturn for instance. Other schemes envisage the use of quotas, auctions or subsidies for investment. After the Third Legislative Package, the EU gives freedom to its member states to adopt the payment scheme of their choice, mainly FIT, tradable green certificates (quotas), tax incentives or auctions. However there seems to be a greater consensus around the efficiency of the FIT or bonus system, which is preferred by the Commission and is, in fact, applied in most member states. Therefore this appears to be the most convincing scheme.

Nonetheless the problem is not so much about where the appropriate regulation is in force as about who ultimately pays the bonus: the MPCs themselves or the EU member states? In the southern Mediterranean, the bonus system is in force in Algeria, Egypt, Israel and Turkey, and is under review in Morocco, Tunisia and Syria. Tunisia, Egypt and Syria offer investment subsidies, while Morocco and Turkey are studying them. Morocco and Tunisia offer tax reductions (on VAT or tariffs). Tunisia and Algeria have national funds for developing RES. However perhaps the major obstacle is the high degree of subsidies for fossil fuels in most MPCs. In Morocco these subsidies have tended to slowly decrease, but are still considerable and damage the competitiveness of RES. In short, it does not seem that Morocco, which has managed to reduce the fossil fuel and electricity subsidies at a significant political cost, could take on overly ambitious commitments in terms of granting a significant bonus to RES. Furthermore, a continuity of subsidized prices is expected in order to moderate Moroccan inflation and support agriculture.

A different aspect is the regulation scheme for green electricity exports to the EU. Within the EU the lowest bonuses are applied to wind energy and hydroelectric energy followed by solar thermal, while the bonuses for PV energy tend to be the highest. At a Community level the convergence of the different models for promoting RES seems difficult, and therefore it might be preferable to develop a 'Euro-Mediterranean' regulatory model that supersedes the different national models applicable to a Mediterranean RES plan. In fact art. 9 of the Community's new Renewable Energy Directive 2009/28 stipulates the treatment of joint projects between member states and third countries for their consideration within the objectives established by such a directive for each member state, always under determined conditions.[3]

One proposal is to establish a bonus somewhat lower than the one prevailing in the destination EU member state. This possibility seems problematic in so far as it entails what could be called 'subsidized protectionism': the fact that discriminatory FITs penalize Moroccan green electricity exports by granting them a lower bonus. It is debatable if such a discriminatory scheme complies with WTO regulations concerning services, but it would not be permitted by Single Market logic and the trading scheme should be competitive and not intended to protect EU producers.

The new directive allows member states to link their domestic support systems to those of other Community countries. More importantly, in terms of this article, it also allows the 'physical ' import of RES (including green electricity, from wind or solar farms, for example) from third countries into Morocco, which is the only country already interconnected to the EU. However 'virtual ' imports (investment in RES in those third countries) cannot be calculated according to the objectives set by the directive. The statistical transfer (the exchange of renewable credits between countries with production surpluses and deficits) is limited to the member states, and only if the selling country has achieved its own objectives and if both countries cooperate in joint renewable energy projects. However Morocco is developing an

Advanced Status with the EU, which entails Moroccan participation in the European Single Market. This could lead to a gradual Moroccan participation in the virtual green electricity market whenever the country progressively converges towards the regulations, standards and policies of the *acquis communautaire's* energy-related chapters. This would be a meaningful incentive to Moroccan energy actors for reforming the energy sector along the model set up by the *acquis communautaire*.

Finally, a pivotal issue in the economics of the Mediterranean Solar Plan is its financing (Marín and Escribano, 2010a). The recent financial crisis has had a serious impact on the real economy, which has in turn resulted in the fall of energy demand and fossil energy prices. This is acting as a disincentive to investment in new energies, in both research and production. In this sense, development cooperation can also contribute by funding installations that help fight energy poverty, as well as through technical cooperation and training programs.

11.6   CONCLUSIONS

From the perspective of the southern Mediterranean countries the development of RES has significant socioeconomic potential (Marín and Escribano, 2010b), mainly for MPCs like Morocco that are highly dependent upon imported fossil fuels. RES can stimulate their economies through the promotion of foreign direct investment, the generation of new local energy sources, the export of green energy to the EU, the creation of employment, the fostering of R&D and the transfer of technology, which may entail the delocalization of certain industrial processes in the MPCs, such as the manufacture and assembly of components in the wind or solar industry. In MPCs without hydrocarbon resources, RES can be a solution to their economic and energy vulnerability in the medium and long term, especially considering the major increases expected in domestic demand. The impact of these energies on economic growth has been accredited for the EU (EmployRES, 2009) and could also be a driver for the development of its Mediterranean neighborhood.

RES provide, in addition to helping solve environmental problems, a source of wealth for the countries that develop them. In so far as the integration of RES entails an adaptation of institutional and regulatory frameworks, their development also constitutes a modernizing factor for the Moroccan energy system. Moreover these reforms involve a certain regulatory convergence that makes regional integration, at least of electricity, possible at both Euro-Mediterranean level and a South–South one. This integration is furthermore consistent with the logic of comparative advantage, as it would allow Morocco to exploit abundant factors until now in disuse, such as the large desert spaces, insolation hours, wind hours and speed. The promotion of RES is, therefore, a key vector for the economic, physical and regulatory integration of the Euro-Mediterranean space and the European energy policy.

Along these lines, the EU should ensure that all projects related to RES in the southern Mediterranean constitute a factor of sustainable development for these countries. This requires technology cooperation and local capacity-building so that the MPCs can benefit from the deployment of RES to boost their socioeconomic development. Southern Mediterranean countries have expressed their interest in RES, but have also clearly pointed out what kind of European support they require. There is a lot to do in terms of technology cooperation, and the EU has the potential to act in this field, from using current cooperation programs to the launch of specific instruments against climate change that can be applied to the Mediterranean region. At the level of multilateral cooperation there can also be funding opportunities for the fight against climate change. The UfM could agglutinate all these elements and turn the Solar Plan into a major Euro-Mediterranean sustainable development project incorporating elements of technological development, generation of local capacities in terms of RES, the fight against climate change, eradication of energy poverty and regional integration.

The Moroccan example clearly illustrates the case for approaching the Mediterranean Solar Plan as a comprehensive sustainable development strategy. When designing regulatory, trading and financing schemes, the focus should be on Moroccan development. If the benefits are not to be reaped by EU companies and their Moroccan partners, several measures should be adopted. One of them is the focus on the alleviation of energy poverty in rural households, with its positive impact on sustainability and human development: this calls for supporting individual decentralized photovoltaic systems, as well as delivering modern energy services not necessarily related to RES. Another prerequisite is supporting the training of Moroccan manpower to attract investments. However, training should not be exclusively provided for the purposes of maintenance, which is the activity that generates least jobs and added value. A meaningful participation in the construction and operation phases should be attained in the medium term. At the same time, the EU should establish a long-term mechanism for promoting technology transfers and enhancing local innovation capabilities.

Without such prerequisites in mind, the whole discussion on the Mediterranean Solar Plan risks deviating from its principal objective. As a project under the UfM, it should aim to create an area of shared prosperity in the Euro-Mediterranean region (that is the consolidation of the EU as a 'green-energy' exporter towards the Mediterranean). This can be achieved only by supporting MPCs' reform efforts and strengthening their economic opportunities, such as green electricity exports. This chapter has tried to show that, without upgrading Moroccan institutions, human resources and the country's rural energy poverty situation, the Solar Plan risks being reduced to a EU strategy for achieving its own energy objectives and promoting European renewable-energy industries, energy companies and engineering firms. This scenario would add very little to Moroccan development (and arguably that of other MPCs) and therefore should be neither defended nor pursued as a development strategy (that is against the EU role as a 'green-energy' model exporter).

NOTES

1. This chapter is one of the results of a research agenda conducted by the Spanish Open University's (UNED) International Political Economy of Energy Research Group. The research behind it has benefited from the REACCESS (Risk of Energy Availability: Common Corridors for Europe Supply Security) Project, VII Framework Programme of the European Union (Subject: Energy-2007–09. 1–01; Grant Agreement no. 212011). It has also benefited from the research project Renewable Energies as a Euro-Mediterranean Vector of Integration, funded by the Instituto Europeo del Mediterráneo (IEMed) in the context of the preparation of the EU's Spanish Presidency. It also profited from the research conducted by Professor Escribano on the 'Moroccan Strategic Economic Horizon' for the Real Instituto Elcano de Relaciones Internacionales. However, its contents are the sole responsibility of the authors and do not represent the opinion of the above-mentioned institutions.
2. For a more detailed discussion on the economics of the Mediterranean Solar Plan for the whole Mediterranean region, see Marín and Escribano (2009).
3. Directive 2009/28 on the promotion of the use of energy from renewable sources, 23 April 2009.

REFERENCES

Barnes, D. and W. Floor (1996), 'Rural energy in developing countries: a challenge for economic development', *Annual Review of Energy and the Environment*, **21**, 497–530.
Brand, B. and J. Zingerle (2011), 'The renewable energy targets of the Maghreb countries: impact on electricity supply and conventional power markets', *Energy Policy*, **39** (8), 4411–19.
Colombo, S. and I. Lesser (2010), 'The Mediterranean energy scene: what now? What next? Summary report', Instituto Affari Internazionali; Documenti IAI 10/06, April.
DLR–German Aerospace Center (2005), *MED-CSP: Concentrating Solar Power for the Mediterranean Region, Final Report*, April, DLR Institute of Technical Thermodynamics, Stuttgart: Germany.
EmployRES (2009), 'The impact of renewable energy policy on economic growth and employment in the European Union', April, Karlsruhe, Germany.
Escribano, G. (2010), 'Convergence towards differentiation: the case of Mediterranean energy corridors', *Mediterranean Politics*, **15** (2), 211–29.
Escribano, G. and A. Lorca (2008), 'The Mediterranean Union: a union in search of a project', Real Instituto Elcano de Relaciones Internacionales, working paper no. 3, Madrid.
Escribano, G., E. San Martín and A. Lorca (2006), 'Energía y política exterior: la UE,

Rusia y el Mediterráneo', in A. Sánchez, A. (ed.), *Gas y petróleo en Rusia: impacto interno y proyección exterior*, Valencia, Spain: Universidad de Valencia, pp. 91–110.

ESTELA (2009), *Solar Power from Europe's Sun Belt: The Solar Thermal Electricity Industry's Proposal for the MSP*, June, Brussels.

European Commission (2007), *Energy Corridors: European Union and Neighbouring Countries*, Directorate General for Research, Brussels.

Greenpeace, ESTELA and Solar Paces (2009a), *Global Outlook 09, Concentrating Solar Power*, June, Amsterdam, Netherlands; Tabernas, Spain; Brussels.

Marín, J.M. and G. Escribano (2009) 'Renewable energies as a Euro-Mediterranean vector of integration', paper presented at the Barcelona Euromed Forum Union for the Mediterranean: Projects for the Future, November 5, Barcelona.

Marín, J. M. and G. Escribano (2010a), 'El Plan Solar Mediterráneo y la integración energética Euro-mediterránea', *Revista de Economía Industrial*, **377**, 118–126.

Marín, J. M. and G. Escribano (2010b), 'The Mediterranean Solar Plan as a Euro-Mediterranean vector of integration and economic development', paper prepared for the Ministry of Industry, Trade and Tourism and the Conference on the Mediterranean Solar Plan, 11–12 May, Valencia, Spain.

OME (2007), *Renewable Energy in the Southern and Eastern Mediterranean Countries: Current Situation*, June, Nanterre, France: OME.

OME (2008), *Mediterranean Energy Perspectives 2008*, Observatoire Méditerranéen de l'Energie, Nanterre, France: OME.

Plan Bleu (2007), *Mediterranean and National Strategies for Sustainable Development. Energy and Climate Change*, Sophia Antipolis, France, March.

Plan Bleu (2008a), *Changement Climatique et Énergie en Méditerranée*, Sophia Antipolis, France, July.

Plan Bleu (2008b), 'Changement climatique en Méditerranée: l'efficacité énergetique et les énergies renouvelables au coeur des solutions', *Les Notes du Plan Bleu*, **10**, Sophia Antipolis, France, November.

REACCESS-UNED (2009), 'Characterisation of electricity import corridors – export potentials, infrastructures and costs', REACCESS project, technical note 2.3, March, Athens.

REACCESS-DLR (2009), 'The Europeanization of MS energy security policies', REACCESS project, deliverable 4.1.2, March, Athens.

Sagar, A.D. (2005), 'Alleviating energy poverty for the world's poor', *Energy Policy*, **33** (11), 1367–72.

San Martín, E. (2010), 'El "giro al este" en el suministro de energía de la UE y la evolución del riesgo energético de carácter socioeconómico en el período 1995–2005', 5th Congress of the Spanish Association for Energy Economics (AEEE), Vigo, Spain, 21–22 January.

Trans-Mediterranean Renewable Energy Cooperation (TREC) (2007), *Clean Power from Deserts: White Book*, Berlin: TREC/Club.

12. Conclusions: bridging over environmental and energy policies

Francesc Morata and Israel Solorio Sandoval

12.1 ENERGY: AN INTEGRATIONIST DRIVER

After almost 60 years of European integration, the member states of the European Union (EU) have not been able to agree yet on the need to develop a common energy policy. They did not do so in the 1950s, despite the creation of the European Coal and Steel Community (ECSC) and, later on, EURATOM, nor in the 1970s, ignoring the initial proposals of the European Commission in the midst of the strong economic shocks caused by successive oil price increases.[1] They chose instead to strengthen their protectionist policies on behalf of the sovereignty-rooted principles of independence and energy security. Certainly, the heterogeneity of the energy structures of the member states has not made things easy. However, it is worth emphasizing the determining weight of domestic considerations, including the maintenance of free-market barriers to protect the national energy champions.[2] Consequently, the development of the internal market has suffered the limitations resulting from the lack of a common energy policy; and internationally, the EU, heavily dependent on external supplies, has not been able to speak with a single voice when negotiating agreements with its major suppliers of oil and gas, and with transit countries.

Clearly, liberal intergovernamentalism is the best theoretical approach to account for the shortcomings identified to the extent that energy policy, particularly security of supply, forms part of the hard core of state sovereignty ('high politics'). As Ciambra explores in this volume (Chapter 9), concerns about energy supply remain 'hostage' to the geopolitical and bilateral preferences of the member states. Against this historical background, as already noted in Chapter 1, the Lisbon Treaty (art. 176a) introduces a significant move by linking energy policy with the environment while emphasizing the 'spirit of solidarity between Member States'. This formulation reflects obviously the growing concern of the member states and supranational institutions about the common energy challenges. However, recalling our analytical framework, it also expresses implicitly the incremental transformations energy policy has been experiencing over the last 20 years. As a result of increasing public awareness to address climate change threats and member states' reluctance to transfer national economic and foreign policy making authority, the European Commission's strategy has focused largely on sustainability and climate change as 'policy subterfuges' (Héritier, 1999) or legitimate drivers aimed at promoting a true European energy policy. Accordingly, member states have taken some significant steps toward further liberalizing the EU-wide energy market and have broadly endorsed increased foreign policy coordination on securing energy supplies (Belkin, 2008).

Despite the obvious (and growing) interdependence between energy and environment, the interrelationships between these two policy fields have remained relatively unexplored at the European level (Buchan, 2010; Solorio Sandoval 2011). Following our three-steps model, this volume has attempted to fill this gap by addressing two specific dimensions: on one hand, the internal interactions between energy policy, sustainable development and climate change; on the other, the external impacts of the latter two on the security and diversification of energy supply. As Adelle et al. argue (Chapter 2), focusing on energy security issues makes more evident the synergies between energy and climate change objectives.

In the next pages this concluding chapter, following the overarching analytical framework of this book (the three-step model on the 'green Europeanization' of energy policy), draws general conclusions regarding the different patterns and driving forces behind the Europeanization of energy policy for the internal as well as the external dimension. In doing so, these conclusions aim to round off the main contributions of this book on both the theoretical (Europeanization literature) and the empirical levels (the European energy policy).

12.2   'GREEN EUROPEANIZATION' OF ENERGY GOVERNANCE: INTERNAL DRIVERS

Chapters 2 and 3 provide a number of interesting inputs to the debate on the ability to integrate the environmental considerations into the emerging EU energy policy, including the fight against climate change. Recent literature has highlighted the strong normative connotations of the principle of EPI in connection with sustainable development (Persson, 2007). However, as noted in Chapter 1, we still find differing interpretations of the practical implications of the concept. In short, while some scholars (notably, Lafferty and Hovden, 2003; see also Adelle et al. in Chapter 2) give priority to environmental considerations in sectoral policies, others (e.g. Lenschow, 2002; Jordan and Lenschow, 2008; Russel and Jordan, 2009) emphasize the need to maintain a balance between the three components – environmental, economic and social – of sustainable development. The development of institutional capacities has also been stressed as a precondition for improving EPI multi-level coordination between public actors and between these and private actors, particularly in a system such as the EU that is strongly impregnated with network governance (Schout and Jordan, 2008). These capabilities are seen as mechanisms aimed at facilitating coordination between networks of interdependent actors. Schout and Jordan (2008, p.8) argue that these mechanisms provide capacities for 'helping the participants exchange information among them; lowering transaction costs; identifying issues requiring coordinated solutions; and arbitrating when conflicts cannot be settled informally and bilaterally'. Procedural aspects of EPI are also seen as highly relevant in order to ensure coordination both horizontally within the governments and vertically within the sectoral ministries (Lafferty, 2004; Mickwitz et al., 2009). So far, empirical research has shown that most of these requirements are fully met neither at the national level nor at that of the EU (Jordan and Lenschow, 2008).

Looking at the application to the EU's EPI evaluation framework put forward by the EEA in 2005, Chapter 2 reveals issues of concern related to some of the former considerations, in particular regarding the priority of EPI on the agenda, conflict management between objectives and sectors, and the pervasiveness of the concept in the policy sectors involved. A significant finding is the high-level political commitment to climate change and its implications for energy policy at the EU level, reflected also in the leadership of the policy process. In fact, the package on Energy and Climate Change was negotiated and approved by the European Council, not by the Environmental Council. Thus the issue became a major priority on the political agenda as a result of changes in both the international (Intergovernmental Panel on Climate Change, Stern Review) and the European arenas (energy security and climate change concerns). It was also a clear indication of the EU's determination to take the lead of post-Kyoto negotiations ahead of the 2009 Copenhagen summit. This set of factors seems to have reinforced the willingness of member states to delegate powers to the EU on energy issues, allowing it to assume also a stronger international leadership role to promote its positions. Another important development from the institutional point of view was the creation of a new Climate Action DG in the Barroso Commission II established in November 2009. However, as Adelle, Russel and Pallemaerts point out, the separation of DG Environment from climate issues may not necessarily produce a better horizontal integration of climate change issues in other policy areas. This is especially accurate since climate change and energy issues were not amalgamated into one large 'super-Directorate' as originally anticipated.

As regards EPI's *ex ante* environmental assessments and consultation procedures geared to improving coordination between the different policy sectors, in recent years the European Commission has carried out a more systematic implementation of impact assessment. However, with regard to energy issues, economic considerations still seem to prevail over the environmental ones. As to consultation with stakeholders, despite the existence of institutionalized procedures, there is a tendency to give priority to informal contacts with some economic sectors. When it comes to policy instruments, the same chapter reveals the difficulty of integrating cross-sectoral EPI initiatives into the bureaucratic practices of the units responsible for energy policy at the EU level. Neither the Cardiff Process nor the European Strategy for Sustainable Development has played a significant role in this process. In contrast, sector-specific adaptations have led to better results in promoting the mutual integration of energy and climate issues. From the policy-making perspective, the use of command-and-control policy instruments by the European Commission responds largely to the scarce interest shown by member states towards non-regulatory instruments (e.g. EMAS, Ecolabels and VAs). However, one should also remember the decision-making restrictions related to the need to reach unanimity when fiscal measures are under review, along with the preservation of the 'energy sovereignty' in the Lisbon Treaty. Finally, a positive sign can be detected in the increasing integration of non-ETS sectors like transport, residential housing and agriculture.

Chapter 3 draws on multilevel governance, policy networks and policy-learning as analytical dimensions to assess how EPI has been applied in the Nordic countries to the promotion of renewable energies, especially in the electricity sector (RES-E). According to Knudsen, contextual/domestic factors are a key explanatory variable to understand the behavior of public and private actors all along the policy process, including the choice of policy instruments. From a multilevel perspective (the EU and the four Nordic countries), the chapter raises the question of the strategic relationship between the Energy and Climate Change Package, the RES directive and EPI, especially when energy concerns dominate. Concerning the new RES directive, it underlines the growing use by the European Commission of formal and informal networks as an alternative mode of governance with the aim of involving experts, think tanks and the industry. Beyond facilitating communication between different actors, these mechanisms anticipate the assessment of the advantages/disadvantages of the various national experiences at the European level. The analysis reveals unprecedented lobbying activity as a reaction to the Commission proposals aimed at regulating the promotion of RES. While the organization representing the energy producers (Eurelectric) initially demanded a common scheme of support at the EU level through tradable RES certificates, small producers, in alliance with environmental organizations, supported a regulation based on the feed-in tariffs (FIT) scheme in line with most member states (Nilsson et al. 2009). Regarding the impact of EPI in the RES-E policies of the four Nordic states – which share a single electricity market – Denmark and Sweden are showing the highest level of performance. Both countries, though in different ways, are interesting examples of how EPI can facilitate the promotion of RES-E. However, in terms of downward Europeanization these outcomes seem to result more from political commitment and the political, legal, economic and technology conditions of each country than from the EPI approach backed by the EU.

Chapter 4 takes a critical look at the diffusion of RES in the electricity sector in the EU and the OECD's members. Busch and Jörgens translate the concept of Europeanization as cross-national policy clusters resulting from cross-national policy coordination modalities (mutual adjustment of domestic policies prompted by interdependence) leading to policy convergence. Drawing on the concept of diffusion (Radaelli 2003; Grabbe 2001), understood as 'international spread of policy innovations driven by information flows', the study focuses on the use of economic incentives for the promotion of electricity from renewable RES. As we have already noted, the issue revolves around the debate between the feed-in tariffs (FIT) and the green certificate systems. The authors show the influence, in both cases, of international driving forces upon the proliferation of RES-E Policies. Regarding the FIT, over the years, the German model has influenced their adoption in many member states and beyond. In contrast, the green certificate systems have been promoted more directly by the European Commission since its (failed) draft proposal of 1998 on legal harmonization of RES policies aimed at the creation of a European green certificate system along with a European market of renewable energy certificates. Support for the green certificate system at the EU level certainly encouraged their worldwide spread (e.g. the international Renewable Energy Certificate System). The two instruments provide interesting lessons in terms of Europeanization. During the 1990s, the lack of a specific European regulation didn't prevent the proliferation of the FIT system by imitation and learning (direct diffusion). At the same time, despite the failed harmonization attempt by the European Commission, there was also a diffusion process in many member states based on voluntary adaptation of domestic policies to incentives promoted at the EU level (mediated diffusion).

A further example of Europeanization arises from the promotion of the carbon capture and storage (CCS) policy under the EU Energy Strategy (Chapter 5). Here, unlike in the previous example, the most striking aspect is the high diffusion speed among the member states. The explanation of this 'success story' offered by Severin Fischer is based on international commitments by the EU to reduce its levels of CO_2. Given the obvious impossibility of reducing emissions by 2050, the promotion of CCS appears as a window of opportunity to reduce greenhouse emissions. The argument also takes into account the growing trend of highly energy-demanding countries – such as China – to exploit their coal and lignite energy resources. This reasoning applies also to some member states, like Poland, concerned about avoiding any further reliance on Russia. The appealing paradox posed by the chapter is the success of a new technology whose effects have not yet been tested in depth. Following a typical Europeanization pattern, the entry of CCS in the EU agenda resulted initially from the pressures of an advocacy coalition of member states with depleted gas fields (UK, Netherlands) and a non-member state (Norway) interested in exporting its technology potential, supported by some members of the European Parliament. Later on, this coalition expanded to two key countries, Germany and Poland, large consumers of solid fossil fuels. The discussion highlights two relevant aspects that further help explain the rapid implementation process: the choice of the method of regulation by the European Commission and financial incentives for CCS-supporting invest-ments. In the first case, the Commission's strategy was to offer a wide regula-tory framework at the European level, leaving to the member states the responsibility for translating the guidelines of the directive into national legis-lation (while domestic resistance to CCS technology was increasing in some member states). The second aspect is related to the decision to exclude CCS from ETS installations. Here, the Commission, backed by the industry, launched a funding strategy based on competitive European incentives from the European Economic Recovery Plan that called for the rapid adoption of complementary measures by national governments to take advantage of fund-ing opportunities at the supranational level.

In Chapter 6, Solorio Sandoval and Zapater argue that 'the study on the Europeanization of energy policy has been largely neglected and this policy area has been persistently excluded from the main Europeanization hand-books.' In an attempt to fill this gap, they review the set of energy governance tools implemented in recent years at the EU level with an analytical focus based on the new institutionalism. At first glance, the green dimension and the internal energy market emerge as the main drivers of the Europeanization of energy governance. However, the results diverge if one distinguishes between legislative acts in force and preparatory legislation. The frequent use of soft law instruments (i.e. Green Papers and strategic communications) allows us to conclude that 'a basic characteristic of "green Europeanization" has been its capacity to activate the debate at the EU level on the need for a coherent EU energy policy and its ability to facilitate consensus between the Member States and the EU institutions around energy issues.' This takes the form of a soft 'green Europeanization' of domestic energy policy based on flexible regula-tory instruments as a way to overcome member states' reluctance. Hence, we are still far from any consistent harmonization in the energy sector. As already noted, the change could come from the inclusion of energy policy in the Lisbon Treaty and, in particular, from the application of the ordinary legislative procedure to the decision-making process, with the consequent involvement of the European Parliament. In conclusion, as argued in this volume, there is a direct increasing relationship between the development of environmental policy and the Europeanization of energy governance. At the same time, the green dimension is having a clear influence on the process of institutionalization of a European energy policy. With all the necessary reservations, the recognition of a formal EU competence in this policy field may act as a main driver for further Europeanization.

12.3   TESTING THE EU AS A 'GREEN-MODEL' EXPORTER THROUGH ENERGY POLICY

Despite its latecomer position, energy security stands as one of the three main pillars of EU energy policy along with market competitiveness and sustainable development (Buchan, 2010). How has this affected the promotion of the environmental objectives abroad? The second part of the volume looks at this policy issue from different perspectives covering a number of strategic geographical areas.

Chapter 7 raises some relevant questions related to the Europeanization of energy policy in the new central and eastern European (CEE) member states and, in particular, the differences between these countries and the rest of the EU concerning the adoption of market-based instruments. From this perspective, Dobbins and Tosun argue that a number of common elements (lack of institutional capacity, weak environmental organizations, enhancing pollutant transport infrastructures and prevalence of economic interests) account for the greater tendency of these countries to use market-based instruments with a view to mitigating the environmental impacts of the pollutant-intensive development model. Ironically, such a preference would be favored by pre-existing – pre-democratic – regulatory systems of market-based instruments, although, in practice, these are little used. To some extent, relying on these instruments would offset institutional shortcomings while increasing the level of fiscal resources devoted to the environment. The relatively higher weight of environmental taxes on fuel consumption in the new member states compared with the EU-15 confirms the hypothesis of differentiation. However, this does not mean greater energy efficiency, but rather the opposite, owing to the prevailing patterns of production and consumption. The main objective of the CEE member states remains to recover the development gap with respect to the EU-15, taking advantage also of the European Greenhouse Emissions allowance scheme.

Herranz-Surrallés and Natorski (Chapter 8) underline the enormous complexity of building a European foreign policy in this area, characterized as it is by contradictory and conflicting interests that may undermine its compatibility with the two other pillars of the European energy policy. Their contribution tackles the impacts of energy security on the EU's energy foreign policy by looking at the EU's relations with its eastern neighbors, given the relevance of this region to the EU, both in terms of supply and transit, especially of natural gas. The analytical approach relies on three theoretical models of external energy policy that incorporate different levels of politicization: technical and market-oriented proposals, 'Europeanization beyond the EU' (exporting EU's regulative standards) and the securing of energy supply (developing bilateral and regional relations). It is assumed that the evolution or the relative prevalence of each model will depend on internal and external variables mirroring preferences and power relations between different actors. With this background, the chapter illustrates the extent to which energy relations with this set of countries result from different combinations of the three models according to factors related to each single country or each regional group. Thus, from the mid 2000s, the growing importance of energy policy on the European agenda, influenced by rising oil prices and the gas crisis between Russia and Ukraine, led the EU to step up from past practice seeking to export internal rules in the framework of the new ENP (mainly regarding the internal market legislation). This strategy included measures aimed at improving competitiveness, environmental sustainability (energy efficiency and RES development) and security of supply through joint management of potential crisis. Furthermore, the issue of security of supply has been reinforced from 2008 with the *Second Strategic Review of the Energy Sector*, which explicitly addressed energy security 'in the context of a real external energy policy' (European Commission, 2008) and the second Russia–Ukraine crisis of 2009. Empirical analysis shows that the evolution of the three models over time depends on the internal coherence of the EU in formulating its priorities and harmonizing its political, economic and environmental interests (legitimacy). However, as expected, there is also evidence that the responses of each country or group of countries are more influenced by variables such as internal stability, financial incentives, access to the European market or the ability/willingness to implement EU legislation. All things considered, the predominant model of convergence is Europeanization (Herranz-Surrallés and Zapater, 2010), which, as such, incorporates also environmental concerns. Russia, the regional gas superpower, is the main exception for two reasons. The first one has to do with Russian disagreements with the EU about the domestic implementation of the European energy market rules since it would require market liberalization and deregulation. The second reason derives from the larger member states's reluctance to endorse initiatives at the EU level that may condition their negotiation power with producing countries.

The analysis of EU energy relations with the Balkan countries provides a rather different picture (Chapter 9). Since they are candidate or potential candidate countries, the power of influence of the EU is considerable and, therefore, Europeanization – by way of the *acquis* and the conditionality principle – more effective and consistent (Schimmelfenning and Sedelmeier, 2008). Drawing on sociological institutionalism, Andrea Ciambra focuses on the Energy Community Treaty (EnC) as a stabilization process of the European external energy market through the integration of candidate and potential candidate countries with an institutional framework very similar to that of the ECSC. This is reflected in the leadership of the European Commission and the relatively minor role of the member states, of which 14 sit in the Council of Ministers along with 9 EnC external participants. One of the most innovative aspects is precisely the progressive institutionalization of a flexible and asymmetrical mode of external shared governance of energy issues to facilitate the implementation of the energy *acquis* and make legal decisions. The chapter focuses on the implementation of the environmental, RES and competition *acquis*, together with the regulations relating to electricity and gas. Partnership with the EU, even for countries with no immediate access expectations, seems to be an important driver towards fulfilling commitments. However, there are further explanatory keys. Financial incentives for the construction of an integrated regional energy market and benefits in terms of good reputation *vis-à-vis* the other partners and the European institutions also play an important role. Unlike in relations with eastern neighboring countries and the Caucasus, here the structure of incentives is based on recognition of these countries as special partners of the EU, with which they share ideas and basic values ('a common notion of Europeaness'). In sum, in terms of costs and benefits, the opportunity to participate in a joint project overcomes the drawbacks associated with sovereignty limitations.

One of the most interesting current approaches to analyzing Europeanization beyond the EU's borders is rooted in the notion of external governance as a process of institutionalized interaction or coordinated interdependence through which the EU exports its rules to third countries (Schimmelfening and Sedelmeier, 2008; Lavenex and Schimmelfening, 2009). This notion can be supplemented with the concept of diffusion, according to which ideas cross borders and are transferred to other countries (see Chapter 4). Like other instruments of external governance (e.g. regulations and procedures), the effective impacts of ideas depend on factors that mediate policy change – in particular, the consistency of European standards and ideas with the cultural and institutional structures of recipient countries. Therefore, from this perspective, the diffusing capacity of EU policies will be greater when they match institutional structures, rules and procedures that encapsulate domestic governance. Luigi Carafa (Chapter 10) uses the sociological institutionalism lens to examine

Turkey's adaptation in the three subfields of European energy policy (competitiveness, security and sustainability). In addition to its status of candidate country and its geo-strategic position, Turkey is of special interest for these issues because it is one of the largest emerging economies, with a rapidly growing energy market as well as CO_2 emissions. Empirical analysis detects three dominant outcome patterns in the energy sector reforms undertaken by Turkey (though negotiations on the energy chapter had not yet started in 2011). The first one refers to the dominant weight of the Community *acquis*, especially in the case of energy security. Clearly, the more established is the *acquis*, the stronger will be the power of influence of the EU. Diffusion capacity is further reinforced through institutionalized transgovernmental networks. The second pattern concerns the influence of domestic factors on the transformative power of the EU. This includes the need to address the problems of the energy market (liberalization of the energy sector and adaptation to the *acquis*), as well as energy supply security (the Nabuko pipeline), and the promotion of renewable energies sources (RES) and energy efficiency. The domestic resonance of the European rules is enhanced when they are coupled directly to the internal needs. Finally, Turkey is progressively adapting its legislation to the EU sustainable energy policy according to its specific needs, which are very similar to the European ones: reducing dependency by increasing energy efficiency and the RES potential.

RES have recently joined the external dimension of EU energy policy, especially after the 2006 Green Paper (European Commission, 2006). Chapter 11 discusses the Mediterranean Solar Plan (MSP), one of the flagship projects of the Union for the Mediterranean (UfM), which aims to promote the development of RES on its southern shore. Escribano-Francés and San Martin review the characteristics of the initiative to evaluate its social, economic and environmental impacts both for Morocco and the EU. Unlike the previous chapters, the evaluation refers only to potential impacts since the project has not yet been implemented. Nevertheless, the case study provides an understanding of the raison d'être and the complex network of interests behind the project. The choice of Morocco was due to its geographical position (distant 14 km from the European shore), but also to its model of development which entails increasing energy costs (20 percent of total imports). In this context, RES appear as an alternative to reduce the level of dependence on fossil fuels and an instrument to promote local development and poverty eradication in rural areas. In addition, RES can also help improve sustainability in a country with high growth potential for the production and export of green energy. Hence the MSP is expected to play a role as a comprehensive strategic driver for sustainable development.

Whether this expectation becomes a reality will depend on a complex set of factors that are illustrated in the chapter. The central question is to what extent the MSP may benefit Morocco as a key vector for economic, physical and regulatory integration of the Euro-Mediterranean space. Opportunities and mutual interests are obvious. However, as the chapter points out, the project's feasibility will depend upon a number of prerequisites, including the EU's willingness to cooperate on technological and financial issues and the political capacity of the UfM – whose future is closely related to democratic change on the southern Mediterranean shore – to make the MSP an example of sustainable development for the whole region. If these preconditions are not fulfilled, the main risk is that the Solar Plan becomes an instrument to meet the EU's environmental and economic interests without actually contributing to human development in Morocco.

12.4   THE THREE-STEP MODEL ON THE 'GREEN EUROPEANIZATION' OF ENERGY POLICY

While in the past years Europeanization has become a 'booming industry' for European studies, energy policy has remained largely excluded from this expansive trend (Solorio Sandoval, 2011). At first glance this is somewhat difficult to understand, considering not only the growing importance of this policy for European affairs but also the attention paid to related areas such as the environment and the internal market. This book has aimed to close this gap, bridging the literature on EPI, Europeanization and external governance. In doing so, the introductory chapter proposed a three-step model, looking basically to explore: (1) the relevance of environmental policy in the overall construction of the European energy policy; (2) the 'unintended' Europeanization of energy policy stemming from the environmental concerns at the EU level; and (3) the relationship between the internal and external dimension of European energy policy.

The first step of our explanatory model is perhaps the most uncontested one. Few can still doubt the importance of environmental concerns in the fight against climate change for the redefinition of energy policy in Europe. Given the sector-based origin of energy policy at the European level this is not at all surprising. However, the underlying lesson from the first part of this volume refers to the fact that, in contrast with other related areas, environmental policy has, by means of EPI, substantially shaped the European energy policy. Hence, Europeanization has followed an indirect trajectory. Accordingly, our explanatory model allows the better conceptualization of the progressive 'green Europeanization' of energy policy. To be clear, as far as the internal dimensions of the energy policy are concerned, it is possible to argue that the environmental policy has been a key driver for the energy policy at the EU level.

Is it possible to replicate this explanation for the development of the external energy policy? The third step of our model copes with this question. While the chapters in the second part of this book have demonstrated that there is not always a negative relationship between environment and security concerns regarding energy, it remains clear that the external dimension has not followed the same logic as the internal one. In fact, from the empirical findings of this volume we can conclude that energy security concerns have prompted the emergence of the EU as a 'green-energy' model exporter. All in all, looking for alternative governance approaches to knit its external ties, the EU has explored the possibilities of exporting RES and energy efficiency as a path to influence its energy partners (for example exporting the 'green-energy' model). This has come to reinforce the EU as a leader in the international negotiations on climate change, although it still has a long road ahead before speaking with a common and coherent voice in the external energy arena, including the climate-related issues. The chapters in the second part of this book have altogether captured this challenge.

To sum up, the three-step model of the 'green Europeanization' of energy policy appears as a useful analytical tool to explain the 'rareness' of energy policy-making in the EU and the changes this dynamic has been producing. However, it is worth reminding ourselves that its scope is limited exclusively to the environmental field while – as is clear from most of the chapters – the internal market has also been a strong key driver for the Europeanization of energy policy. Hence, once the 'green heritage' of the European energy policy has been established, we are still missing the big picture of the transformation of this policy area at the EU level. Last but not least, the three-step model has succeeded in providing coherence to the explanations given for the internal as well as for the external energy policy in Europe. Nevertheless, this does not necessarily mean that there is a causal bond between what moves the EU energy policy within and outside its borders. As a matter of fact, policy coherence is one of the biggest challenges for the new European energy policy.

12.5   FUTURE RESEARCH IN THE ENERGY POLICY FIELD

Along these lines we have explored the emergence of the European energy policy as a critical variable in the definition of national practices in the field. Moreover, the various contributions have demonstrated that the EU relevance is not only traceable for its member states, but also, increasingly, for the neighboring countries. Hence, this volume has shed light on the transformative capacity of Europe in the energy field in spite of the fact that energy policy is a newcomer in the 'family' of EU policies. That said, research on the European energy policy is still in the early stages of its development and it certainly represents an important challenge for European studies. On what should further research be concentrated?

In the first place, this book has focused on the Europeanization of energy policy mainly as an independent variable influencing change at the national level. However, as noted in Chapter 1, Europeanization can also be understood as changes at the domestic level brought about by the regional integration process. In this sense, while recent years have witnessed an unprecedented take-off of the Europeanization literature, little empirical research has been undertaken to explain the developments in the energy field (see Chapter 1). Therefore, an important task for European studies in the near future is the construction of an overall and comprehensive picture about how the EU has modified – or is modifying – national energy policies. These efforts have to take into consideration not only recent developments regarding the European energy policy but also the sector-based origin of the EU's action in the field.

Against this backdrop, when studying the Europeanization of energy policy one should be careful not to confuse this concept with European integration as such. Indeed, energy policy presents an interesting case of an integrationist dynamic. In this sense, as shown throughout this volume, climate change appears as the likeliest explanation for the emergence of European energy policy. Therefore, another pending item for the research agenda is the investigation, on the basis of neo-functionalist theory, of how the need for further cooperation on issues such as climate change and the internal market has led to the pooling of sovereignty in a field as significant for the national governments as energy policy.

Last but not least, as already mentioned before, the European energy policy presents the challenge of giving coherence to the overall EU action in the field. If integration theorists have been permanently challenged by the problem of the complexity of institutional engineering, the recent emergence of European energy policy introduces a unique scenario of 'disorder' in the post-Lisbon EU which definitely needs further attention. More specifically, European energy policy is affected by several related policies that force better coordination of the institutional machinery to avoid suboptimal trade-offs in the EU action. Gaining insight into this public policy challenge is a subject that definitely requires further attention from political scientists dealing with the European integration. Against this backdrop, reviving EPI approaches appears to be a useful path towards building a positive relationship between the different elements of the European energy policy so as to achieve, over time, a real European low-carbon/green economy.

NOTES

1. The Commission only achieved to approve, in 1967, the first directive on 'security of supply' which required Member States to maintain strategic stocks of oil products.
2. In 2011, only 3 per cent of the electricity produced in Europe was traded beyond the borders of a member state (Barroso, 2011).

REFERENCES

Barroso, J.M. (2011), 'Energy priorities for Europe', presentation to the European Council of 4 February 2011, Brussels.
Belkin, P. (2008), 'The European Union's energy security challenges', *Connections (The Quarterly Journal)*, PFP Consortium of Defense Academies and Security Studies Institutes, Spring issue.
Buchan, D. (2010), *Energy and Climate Change: Europe at the Crossroads*, Oxford: Oxford University Press.
Eikeland, P.O. (2011), 'The Third Energy Internal Market Package: new power relations among member states, EU institutions and non-state actors?', *Journal of Common Market Studies*, **2** (49), 243–63.
European Commission (2006), *Green Paper: A European Strategy for Sustainable, Competitive and Secure Energy*, 8 March, Brussels, accessed 10 September 2011 at from: http://ec.europa.eu/energy/strategies/2006/2006_03_green_paper_energy_en.htm.
European Commission (2008), *Second Strategic Energy Review – Securing our Energy Future*, accessed 3 September 2011 at http://ec.europa.eu/energy/strategies/2008/2008_11_ser2_en.htm.
Grabbe, H. (2001), 'How does Europeanization affect CEE governance? Conditionality, diffusion and diversity', *Journal of European Public Policy*, **6** (8), 1013–31.
Héritier, A. (1999), *Policy-Making and Diversity in Europe: Escaping Deadlock*, Cambridge, Cambridge University Press.
Herranz-Surrallés, A. and E. Zapater (2010), 'A toda luz y a medio gas: relaciones energéticas entre la Unión Europea y su entorno próximo', in E. Barbé (ed.), La Unión Europea más allá de sus fronteras, Madrid: Tecnos, pp. 61–84.
Jordan, A. and A. Lenschow (2008), *Innovation in Environmental Policy?*, Cheltenham, UK and Northampton, MA, USA: Edward Elgar.
Lafferty, W.M. (2004), 'From environmental protection to sustainable development: the challenge of decoupling through sectoral integration', in W.M. Lafferty (ed.), *Governance for Sustainable Development*, Cheltenham, UK and Northampton, MA, USA: Edward Elgar, 191–220.
Lafferty, W.M. and E. Hovden (2003), 'Environmental policy integration: towards an analytical framework', *Environmental Politics*, **12** (3), 1–22.
Lavenex, S. and Schimmelfennig, F. (2009), 'EU rules beyond EU borders: theorizing external governance in European politics', *Journal of European Public Policy*, **16** (6), 791–812.
Lenschow, A. (ed.) (2002), *Environmental Policy Integration*, London: Earthscan.
Mickwitz, P. et al. (2009), 'Climate policy integration, coherence and governance', Partnership for European Environmental Research report no. 2. Helsinki.

Nilsson, M., L.J. Nilsson and K. Ericsson (2009), 'The rise and fall of GO trading in European renewable energy policy: the role of advocacy and policy framing', *Energy Policy*, **37** (11), 4454–62.

Persson, Å. (2007), 'Different perspectives on EPI', in M. Nilsson and K. Eckerberg (eds), *Environmental Policy Integration in Practice: Shaping Institutions for Learning*, London: Earthscan, p;p. 25–48.

Radaelli, C.M. (2003), 'The Europeanization of public policy', in K. Featherstone and C.M. Radaelli (eds), *The Politics of Europeanization*, Oxford: Oxford University Press, pp. 27–56.

Russel, D. and A. Jordan (2009), 'Joining up or pulling apart? The use of appraisal to coordinate policy making for sustainable development', *Environment and Planning A*, **41** (5): 1201–16.

Schimmelfenning, F. and U. Sedelmeier (2008), 'Candidate countries and conditionality', in P. Graziano and M.P. Vinck (eds), *Europeanization: New Research Agendas*, Basingstoke, UK: Palgrave Macmillan, pp. 88–101.

Schout, A. and A. Jordan (2008), 'EU-EPI, policy coordination and new institutionalism', *Quadern de Treball*, **48**, Bellaterra, Spain: IUEE.

Solorio Sandoval, I. (2011) 'Bridging the gap between environmental policy integration and the EU's energy policy: mapping out the "green Europeanisation" of energy governance', *Journal of Contemporary European Research*, **7** (3).

Index

Van der Linde, C. 133
Vasileiadou, E. 39
vertical coordination, EPI 28, 49, 51,
    56–8, 60
Vink, M. 11, 13
'virtual' imports 205–6
Voluntary Agreements (VAs) 41, 43

White, B. 157

Wilkinson, D. 38, 53
wind energy 197, 198, 200–201
Wurzel, R.K.W. 14

Yin, R.K. 159

Zakkour, P. 88, 90
Zapater, E. 3, 171, 217
Zingerle, J. 193